Truth Is Stranger than Dogma

Truth Is Stranger than Dogma

Rev. John O. Fisher

VANTAGE PRESS
New York / Los Angeles / Chicago

FIRST EDITION

Copyright © 1988 by Rev. John O. Fisher

Published by Vantage Press, Inc.
516 West 34th Street, New York, New York 10001

Manufactured in the United States of America
ISBN: 0-533-07747-8

Library of Congress Catalog Card No.: 87-91779

To Dorothy Stallworth Fisher,
wife, partner, enthusiastic supporter

To search for the simple gospel of the greatest men of insight is to find eventually the basic factors of religion.

—Archer

During the comparatively long intermissions between creative outbursts, the church, instead of serving as a field in which the Spirit can work effectively, seeks to prevent the Spirit from stirring up the souls of men.

—Rylaarsdam

CONTENTS

BOOK I. FUNDAMENTALS OF RELIGION

BOOK II. THE TRUTH THAT MAKES US FREE

Truth Is Stranger than Dogma

BOOK I
FUNDAMENTALS OF
RELIGION

PREFACE

Here is an attempt to convey to the reader a basic working knowledge of the world's living religions, at least in part. The approach is that of an interested student, rather than of a scholar. If this book becomes the key that will unlock the treasures of world religions to the interest of the reader, then it will be worth the effort.

This is an attempt to promote the understanding of, and respect for, those non-Christian religions which the Christian does not know; those non-Hindu religions which the Hindu does not understand; those strange doctrines which ignorance labels heathen. Although the writer is within the Christian tradition, there is no attempt to bias the treatment of the subject matter in order that Christianity may be viewed in a more favorable light than it deserves.

This book is written primarily as a textbook or study guide, and the assumption is made that the reader will have access to a religious library or, at the least, to a good religious encyclopedia. This is but an introduction to a tremendous field of information that has been too much ignored by most of us.

My interest in this field was aroused by Dr. Edmund D. Soper through his lectures at Ohio Wesleyan University when he was president of that institution. Later, the dean of the School of Religion at Oklahoma University encouraged me to write down some of my findings in the field.

The writing has been accomplished under the guidance of Dr. Robert H. Pfeiffer and Mr. Ralph Lazzaro of the Harvard Divinity School faculty, both of whom have given invaluable help and suggestions. Any contribution this book may make to the field of comparative religion is due to the patience and interest of these two gentlemen in guiding my reading and writing.

The only original part of this work is the new approach that has been adopted. The sources of the material used are listed in the bibliography and footnoted in the text. My one desire is to make the facts of the worth of religion more readily available to the general reader and to the student who is just embarking upon the adventure of religious exploration.

INTRODUCTION

Some of the conclusions reached by J. C. Archer in his book, *Faiths Men Live By,* serve to introduce the thoughts set forth in this thesis: "A faith may have peculiar values for its followers, but truth is one, and contradictions in essentials must appear unreasonable, immoral and spiritually deficient. It is fundamental that the followers of any faith, if they would deal at all with the followers of any other faith, should first seek for their convictions. It is fundamental, also, that religion has to do with human welfare."[1]

In this comparative study of the world's eleven living religions we have made rather arbitrary selections of materials, choosing the positive elements rather than the negative. Comparison is made, not to prove one religion better than another, but rather to show that the fundamental elements of religion are common property, observed and utilized by the founders and leaders of every faith.

Truth is indeed one, and whenever a religious group portrays truth it advances the cause of human welfare. No group or sect has a monopoly on truth, but each religion has a distinct contribution to make to the total of truth and goodness which is available for our use. In our search for truth we cannot ignore that which has been discovered and preserved for us in the sacred writings of this world.

For the purpose of this study the comparisons are made from the writings and sayings of the founder of each religion, or from those of his early followers, as far as possible. This arbitrary method is employed in the belief that the strength and survival of the religions depend upon the basic values delineated by the originators, rather than upon the accretions of the centuries.

The liturgics and creeds of later centuries are avoided unless they illustrate a distortion of the basic principles taught by the founder. It is the fundamental idea of the religious leader which is important to us, rather than the ceremonial cloak that has been drawn around the basic statement of faith and belief.

We speak of the fundamentals of religion. By this we mean the basic concepts at the root of all religion: the interest in fertility, in self-preservation, the need for God, fear, hope. We mean also the primary values, such as those discussed in the different chapters of this study. We mean the absolutes, or nonrelative elements, which cannot be qualified or interpreted or ignored, such as life and death, thought, speech, actions, the fundamental elements out of which religion grows.

What is religion? There is no easy definition, nor any single definition that would be acceptable to every student of religion. The simplest definition is "religion is life," but that leaves life undefined. We list here a few of the definitions that have appealed to us as being good, even though they are all incomplete. A minister gave us the best explanation that we have heard of the reason why religion cannot be defined. He said: "Religion is like love. You cannot define it nor analyze it, but when you experience it yourself you know that's it!"

The following definitions are gathered from the work of writers in many different fields:

There is no ground for assuming a simple abstract "religious emotion" to exist as a distinct elementary mental

6

affection by itself, present in every religious experience without exception. . . . Religion, whatever it is, is a man's total reaction upon life, so why not say that any total reaction upon life is a religion?

—William James

Whatever religion adds to human wealth is not poured in, as an extraneous gift: it comes in continuity with what the individual has known before.

—W. E. Hocking

It is possible to make the definition of religion so broad and inclusive as to empty it of all particular meaning. If religion is everything it will cease to be anything. . . . Religion is not theology. . . . It is to be lived rather than reasoned about.

—J. B. Pratt

Religion involves a subject and an object and a relation of subject to object. . . . It is loyalty of heart, will and thought to that ultimate goodness which is ultimate reality; it is allegiance to the cosmos in its deepest meaning. . . . Religion cannot rest satisfied with any ultimate dualism of sacred and secular. It makes for ultimate harmony and complete unification. . . . Religion is not departmental, but pervades all interests and sweeps all life into its orbit; yet in spite of its all-pervasiveness, religion cannot surrender its self-identity and supremacy by losing itself in other interests, for it has its own unique contribution to make to human experience.

—D. M. Edwards

Humanity is asked to place itself at a certain level, higher than that of animal society, where obligation would be but the force of instinct, but not so high as an assembly of gods, where everything would partake of the creative impetus. Moral life will be rational life.

—Henri Bergson

Religion is a consciousness of the highest social values.

—E. S. Ames

A religion is a unified system of beliefs and practices

relative to sacred things. That is to say things set apart and forbidden—beliefs and practices which united into one single moral community called a church all those who adhere to them.

—Emil Durkheim

To be religious is to take a total attitude toward the universe . . . to sense or comprehend one's relation to the divine however the divine be conceived. It is always an awed awareness on the part of the individual of his relation to that "something not himself," and larger than himself with whom the destinies of the universe seem to rest.

—Irwin Edman

Religion at its highest and best is the devotion of the total self through search, service and adoration to the highest cause of which one is now conscious, providing that cause is deemed worthy of the devotion of all men and is symbolic of every higher unexplored value.

—H. N. and Regina Wieman

It [religion] is a relationship of conscious dependence on higher powers; it makes a demand on the whole of man's life, intellect, emotion and will; it is both individual and social; it is worship, yet it is more than worship; and it conserves all the values which give worth and meaning to human life.

—E. D. Soper

With these definitions in mind, let us consider briefly some of the fundamentals of world religion as they are outlined for us in the sacred writings of the centuries.

NOTE

1. Archer, J. C., *Faiths Men Live By* (New York: Nelson, 1934), p. 470.

OUTLINE OF THE WORLD'S LIVING RELIGIONS

The following brief outlines of the world's eleven living religions are given for the sole purpose of placing them, historically and geographically, for the benefit of the reader. For this reason the more detailed outline is preferable to the simple tabulation of names, dates, and places. (For complete discussion of these religions see G. F. Moore, *History of Religions*, 2 vols.)

NEAR EAST

Four of the living religions of the world had their origin in the area east of the Mediterranean Sea, in Palestine, Persia, and Arabia.

Judaism

Historical Judaism as we know it today did not appear in history until about 540 B.C., following the period of the Babylonian Exile. The religion of the Jewish peoples prior to that time is variously designated as Hebraism, the religion of the Israelites, or Semitic religion.

Although legalistic Judaism dates from about 540 B.C.,

9

it is the direct outgrowth of the earlier religious organization of Jehovah worshipers who followed the Law of Moses, known most widely as the Israelites. The Mosaic Code was given to the people about 1200 B.C. by Moses after he had secured their release from Egyptian bondage. Consequently, Moses is considered the founder of Judaism even though the great voice that established what we know today as Judaism was that of Second Isaiah.[1]

The sacred scriptures of Judaism are a collection of documents grouped into three classifications: the law, the prophets, and the writings. These are known to Christians as the Old Testament of the Bible.

Judaism is the parent religion to both Christianity and Islam and, through Islam, has had definite influence on the Indian religion known as Sikhism. It upholds a strict monotheism and maintains that there is a direct relationship between God and man. The primary emphasis is upon individual righteousness, and the great hope is in the coming of a Messiah who will bring about the consummation of God's plan for mankind.

Zoroastrianism

Zoroastrianism was founded in Persia by Zoroaster, who is believed to have lived between 660 and 538 B.C., although some authorities place him much earlier. The religion revitalized Persia and inspired the nation to become an empire that had much influence upon world history.

Some Zoroastrian influence is believed to have been exerted upon both Judaism and Christianity. Cyrus, the Persian king who was also a Zoroastrian, released the Jews from exile and allowed them to return to Palestine. It was after this return that legalistic Judaism was established, with some indication of a religious dualism that may have been adapted from Zoroastrianism. This dualism is much more clearly evidenced in Christianity, and the New Testament book of Revelation has close parallels to the teachings of Zoroaster.

The sacred scripture is the Avesta, of which only the Gathas are directly attributed to Zoroaster himself. The key thoughts are expressed in the Amesha Spenta. The religion is based upon a definite dualism with Ahura Mazda as ruler of the excellent kingdom and Angra Mainyu as the ruler of the kingdom of darkness.

Zoroastrianism teaches the ultimate triumph of good over evil in the world, urges its followers to make the best use of the land, and emphasizes personal choice and responsibility. It has definite social and ethical principles, which gave it the early strength and inspirational quality to fire the imagination of the Persian people.

Today Zoroastrians are the smallest among the eleven great religions because they lost the missionary zeal and prophetic vision of their founder and early leaders. They were driven from Persia by the Muslims in the seventh century of the Christian era and now are found only in India.

Christianity

One of the three great missionary religions of the world, Christianity was founded by Jesus of Nazareth in Palestine during the first century of the Christian era.[2] Jesus was born about 4 B.C. and was crucified about thirty-three years later because he was a disturber of the people, a subversive influence who was endangering the status quo.

Jesus preached self-denial and loving service, as well as loving obedience to one supreme, loving, merciful God and Father of all the world. He founded his teachings upon the Law of Judaism and sought only to reform his own religious heritage, having no intention or desire to depart from the established religion of his people. His followers found that it was necessary to break away from Judaism completely, and organized independent churches or communities that became known as Christian.

The sacred scriptures of Christianity are primarily the New Testament of the Bible, although most Christian sects use the Old Testament (Jewish scripture) as well. Jesus wrote none of this scripture, but many of his teachings and sermons, as well as much of his conversation with his disciples, have been recorded by his followers. These words of Jesus are found in the first section of the New Testament, known as the Gospels, the most accurate of which is generally believed to be the Gospel according to Mark, which was written down earlier than the others.[3]

The religious and ethical teachings of Christianity can be summarized in six words: Love to God, Love to Man. Jesus stressed individual responsibility toward neighbor as well as toward self, which became the major factor in the great zeal with which Christians became missionaries for their faith.

One fact of great historical significance is that Christianity moved westward, while all other religions moved eastward. It is true that Islam moved westward along the northern coast of Africa and crossed into Spain, but this expansion did not continue and the strong movement of Islam has been toward Asia. Christianity, therefore, became the primary religion of Europe and of the entire Western Hemisphere.

Islam

Islam means "submission" and Muslim means "those who submit." This fourth great living religion of the Near East is known also as Muhammadanism, making use of the name of its founder, Muhammad. Like Christianity, Islam is a personally founded, universal, monotheistic religion.

Muhammad, who lived from A.D. 570 to 632, was the founder of Islam. He considered himself the last of the prophets who succeeded Abraham and the messenger of the truth, which came directly from God. His revelations are gathered into the holy book of Islam, the Koran, which is final authority in all matters and from which there is no appeal, since it is the revealed word of God.

The ancestry of Islam is threefold. Judaism plays a large part in the background of the religious teaching, and Christianity has contributed the ideas of resurrection and last judgment. The third source is the Arabian mythology, many parts of which are seen in the religious practices of Islam, especially the pilgrimage to Mecca and the rites performed there by the faithful.

Muhammad gave the Arab tribes a common cause that served to unite them into an uneasy coalition under a theocratic leadership. The discipline that Muhammad introduced made it comparatively easy for the Muslims to overrun all of North Africa to the west, as well as all of the countries eastward to India within a hundred years of the founding of Islam.

Muhammad set out to replace, rather than to reform, the existing religion of Arabia. For idolatric practices he substituted allegiance to one supreme deity who is also merciful and compassionate. He placed a great emphasis upon the importance of prayer and the giving of alms, and instilled in his followers a definite missionary aggressiveness, as well as a feeling of unity which held them together despite the rise of sects.

MIDDLE EAST

Four of the world's living religions are native to India, although Buddhism spread far beyond the borders of its native land.

Hinduism

The oldest living religion in India is Hinduism, which was developed by the Aryan invaders who came over the Hindu Kush mountains and settled in the valley of the Indus about 2000 B.C. Hinduism began as a nature worship, an advanced form of animism, with the sun and sky among the more important spirits.

As the tribes became merged, the various tribal gods were amalgamated, priests took over the duties of the family heads as cajolers of the gods, and a ritual legend grew which culminated in the Vedas. The Vedas, the principal one being the Rig Veda, were the first sacred literature of the Hindu religion. They were hymns which contained instruction, supplication, worship and praise, and which gave history an idea of the religious development of the Aryan peoples in the Indus valley.

Eventual overcrowding of the Indus valley forced a migration to the valley of the Ganges. As the population increased, the caste system grew more and more complicated in a vain effort to keep Aryan and native black people separated. Caste became an insurmountable barrier among the Aryans themselves during this process.

14

The second significant body of Hindu religious literature was the Brahmanas, writings of the priestly caste to insure the maintenance of their favored position in the caste system. This was the emergence of apologetic theology in Hinduism.

The Upanishads, dated from about 800 to 600 B.C., comprise the third scriptural contribution to the Hindu literature. These writings discard the majority of the old gods and uphold the Brahma as the one absolute. Transmigration was introduced and Nirvana (nothingness) became the goal of life.

The fourth great contribution to the religious literature of the Hindus is probably the best known outside India, because it has been more widely translated than any other Hindu sacred writing. This book of devotion is known as the Bhagavad Gita, and it stresses the way of faith or devotion as the way of salvation that is open to all.

Time has brought much change in Hinduism, as well as many attempts at reform, of which three have survived as separate religions in India. Yet there is little change in the caste sytem, although as recently as 1947 there was an attempt to eliminate the outcaste group as a classification, nor has Hinduism relinquished the veneration of the Vedas.

Jainism

One of the first of these major attempts to reform Hinduism was that of Mahavira, who lived 599 to 529 B.C., but he did not succeed in changing the course of the Hindu traditions. He did establish a strong sect which became a separate religion in India known as Jainism.

Mahavira, through twelve years of self-denial, became a complete ascetic. He preached abolition of the gods and

15

the complete eradication of caste, the latter point being the primary cause of his rejection by the Hindus. He forbade killing anything. His three jewels were Right Faith, Right Knowledge, Right Living.

His followers were urged to attain complete poverty and absolute meekness. They were expected to carry out a willful annihilation of the self so that there would be no temptation to forget the true purpose of existence.

The followers of Mahavira called him Jina, meaning "Conqueror," and called themselves Jains, or followers of the Jina. They deified their founder, but speedily forgot his teachings and admonitions.

There are many sacred scriptures, only a few of which have been translated into English. Called the Agamas or the Siddhantas, none of the scriptures came into being within two centuries of the death of Mahavira. At the present time the sacred scriptures are used more for ritual recitation than for instruction or guidance. Most of the Jains at the present time are not familiar with the language in which their scriptures are written, although a few of the books have been translated into present-day vernaculars.

Buddhism

The second reform movement within Hinduism to become a separate sect was Buddhism, founded by Siddhartha Gautama, who lived from 560 to 480 B.C. Instead of reforming Hinduism, Gautama established a distinct religion that became the first of the three universal religions, the other two being Christianity and Islam. The development of Buddhism from Hinduism and of Christianity from Judaism is strikingly similar in many points.

Gautama, a rich Indian prince, renounced his heritage and sought peace of mind by consulting the hermit philosophers. He found that they spoke nothing but wind. Then he tried the severe asceticism preached by Mahavira, but decided that self-affliction was not enough. One day, while sitting under the shade of a banyan (bay) tree, he received an inspiration.

He saw the folly of all excess. He preached the middle path of decency and self-control, which was attained by the noble eight-fold path of right belief, resolve, speech, action, livelihood, effort, thought, meditation. The three cardinal sins were sensuality, ill-will, and stupidity.

Gautama had no use for gods nor for caste but, unlike Mahavira, he replaced them by emphasizing social ethics. Karma is the "law of the deed," and the fate of man depends upon what he does. His disciples, when convinced of the truth of his doctrine, hailed him as the Buddha, meaning "enlightened one."

The sacred scriptures of Buddhism are the *Tripitaka*, or "Three Baskets," and have made a distinct contribution to the religious literature of the world.

Sikhism

The latest of the world's eleven religions was founded by Guru Nanak, who lived from A.D. 1469 to 1538 in the Punjab. Nanak was influenced greatly by the philosopher Kabir of Benares, the area of India in which both Mahavira and Gautama lived and taught.

Sikhism is the only religion among the eleven that is clearly synthetic in origin. Its establishment resulted from an attempt to harmonize Hinduism and Islam, which were

17

the two major religions in India at the time. Islam had great appeal for the followers of Buddhism, and had supplanted that religion to a great extent in India itself.

It is a point of interest that Nanak was carrying out his reform movement in India at about the same time that the great German reformer, Martin Luther, was active in Europe. However, Nanak did not have the success that Luther had. His reform did not reach beyond India, in fact was not effective beyond the area of the Punjab, where over ninety percent of the Sikhs are found today.

The sacred scripture of the Sikhs is the Granth, an anthology of poetry in several languages and dialects, which combines meditations upon God with admonitions concerning life and conduct. The central point of belief is in the one, true, sustaining, omnipotent God.

The central shrine of the Sikhs at Amritsar is one of the most beautiful sights of India, second only to the Taj Mahal in the opinion of some observers. Within this shrine the Granth holds the central place, and is an object of worship.

FAR EAST

Three of the world's living religions originated in the Eastern portion of Asia, two being native to China and one to Japan.

Taoism

The older of two Chinese religions established in the same century, Taoism was founded by the teachings of the philosopher Lao-tze, who lived from 604 to about 517 B.C. in central China.

Lao-tze had an inquiring mind and was not satisfied with ancestor worship. He sought to know the way of the universe through the discovery of the why of things. It is reported that Lao-tze, as a venerable philosopher and keeper of the archives of the Chou dynasty was visited by the young reformer Confucius, who was searching out the ancient history of China. Lao-tze urged the young man to search quietly for the Tao if he would find the key to religion and life, but Confucius did not follow his advice.

The sacred scripture of Taoism is the Tao Teh King; *Tao* meaning the way, the why of the universe, and *Teh* meaning the how of life. The book is a collection of counsels and general observations, and is regarded as an important contribution to the ethical and religious literature of China. At one time its study was obligatory for all students in China who wished to become graduates of the second degree.

The followers of Lao-tze organized themselves into orders, acquired great monasteries, distorted his teachings, and deified him. Taoism has been ruled by a kind of pope since about the beginning of the Christian era. The three jewels of character which were stressed by the founder were inactivity, humility, and frugality. The fact of his veneration by his followers would be a matter of distress to him.

Confucianism

The chief religion of China was founded by Confucius (Kung-fu-tze) who lived from 551 to 479 B.C. in Shantung province, which has since been considered holy ground by the followers of his teachings. Confucius did not found a religion by intent. He was interested in establishing an ethical code of state-centered morality, and it was not until long after his death that his teachings became the state religion.

He formalized and regularized the ancestor worship of his people, having made himself an expert in ancient ritual customs. He also collected and edited the old writings. His desire was to regiment everyone, and he popularized the elaborate etiquette of tradition. He was not religious, but had an intense interest in the field of ethics. To him, filial piety was the greatest virtue that could be attained by man.

Confucius supplied the sacred texts of Confucianism himself, being the exception among the founders of religious groups in that he wrote down his teachings at great length in the Analects and other documents. His disciples, especially Mencius, saved his teachings and spread his ideas. Confucius was canonized in the year A.D. 1, and he reached the heights in A.D. 1907 when he was raised to the first grade of worship, ranking with the deities of heaven and earth.

Shinto

The religion of Japan was established with the coming of the first Mikado in about 660 B.C., according to the traditional story. Shinto, the way of the gods, had no personal founder, and its origin is shrouded in the mists of tradition. It is a religion of nature worship and emperor worship, furnishing the religious basis for the reigning dynasty, which is the oldest continuing one in the world.

The Shinto teachings establish the position that the islands of Japan were the first divine creation, the center of the world and of the universe. The first Mikado descended to earth from the sun goddess in heaven and established the divine succession of Japanese rulers. Thus Shinto is more of a patriotic cult than a religion, maintaining one paramount principle—that of political loyalty to the Mikado.

Shinto exists beside, and tolerates, other religions such as Confucianism, Taoism, and Buddhism. The people of Japan all observe the Shinto ceremonials and festivals connected with the crops or natural manifestations. Shinto requires physical and ceremonial purity, giving little heed to the necessity of mental or moral purity.

There are two primary sacred scriptures of Shinto; the *Ko-ji-ki,* or records of ancient matters, and the *Nihon-gi,* or chronicles of Japan. In addition there are oracles and traditions, as well as later collections of sacred writings. The scriptures are collections of legends, poems, songs, and chronicles that tell of the divine origin and early history of the empire.

NOTES

1. Second Isaiah is Isaiah 40–66, sometimes considered 40–55.
2. Paul was the organizer of Christianity.
3. See Appendix.

21

CHAPTER I
GOD

Morgan gives a definition of God which is positive and brief: "For what is God but the reality on which we depend, the ultimate might in the universe, interpreted through the highest that has come within our experience."[1]

What, or who, is God? Theoretical answers to such a question would fill volumes, as such answers already have done, and definitions are found wherever a theologian has inscribed his conclusions. Man has tried to explain God to himself and to his fellow men for at least five thousand years; nor is the process at an end. We here hesitate to attempt a further explanation. It is enough for our purposes to say that, to some, God is tangible and visible; to others intangible and invisible.

We speak of God as He. In so doing we personalize God and create a mental image. The next logical step is to create a physical image, and to worship the image as the embodiment of the idea. Being ourselves finite, we find infinity difficult to comprehend. Picturing our thoughts in concrete terms, we are uncomfortable in the presence of any abstraction.

To the writer, God is the creative force, the cosmic mind, author of natural law and universal order. How can one picture such a concept? How can one describe totality of knowledge or of power, or simultaneous presence in every part of our universe? The bright child can imagine

23

such a force, but the matter-of-fact, rational adult has become so used to finite experience that he can only grope blindly toward some facet of the whole idea.

It is the purpose of this chapter to illustrate such groping through examples, and to show the steps by which man's idea of God has grown through the centuries, as man has progressed toward a more adequate understanding of himself and of his environment. Further information in any field or phase which particularly interests the reader may be found in the books mentioned in the bibliography, where there is also reference to other works.

Forces, or a single force, in the world capable of influencing natural events are recognized in every expression of religion. The concept of these forces, or this force, varies from merely the supernormal on the one hand to the idea of the supreme and controlling power in the world on the other. The names used to indicate this force are many, the term "God" being chosen here because it is the familiar term to people of the Western world, although it is no more accurate than any other appellation.

The idea of this force, or "God," is the cornerstone of religion. Other fundamental concepts are just as basic to the structure of religion, but without "God" there would be no enduring structure at all. As Voltaire once said, "If there were no God it would be necessary to create one." The belief that there is an immortal force that influences or changes the course of human events motivates the making of ethical and religious codes for the protection and improvement of humanity. God is, therefore, the first fundamental of religion to be considered.

It is difficult to determine how early religion entered the conscious experience of man, because it has been an evolutionary development within each cultural group. The first appearance of belief in ghosts or spirits is placed more logically within the realm of magic than of religion. Such ghosts were the invisible extension of personalities or powers within the experience of the individual, a continuation that was maintained for the purpose of bringing distress or retributive justice to the living. Gradual development of this belief in ghosts brought about the idea that good ghosts could offset evil ghosts, followed by the idea that there is a reservoir of good that can be drawn upon to gain protection from the lurking evil.

It is almost impossible to determine accurately when a mysterious external force was recognized and first worshiped. One can imagine a primitive man walking along the bank of a river. Suddenly he trips and falls. Recovering from his astonishment, he notices that a crooked stick, half embedded in the mud, has tripped him. Knowing that the stick cannot have done such a thing without help, the savage decides that the spirit within the stick has been offended. So he places the stick upright in the mud and bows down before the spirit within it to propitiate the spirit so that he can safely resume his walk.

Our earliest records of worship are almost that elemental. God as the ruler of the world was not a part of early religious worship, such a comprehensive idea being the product of a long evolutionary process. The mind of man had to expand gradually, through experience and thought, from sense perception to metaphysics. The first consciousness of an outside force was probably the feeling illustrated by the emergence of the idea of ghosts. Some primitive cultures developed the belief that their dead ancestors and relatives might be responsible for the good or bad fortune of the living. They developed a ritual that would propitiate the ghost of their departed relatives, persuading them to intervene only on the side of good fortune.

It is a comparatively short step, but an important one, from ghosts to spirits. Indeed the two ideas are sometimes used synonymously in the accounts of primitive cultures, although there is a distinct difference between them in most cases. Ghosts, as outlined above, were the continuance of an individual person or animal, known to the living when they were alive and haunting the area where they had lived. Spirits, on the other hand, were not necessarily the continuance of any physical beings but had always been spirits and would continue to be. A ghost had control over only one family or a single person, while a spirit was in control of the destiny of a whole tribe or clan of many families.

The important factor for us is not so much the existence of spirits, whether in fact or fancy, as it is the idea that the spirits had power to influence forces or events. This power or influence has different names in the various regions of the world. The Japanese call it *kami;* the Algonquin Indians of North America call it *manitu,* while the Sioux Indians call it *wakanda,* and the Iroquois Indians call it *orenda.* The term used most frequently in the discussion of the history of religion is *mana,* which originated in the Melanesian area of the Pacific. All of these terms refer to an occult power or an influence in nonhuman nature and in the dead. *Mana,* for example, is a force, influence, or potency the spirits have and which they can impart or convey to the living, either directly or through objects and forces of nature.[2]

Thus we see the idea of spiritual and nonmortal power begin to assert itself in the thought of man, who felt the presence of an influence which he could not understand and so tried to make it as concrete as possible. Perhaps the most concrete expression of this attempt is found in Totemism, which flourished particularly along the Pacific coastline in Canada and Alaska, North America. There the family spirits were made comfortable in the totem log or pole, which guarded the home and, whenever the family moved, was taken with them to their new habitat.

An even more primitive expression of the presence of this power is the practice of Voodoo among African jungle tribes. Whether the Voodoo rites can be called religious is more than doubtful, although the ability of spirits to do damage has been accepted without question. One need go no farther than the Southeastern United States to find evidence of these rites among some blacks.

Animism populated the world with spirits and it was natural for man to begin making distinctions between greater and lesser spirits in his worship. Fertility was of paramount importance during this period because the abundance of the yield meant the difference between feast and famine, just as the number of children determined the continuance or extinction of the family. So the spirits of the sun, moon, earth, rain, and wind were more important than the spirits of trees, stones, mountains, and the minor household spirits. The major spirits tended to become gods, served by the minor spirits as well as by man, causing the development of a definite form of nature worship, with many variations according to climate.

One illustration of this development is found among the ancient Semites, where the nature cult of Baalism placed its main emphasis upon fertility, as was true in most of the ancient religions. In Baalism, as we find it in the Ras Shamra poems of the fourteenth century before the Christian era, El was the father of the gods and Asherah was the mother-goddess. Baal was the god who controlled the rain and his consort, Anat, was the goddess of fertility. Mot, death, was the enemy of Baal. He dried up the water of Baal and killed him each summer during the season of heat and dryness. After the harvest, Baal was restored to the atmosphere.[3]

Two illustrations of a similar development can be found in the religious history of the Western Hemisphere. The American Indian had his fertility and nature gods, whom he propitiated with dances and ceremonies of a religious nature. Yet, above all the rest, he worshiped the Great Spirit who was chief of the happy hunting grounds. So great is the difference between the concept of the lesser gods or spirits and that of the Great Spirit that the American Indian can be termed monotheistic.

The other example is that of the Inca civilization in northwestern South America. The Spanish explorers and conquerors found evidences of a highly developed religious consciousness among the Incas. These people worshiped the sun god with elaborate ritual and sacrifice, and their king was the earthly representative of the god.[4] There are some interesting points of similarity between the worship of the Incas and that of the early Egyptians, although no connection is probable.

One other early religion should be considered because of its influence on later developments. The ancient Greeks believed that a family of gods, through its actions and interventions, influenced the welfare and destiny of man. From Mount Olympus, the abode of the gods, Zeus ruled both Olympus and the world. He was the one above all and governed the destiny of all, being the final authority in all disputes and sitting in judgment over gods and men alike. In Homer, Zeus and the other deities were glorified human beings who were immortal. The deities were driven by human moods and passions, plotting against each other and taking sides in the strivings between men. In all this Zeus was the final judge, and the last court of appeal.[5]

At this point it might be well to give a brief summary of the evolutionary development of the idea of God, outlining the different theological positions. A few scholars maintain that monotheism antedates every other form of religious thought, but that it was lost to view and has been regained only in comparatively recent times. Most of the material available does not substantiate this position. On the other hand the research outlined in most books concerned with early religious history indicates a definite pattern of progress.

From the earliest period, when magic and religion were intermingled, through animism to polydaemonism and then to polytheism, most religious cults had a comparable development. We have endeavored to show that there is a progressive development from spirits that inhabit objects to spirits, both good and evil, that are free agents. The next step tends to transform the good spirits into gods and the evil spirits into fallen gods or devils, which is the passage from polydaemonism to polytheism.

Henotheism becomes the intermediate stage between polytheism and monotheism. Henotheism is tribal or national monotheism, and the religion of Israel was henotheistic from the time of Moses to the period of the exile. The henotheistic group worships only one god, but accepts the fact that the neighboring group worships an entirely different god as perfectly natural and right. Thus the Israelites worshiped Jahweh and the Babylonians worshiped Marduk, although both nations were of Semitic background.

Some scholars place henotheism before polytheism in the scale of development, but such placement is open to serious question. While it is perfectly possible for henotheism to spring directly from an advanced form of polydaemonism, thereby cutting out the polytheistic step, it does not seem probable that polytheism would be the logical outcome of henotheism. Grafting a number of henotheistic cultures into one political entity is one thing;

forming a polytheistic religion from that graft is quite another. The Israelites did not place Marduk on the same level with Jahweh during their period of exile in Babylonia, although both gods were worshiped in the same area by different people. Evidence to the contrary evolutionary position can be drawn from the fact that the people under the Greek polytheistic mythology chose a particular god or goddess as the protector of their city, and worshiped that one deity to the virtual exclusion of the rest, as shown in Ephesus when the citizens of that city chose Diana as their patron goddess.

The highest stage of development in the idea of God followed henotheism in Judaism in the form of monotheism as expounded by the Second Isaiah in about 540 before the Christian era. Monotheism is the belief that only one God exists in the universe and that He created and ordered all things. Such a concept can be attained through mature philosophical thought or step by step in the development of religious consciousness.

As a parallel to the monotheistic position there has grown up the idea of pantheism, meaning that God is the essence of all created things, which appears in some religious cultures in place of monotheism. In our Christian tradition we have seen pantheism come into the picture at least eight centuries after the Christian beginnings, which, stemming from Judaism, are basically monotheistic. Benedict Spinoza, 1632–77,[7] is an outstanding champion of the pantheistic position.[8]

For a practical demonstration of the development of the idea of God we will turn now to the consideration of the idea as formulated in the eleven living religions. Three of the four religions native to India appear to have an approach to deity which is more pantheistic than otherwise, although the idea of God is so veiled in mysticism as to be

30

almost indiscernible. In fact, both Jainism and Buddhism have been called atheistic, although there seems to be an abstract concept, an upward pull, even in these two beliefs, and one may be permitted to call that mystical soul-force God.

In the Hinduism of the Upanishads and the Bhagavad Gita there is definite indication of the presence of a life-force which is eternal and immortal. Brahma, or Krishna, is the one supreme being, the embodiment of the omni-present and nonmaterial spiritual reality which underlies everything that exists. There is little indication of a personal character, or of moral responsibility for the fate of man, in this supreme being. Yet mystical association with the supreme is attainable through knowledge or faith.[9]

Closely allied to Hinduism are the two religious cultures known as Jainism and Buddhism. The idea of God as an ethereal or tenuous nonmaterial force is brought to such a fine point in these two religions that it almost ceases to be a clear idea and becomes a vague suggestion of a haven for the soul. Both Jainism and Buddhism have been classified as heretical sects of Hinduism by some scholars, even though they have existed as independent forms for twenty-five centuries and both have their own sacred scriptures. They have all the attributes of religion within their own structures and should, therefore, be termed religions, rather than sects.

Many scholars label Jainism and Buddhism atheistic. If one interprets lack of reference to a specific supreme deity as atheism, then such a label is justified. There seems to be no discernible God-consciousness, nor is there any reference to a supreme deity, in either religion, although Jainism had, at first, a class of gods (*devas*) that were participants in the development of the ethical and moral teachings of the order. However, the fact that both Jainism and

31

Buddhism created a kind of God-consciousness in the minds of their followers is assumed because both groups later deified their founders. The very lack of deity brought a substitute through a feeling of necessity, and so eternality was expressed even though the source of it was not admitted or denied.

Yet it seems to me that the idea of God which existed in the parent Hinduism influenced both religions. In Jainism there is definite reference to an indestructible soul, an idea which, in the Uttara-Dhyayana Sutra 29.73, is stated thus: "The soul goes to the highest heaven, and there develops into its natural form; obtains perfection, enlightenment, deliverance and final beatitude; and puts an end to all misery."[10] Could this concept spring from atheism? If so, then there is need for a further definition of atheism. If one fails to say that there is a God, yet implies such existence through the idea of soul and immortality, such failure does not mean atheism as we find the term defined in the dictionary.

The idea of God which can be sensed in Buddhism is more definite than that in Jainism. Gautama refers to a vague totality that is the focus of the realities of life. He makes no attempt to describe such a totality, but points out that it is beyond definition. There is an invisible force within all life, *karma,* which alone links the rebirths, and the state of complete peace, erroneously called nothingness, is Nirvana. This ultimate goal is reached through a life of meditation and contemplation, the final step in Gautama's noble eight-fold path.

Gautama neither affirms nor denies immortality, nor does he attempt to define heaven, or what lies beyond the round of rebirths. There are indications that something does lie beyond, in his opinion, if the text of the Dhammapada is translated correctly because, from Dhammapada 21, we have the following: "Earnestness is the path of immortality; thoughtlessness, the path of death. Those who are in earnest do not die; those who are thoughtless, are as if dead already."[11] There is an element which can be termed "the wholly other," an element which cannot be described or expressed in the speech or experience of the finite world. What it is, and how it affects the consciousness, will be known when the time comes. Whatever it is, and whether it exists or not, man's duty is to reach Nirvana first by the path Gautama charted.

The fourth great religion of India, Sikhism, has a very definite concept of God, holding to a mystical monotheism that is the fusion of the strict monotheism of Islam mellowed by the native Indian mysticism. To the Sikh, God is everything, everywhere. In the Gobind Singh Puran Singh 148 there is a recitation of God's attributes that kindles the imagination:

Nath! [Lord!] Thou art the Hindu, the Moslem, the Turk, and the Feringhi; thou art the Persian, the Sanskritian, the Arabian; thou art the poet, the skilled dancer, the songster supreme. Thou art the speech; and thou art the avdhuta. The adept. Thou art the warrior clad in shining armor, and thou art the peace supreme! Thou art man, woman, child and God! Thou art the flute-player, the herdsman that goes grazing the dumb cows! Thou bestowest love, and thou givest thyself to all! Thou art the protector of life and the giver of all prosperity! Thou art the cure of all sorrow and suffering; thou art the net of the charms of youth, and high summit of all fulfillment! Thou art the form of a beautiful princess and thou art the emaciated form of the Brahmachari with the wooden beads hanging from his neck! Thou art the Muezzin that cries from the roof of the Mosque, the Yogi that lies wrapt in silence of deep thought, unthinking in the soul-lit cave. The vedas art thou, and the

Qur'an! In all shapes and everywhere, thou art dear to me; in every form thou art thyself! Thou art my vow, my Dharma; my beginning and my end.[12]

When we realize that the beginning of Sikhism was within the century of the Protestant Reformation in Europe we might be tempted to accept this idea of God as a matter of no moment. Yet the only definite Western influence came from Islam, which had entered the life of India at the beginning of the second millennium of the Christian era. It seems fair to describe the Islamic idea of God as a catalytic agent which precipitated the Indian idea of God as a relatively definitive concept. Such a ready acceptance of a definite and monotheistic idea of God gives weight to the assumption that a concept of God was by no means foreign to the earlier Indian religious development, no matter how tenuous it might appear from the literature of the time.

The three religions native to the Far East show three different ideas of God. In Japan, Shinto teaches that the sun goddess is the ruler of the lesser gods and of all Japanese, who are a race apart from and above any other. There seems to be no concept of cosmic unity, nor is there any indication of universality. Perhaps the best illustration of the Shinto concept of God is found in the pronouncement of the Oracle of Itsukushima in Aki: "Of old the people knew not My name. Therefore I was born into the visible world, and endured a base existence. In the highest heaven I am the Deity of the sun. In the mid-sky I show My doings. I hide in the great earth, and produce all things. My power pervades the four seas."[13]

Chinese religious culture reached a much higher level than the Japanese; in fact, much of the higher development of the Japanese religion was due to the contact with

Chinese scholarship. Confucianism was the state religion of China and it is peculiarly well fitted for that role. Confucius was the apostle of order and of respect for authority. He believed that the supreme being who created the order in the universe was accessible only to the emperor. The people could reach the supreme being only through the orderly progressions of society, but the link between the gradations of the social and political structure was so strong that the humblest could feel the presence of God through his faithful observance of all the proprieties. Such fealty brought a smile of approval from God "through channels," as an army officer would say.

No two religious forms could be much less similar in their concept of God than Confucianism and Taoism. Lao-tze, founder of Taoism and older contemporary of Confucius, was the antithesis of Confucius in his teaching and practice alike. The Taoist looked upon God as the eternal, impersonal supreme being, to whom each person had direct access. In fact, Lao-tze saw an intimate connection between each human individual and the supreme being. God was an all-pervading force and could not be avoided and the less effort spent seeking God, the better the chance of reaching Him. In the words of the Tao Teh King 51,1,3,4: "The Supreme (Tao) produces all things. Its virtue nourishes them. Its nature gives them form. Its force perfects them. The Supreme, engendering all things, nourishes, develops, fosters, perfects, ripens, tends and protects them. Production without possession, action without self-assertion, development without domination—this is Its mysterious operation."[14]

To this point we have considered seven of the living religions in their attitude toward the existence and nature of God. All seven have been located in Central or Eastern Asia. When we turn our attention to the West, the countries

35

surrounding the Eastern Mediterranean stand out as the most fertile of all religious fields. Many claim that the Mesopotamian valley is the birthplace of religion. Certain it is that Palestine has had more influence on the religious life of man than any other region.

From Western Asia come four outstanding religious cultures, two of which have become the great missionary movements of history. All four have a definite and highly developed concept of God. These religions are culminations of a religious consciousness which began its development at least three, and probably four, thousand years before the Christian era. The Sumerian writings disclose a religious consciousness which was in the process of growth during the third millennium before the Christian era or earlier.

Indications of monotheism in Egypt are discerned by Breasted in the ancient texts as early as 1600–1400 before the Christian era. In 1375 B.C., Amenhotep IV attempted to make the religion of Aton (sun god) universal. Aton was conceived as the creator and ruler of the universe. Amenhotep changed his own name to Ikhnaton (meaning "Aton is satisfied").[15] By 1000 B.C. the omnipotence of God was accepted in Egypt: "The impelling voice within was now unreservedly recognized by the believer to be the mandate of God himself. Conscience became, as it had never been before, the unmistakable voice of God. Under these circumstances there can of course be no concealment or denial of sin, and the believer, conscious that his whole case is known to his God, places himself without reserve in the hand of God, who guides and controls all his life and fortunes."[16]

While some ancient Egyptians were definitely monotheists, the religion of Israel was still in the henotheistic stage of development. Jehovah (in Hebrew, *Yaweh*) was the God of Israel and was the one God above all other gods for them, although the bounds of Jehovah's power were national. He was the special God of the Hebrew tribes, jealous and vindictive, providing strict justice and swift retribution, feared as the foe of all violators of national custom and law.

Jehovah, as the Lord of Hosts, fought Israel's battles, and His ark in the midst of the army encouraged the Israelites and frightened their foes. Obedience to His will was thought to bring victory over superior enemies: "Behold, he that keepeth Israel slumbers not nor sleeps" (Psalm 121:4). Such was the attitude of the Israelites until the Exile in 586 B.C., but it was only a few years after this date that Jehovah was conceived as the sole, supreme and holy God.

With the prophecy of the Second Isaiah there appeared the idea of God as both the moral governor of mankind and the creator of the world. Here was the monotheistic idea of God which Jesus presented to his followers, and also the concept which attracted Muhammad six hundred years later. Jehovah was no longer merely a national deity, but was universal, omniscient, omnipotent, omnipresent, and merciful as well as just.

In nearby Persia, and less than a century before the Second Isaiah, Zoroaster had exhorted his followers to fight in the ranks of Ahura Mazda, the supreme God, against Angra Mainyu and the forces of evil. Ahura Mazda was the champion of the right or divine order, the supreme good, the personal, moral and helpful deity who ruled the excellent kingdom. Angra Mainyu was the prince of darkness who led the evil forces in opposition to the establishment of the excellent kingdom.[17]

The Christian concept of God is the one most familiar to the Occidental mind. The right attitude towards God was summed up by Jesus in his first commandment, which he quoted from Deuteronomy 6:4–5:[18] "Hear, O Israel;

The Lord our God, the Lord is one; and thou shalt love the Lord thy God with all thy heart, and with all thy soul, and with all thy mind, and with all thy strength" (Mark 12:29–30).

In our survey of the idea of God we find the position of Jesus to be almost unique. In no religion except Judaism and Christianity is God so personal that His followers are taught to love Him. That man should fear, obey, respect, submit is general, but the idea that man should love God is unique.

The obverse, that God loves man, is of the same unique quality. Jesus recognized that God was not only omniscient, omnipresent, and omnipotent, but also our loving Father in heaven. Thus God became almost as easily approachable by all of His earthly children as their own earthly fathers. A significant point concerning this concept is that it reversed, in part, the trend of development in the idea of God. The gods of the primitive family were within the home. Then they were taken from the home and, by degrees, placed at an infinite distance from personal relationships so that, in some cases, God became so distant as to disappear from the consciousness of man. Jesus reestablished the personal touch without destroying the universal concept of the supreme creator.

In Islam the concept of God is the culmination of the Jewish and Christian idea. Muhammad said, "Thy Lord—magnify Him!"[19] and presented Allah as the sole, all highest, the supreme deity. Allah is an arbitrary sovereign whose word is the unquestioned law of Islam, the absolute ruler of the world with Muhammad as his prophet. Muhammad's teaching about God is chiefly derived from the teachings of Judaism, although there is some evidence of Christian influence of the Nestorian type. His preaching was adapted to the Arab mind and, in that form, found ready acceptance.

SUMMARY

Voltaire has been quoted as saying that if there were no God it would be necessary to create one. George Foot Moore, in his book *The Birth and Growth of Religion*, seems to argue that man did create his gods as he needed them. From an objective scholarly approach to the history of religion that conclusion is logical but, in my opinion, incomplete. Is it not equally logical to assume from the historical evidence that God exists, and has always existed, and that religion is the progressive growth of the consciousness of that existence? Did not the spherical earth revolve around the sun at the time when man lived upon a flat earth about which the sun revolved? Surely the growth and development of our knowledge in other fields of learning can be compared with our gradual enlightenment in the field of religion and the nature of God.

The existence of a supreme being, or of a central supernatural force, is admitted or more or less vaguely perceived in all higher religions, as we have seen in the development of this chapter. The mass of testimony outlined here has led many to the conclusion that God is. Certainly there is no comparable mass of testimony to the contrary.

We have not reached the final concept of God. While life continues and thought remains unfettered there is continual addition to the evidence concerning this universe and, as our knowledge of the universe broadens, our respect for the creative intelligence deepens. We have now reached the stage where we see God as the creative intelligence, the primary creative force, the cosmic mind which authored the universal laws, establishing order in the universe.

This chapter is not a theological treatise, and is not intended as such. It is the attempt to bring together the

39

simple belief in God which is to be found in the religions of the world, and to give the comparative picture as clearly as possible so that the reader may draw his own conclusions from the evidence presented.

NOTES

1. W. Morgan, *The Nature and Right of Religion* (Edinburgh: Clark, 1926), p. 16.
2. For a detailed discussion of *mana*, see R. R. Marett, *The Threshold of Religion*, (New York: Macmillan, 1914).
3. See *Harvard Theological Review*, April 1945, pp. 77–109.
4. See *National Encyclopedia*, Henry Suzzallo, ed. (New York: Collier, 1935).
5. For detailed discussion of these matters, read M. P. Nilsson, *Greek Popular Religion*, (New York: Columbia University Press, 1940).
6. Scotus Erigena.
7. *Pantheism: The Philosophy of Spinoza*, vol. 2, H. A. Wolfson, ed. (Cambridge: Harvard University Press, 1934), pp. 38–9.
8. The summary given is merely an outline. For an understanding of the various concepts mentioned, the reader should consult J. Hastings, *Encyclopedia of Religion and Ethics* (New York: Scribner's, 1913–22).
9. R. E. Hume, *The World's Living Religions* (New York: Scribner's, 1924, 1944).
10. R. E. Hume, *Treasurehouse of Living Religions* (New York: Scribner's, 1932), p. 71.
11. Ibid., p. 65.
12. S. G. Champion, *The Eleven Religions* (New York: Dutton, 1945), p. 264.
13. R. E. Hume, *Treasurehouse of Living Religions* (New York: Scribner's, 1932), p. 17.
14. Ibid., p. 14.
15. J. H. Breasted, *The Dawn of Conscience* (New York: Scribner's, 1933), p. 280.
16. Ibid., p. 320.
17. For some difference between Ahura Mazda and the God of Christianity see Chapter 2, p. 47.
18. Deuteronomy 6:4,5 reads: "Hear, O Israel: Jehovah our God is one Jehovah: and thou shalt love Jehovah thy God with all thy heart, and with all thy soul, and with all thy might".
19. Robert O. Ballou, *The Bible of the World* (New York: Viking, 1939), p. 1290.

CHAPTER II
FROM DUTY TO LOVE

The distinction between duty and love which will be made in these pages is the difference between compulsion and voluntary action. Although the fulfillment of obligations is the same in either case, there is a difference in spirit, in attitude toward those obligations, stemming from the concept of God held by the various religious groups, as outlined in the preceding chapter.

The sense of duty is found in the earliest forms of religious worship, while the idea of love comes fairly late in the evolution of religion. Duty was impressed upon the people of earlier times through fear of retribution. They must perform certain rights or suffer dire consequences to themselves, their families, or their possessions.

The primitive peoples felt the duty to conform to custom much more strongly than the conservative people feel it today. In fact, the sense of duty was evidently the primary, if not the only, motivating force in their daily life, in which our distinction between religious and secular activities was unknown. They sacrificed a portion of all that they had in order to placate the spirits or gods, or to induce them to grant continued fertility and prosperity. If the crops were poor, the hunting or fishing inadequate, the gods must be angry; and sacrifice was the only known means of appeasing them.

The savage in the most primitive state of existence observed strict taboos in order to protect himself from

41

unknown dangers. These taboos, or prohibitions, could be neglected only at the risk of life and property. The taboo is "a prohibition of acts and contacts immediately dangerous to the doer and through him to his group. The word comes from the Pacific area where taboo was expanded into a technique of social control. When the scientists began the study of religions the term was used generally to indicate the caution signs set up by groups to guard against things and actions inherently dangerous. The attitudes involved in the taboo belong to the earliest phase of culture when man was making his first faltering steps toward group security in a world little understood and filled with potential menace."[1]

One who ignored these taboos was in danger from his community as well as from his gods or spirits. The anger of the spirits against the one who angered them or who neglected them might endanger the rest of the tribe or clan. The tribesman could not chance the result of any infractions and drove out the offending member, or killed him. In such action we can mark the first growth of the sociological concept. The heresy trials which appear in the records of recent years mark the enduring quality of the primitive fear which caused taboo violators to be exiled or killed in the earliest period of our civilization.

The sense of duty that was established under the compulsion of the taboos prompted the people to supply the necessities of life to the gods and, incidentally, to the priests and shamans, who acted as interpreters between men and the spirit world. The sacrificial offerings designated for the spirits, totems or gods, were duties upon which the priests insisted and from which they received their sustenance.

Duty, in the mythological religions, was determined by the state, which set the minimum requirements upon individuals. The Greeks were required to observe two feast days each year, in which some sacrifices were made. However, guilty consciences or the desire for prosperity might bring the individual to the holy places at times other than those specified for the state festivals.[2] However, gods and men worked independently of each other for the most part. If a man was faithful in the performance of his duties, he escaped Moira (Fate); but if he was not faithful, Moira pursued him relentlessly until he received his punishment from which there was no escape.

Judaism, throughout its history, has shown a strict and highly developed sense of duty. Jehovah demanded definite duties of his people and the moral or ceremonial obligations could not be ignored or avoided, since the divine commands were outlined in specific legal codes so that there could be no question concerning man's obligation in any given instance. Judaism was a theocracy and all law was revealed by God, every obligation being equally binding since it was divinely ordained. Consequently, the violation of any law was a flouting of God's will.

The emphasis upon duty in the smaller particulars brought out a characteristic in Judaism which is found, in a similar degree, in only one other religion, Islam. That characteristic is the fulfillment of the law, the maintenance of the covenant relationship between man and God and between man and man. Such a position cannot be attained without strict adherence to a body of revealed law, which is the basis of the covenant or contract. This produced the consciousness of righteousness as an individual responsibility in the acceptance of the covenant.[3]

Perhaps the distinction can be drawn more clearly in this way: righteousness is the prescribed obedience to the law of God; goodness is the voluntary acceptance of the will of God. Such a distinction could be called arbitrary and, perhaps, even academic, since there is no clear-cut distinction in practice, although there is a difference in emphasis.

In Judaism all duties are clearly specified, first in the scriptures, especially in the Torah, and later in the rabbinical definitions found in the Mishna, Midrash, and Talmud. There are the duties toward Jehovah which are most important and include the duties toward His ministers, the priests, who are responsible for the temple worship. Duties toward the family are sharply drawn and family relationships are defined. A list of duties of master toward servant and of servant toward master are included, and even the use and care of domestic animals, with the special attention to work animals and beasts of burden, are the subject of special commandments. An example of the thoroughness of the delineation of the last mentioned duties is the injunction that prevents the farmer from muzzling his oxen while they tread out his grain on the threshing floor.

So far in our discussion we could have used the word "duty" in the plural throughout and, perhaps, have been more accurate, because duty was made quite concrete by the law and customs of the people which outlined the duties of men in the exercise of their religious life. The difference between "duties" and "duty" is made clear when we turn our attention to the religions of Southern and Eastern Asia. In these sections the mystical approach to God makes the operation of duty less specific, although no less important.

There is one exception to this general pattern, which might be said to prove the rule, since the difference is not discernible in Shinto for the reason that the Japanese have never reached the heights of philosophic thought attained by the other Oriental peoples. In Shinto the idea of duty is broken down into many required observances, and religion did not escape the formalization which is characteristic of all life in Japan. The rituals of Shinto must be performed with exactness and close attention to detail, the duties of the worshiper being carefully defined for every act from ceremonial purification to prayer.

Shrines play an important part in Shinto, and every duty concerning the construction, maintenance, and use of any shrine is outlined in detail. Each household maintains its family shrine, before which offerings are placed and prayers recited. Wayside shrines are the responsibility of the community, unless they happen to be constructed by one of the ruling families as a public demonstration of devotion to the emperor, in which case they are the responsibility of the ruling family.

It is in China that we find duty set up as the most important factor in life. Confucius based his whole ethical sytem upon it because, to him, duty was the primary virtue in life and the path of duty was the road along which man's will must be directed. Filial piety, then, was the highest of virtues, because obedience to one's father was the first step in the proper ways of life. Whoever obeyed his father would obey the magistrate, and the governor of the province, and the emperor, and the god of his ancestors. Thus the path of duty was obligatory for everyone from emperor to peasant.

Lao-tze also maintained that duty was central in life. However, his emphasis was different from that of Confucius. In Taoism the supreme duty is self-mastery. When the self has been completely subjugated, nothing is left but the blissful state of inaction. Then duty evaporates because there is no further need for concentrated effort.

India has made little positive contribution to the idea of duty. However, its contribution, even though of a negative nature, is important to our understanding of the whole picture of religion. In a religious concept based upon the relentless moving of fate, duty has little part. Man needs a certain freedom of will if duty is to be operative.

In Hinduism there is a fatalism that makes duty a part of fate. Man's course is set and his caste is determined through no choice of his. Concentrated effort may speed the process of transmigration, but man cannot jump the cycle through any effort on his own part. His duty is to accept his lot and to make it as easy as possible for himself through that acceptance.

The Jains maintained a refinement of the same general attitude. The chief duty for all the followers of Jainism is the maintenance of an attitude of asceticism so that the evils of life could not have a damaging influence. The man who could most completely separate himself from all sense of relationship with the world around him had the best chance of liberation. Attachment to things should be avoided, and the duties of the saint included repentance, renunciation, the practice of equanimity, and the relinquishment of any bodily attachment.

So far we have been considering a phase of duty that is primarily centered upon the individual, and which prompted each person to think of himself. The methods used to enforce the observance of duty were aimed at the individual, appealing either to the impulse of fear through the threat of swift retribution, or to the impulse of hope through the promise of peace or oblivion. As we pursue our investigation we find a variation of this theme that approaches altruism, and which places duty on a higher plane than that of self-interest.

Sikhism has the definite positive duties received from Islam and, although these duties are overlaid with Hindu mysticism, their origin is unmistakable. The duty toward God is that of reverence and worship because God is all-highest. One's duty toward self and fellow men is that which befits a child of God, and herein lies the subtle change in emphasis. Being a child of God places certain responsibilities upon the individual as regards his treatment of other men, not because he will gain anything for himself but because his privileged position demands it. As a child of God he must be willing to forgive injuries, to do no evil to any person, to distress no one's heart, to be compassionate, to give alms, to utter no disagreeable word; duties which befit his station in life, to be done without any expectation of reward or of benefit to himself.

Zoroaster placed a similar emphasis upon duty when he explained it as being responsibility. In Zoroastrianism each man must bring himself into the excellent kingdom through his own efforts, and it was his duty to see that his works deserved the consideration of Ahura Mazda. Ahura was the supreme being and ruler of the excellent kingdom but was not expected to help man after he was instructed in his duties.[4] Man was expected to speak the truth, to be honest in all of his dealings, to keep treaties and promises faithfully, to be generous to the poor, to live industriously, to cultivate the land and to look after the cattle. Duty well done and work accomplished were the only paths of entrance into the excellent kingdom.

Aside from the general duties discussed under Sikhism, Islam has a definite stand on the nature and extent of duty. A good Muslim must face Mecca in prayer five times a day; he must make the pilgrimage to Mecca at least once during his lifetime, and while in Mecca on that pilgrimage he must perform certain ritual duties, which the Koran describes in detail. As a Muslim, moreover, he must give alms to the poor and win converts to Islam; his good fortune must be shared with those around him. The discipline of duty was one of the most valuable features of early Islam because it brought into being the first well-disciplined army of that whole region. This disciplined army made possible the rapid spread of Islam in both East and West within a century after the death of Muhammad. Such discipline was possible because the Muslim believed that duty performed brought a sure reward to the faithful.

In the shift from the compulsion of duty, even at the stage where duty takes on some altruistic aspects, to the voluntary action of love there is an intermediate period in which a part of both positions is in evidence. This position is not to be taken in the evolutionary sense because the shift in emphasis is not to be found within any single religious culture, since such a change in emphasis in one religion would produce a cleavage which would force the establishment of two separate groups, as history has often demonstrated.

To show the way in which the transition is made in religious thought, we turn to Buddhism as a primary example. There are suggestions of change in other religions but the abstract transition from duty to love is most clearly seen in the teachings of the Buddha. The affirmative position is approached through negations, but the harshness of strict duty is softened by attitudes which introduce the more pleasant aspects of cooperation.

Tolerance is the essence of duty to the Buddhist, illustrated in the principle that one should bring no offense or hurt to man or animal. The gentleness implicit in such an attitude relaxes the stern quality of duty and brings the softening touch of mercy into man's approach to life. Tolerance is made a requisite in the fulfillment of the fifth step of "the noble eight-fold path": Right Livelihood. In the explanation of this precept it is decreed that man shall bring hurt to no living thing; further, he shall bring danger neither to man nor other creatures.

Such an injunction has far-reaching social and economic ramifications which are not, however, fully exploited in the Buddhist teachings; but the basis for a fuller social consciousness is there. The position is so broad that the Buddhists in general tend to overlook its implications through limiting interpretations. This habit of limitations is by no means confined to the Buddhists!

The first of the "Eight undying holy precepts" is closely related to the fifth step of "the noble eight-fold path"; "One should not destroy life." Both principles show a respect for any living thing unusual in religious customs prior to the Christian era. The observance of such principles removes compulsion from duty; it makes virtue spontaneous and living a joyful cooperation.

The Buddhists show a spirit of cooperation with the life force, which is carried out in order to preserve that which was created. Life should be held sacred, not because any living thing might be a friend or relative in transmigratory form, but because life is the soul of the universe. Respect for all manifestations of life is respect for the world-soul, which is the only portion of immortality revealed to man. The desire to assist in the completion of the life-plan is prompted by a spirit of courtesy and consideration, rather than by a strict sense of duty. Nonresistance is the natural expression of this point of view.

A suggestion of the transition from duty to love is found in the Judeo-Christian tradition itself. It is not as clearly a median position as in Buddhism but it lends itself to interesting speculation. The prophet Hosea taught that loyalty is fundamental and that it inspires dutiful behavior even when that behavior is not appreciated. However, Hosea was concerned more with God's love than with man's love, but his knowledge of God's love was brought home to him through his own love for his faithless wife. Hosea had married a woman of unchaste disposition, although the evil tendencies that were within her had not yet manifested themselves.[5] He loved her dearly, but his love was not strong enough to prevent her from leaving him, either for a series of lovers or for the licentious rites connected with Baal worship. In spite of all this, Hosea still loved his wife and he sought her out, buying her back and resuming life with her.[6] From this experience Hosea saw the lesson Jehovah wished him to teach Israel, that the love of God was unchanging and that He wanted His people to turn from their evil ways and return to the ways of righteousness.

Jesus substituted love for duty in his concept of religion because he wanted man to come voluntarily to the right way of living. Since God was the loving Father, man should be the respectfully loving son without the necessity of compulsion, and should be willing to cooperate in all points with the Father.

This position evolved from duty as Jesus had learned duty through his lessons in the religion of his people, but it was from the duty as expressed in Deuteronomy and stated in the great commandment (Deut. 6:4–5) which was far removed from the idea of duty that was expressed by the Pharisaic viewpoint of his own time. It was the decadence of the idea of duty in Judaism against which Jesus was struggling, not the law of Judaism itself.

The whole of Jesus' teaching springs out of his Judaistic background and the concept of love he expresses is his interpretation of the sense of duty so plainly marked in Judaism. The change in approach was a part of his effort to reach a higher level than the rigid legalism and the artificial formalism that governed the Judaism of his experience. The law of Moses was the first step and was accepted by Jesus as such, but the law of God is the second step, and a much more difficult one because the law of God is the law of love. Thus love replaced duty in the evolution of religious thought within the Judeo-Christian field.

The seventh beatitude blesses the peacemakers. Jesus saw no reason for hatred or strife, and although he was born into a nation under foreign domination he did not show hatred or fear of the Roman rulers. Nor did he enjoin hatred or demand love. He simply observed that love was the better way, that peace-making was a blessed personal characteristic. It should be the desire of the people, not their duty, to make peace.

Stronger advice came from Jesus when he told his followers to love their enemies. The religions of the East taught submission, as Mahatma Gandhi has demonstrated to the twentieth century. But love for one's enemies, the soft answer that would turn away wrath, the turning of the other cheek—all these attitudes were new with Jesus. He taught that one would profit most by returning good for evil. Incomprehensible!

The radical change in religious disposition which Jesus effected can be understood best when the new dispensation is contrasted with the prevailing attitude of the times in which he lived. His people were Semites, and blood revenge had held a prominent place for centuries among their traditions and had not entirely died out. The Semites, especially the Arab tribes, believed that an indemnity of an eye for an eye and a tooth for a tooth must be exacted. If a tribesman was killed, his friends and relatives had to kill the guilty party or a member of that man's tribe. Blood feuds were the order of the day in the desert, and to ignore the obligation of revenge was a sign of cowardice, which was punished by ostracism or death.

The people who were not members of the tribes, even

51

though there was no question of blood revenge, were fair game for capture and enslavement. The revenue from the pillage of their villages was a means of supporting the government, as was the sale or barter of captives.

Into this atmosphere Jesus came with his teaching of love. To him it was God's wish that men should live in peace and harmony, that neighbor should love neighbor; this he taught as a fundamental concept of the way to live. Here Jesus stated in concrete terms the abstract idea of the Buddhists. By the same statement he threatened the economic structure of the tribes, and the social structure as well.

Jesus upheld love as the greatest of all virtues. He witnessed the workings of fear on the people around him, engendered by the legalistic Jewish system, and knew the corrosive effect of that system upon them. As Paul, writer of many New Testament epistles, said:

"I had not known sin, except through the law: for I had not known coveting, except the law had said, Thou shalt not covet: but sin, finding occasion, wrought in me through the commandment all manner of coveting: for apart from the law sin is dead. And I was alive apart from the law once: but when the commandment came, sin revived, and I died; and the commandment, which was unto life, this I found to be unto death: for sin, finding occasion, through the commandment beguiled me, and through it slew me."[7]

Jesus believed also that the multitude of religious duties outlined in the law cramped the mind and crippled the understanding. To reform the idea of duty which ruled Judaism, and to eliminate the fear which negated the values of religion for the majority of the people, Jesus taught love. In his picture, God was the loving Father, and it was natural to assume tender family relationship between the loving heavenly Father and His earthly children. Wherever the idea took root Jesus was able to bring men into close communion with God through the notion of love, and the same idea brought men together in a common bond of fellowship wherever it was accepted.

The bloody history of orthodox Christianity shows that the followers of Jesus were not ready to accept the idea of love which he taught. However, the contrast between the gospel message and Christian practice emphasizes the tremendous advance made by Jesus in the idea of man's relation to God, as well as the radical change he advocated in human relationships.

SUMMARY

The evolution of the idea of duty shows the changes advocated by religious leaders in the attitude of man toward God, and toward his fellow men. Bigotry and selfishness give way to tolerance and altruism. Hatred and distrust are replaced by consideration and understanding. Religion becomes a pleasant experience rather than a terrifying task. In an historical sense this is inaccurate because the higher plane of religion has been attained more by the recurrent reforms than by the main stream of religious development.

Jesus used the key of love to unlock all of the treasures of religion. These treasures were available to any seeker after truth, but such liberality was distressing to the heirs of the founder. They forged new bonds of duty to keep the treasure within the confines of the community and to keep out of it the best that the other great religious leaders had to offer, all done in the name of duty.

Love means a broad and tolerant sympathy and a willingness to accept truth from every available source. It means the eagerness to share undiscovered truth with all who wish to know. In the teaching of Jesus, love made the world a brotherhood. It was a fundamental virtue and the essence of religious life.

Love is a common denominator in religion. Through love the East can understand the West, and through love the West can learn the truth underlying Eastern mysticism. Love, rather than duty, is fundamental to worldwide understanding and cooperation. The conclusion of this survey may be stated thus: Duty is the pathway, love the goal, of man's relationship to God and to his fellow men.

NOTES

1. *An Encyclopedia of Religion* (New York: Philosophical Library, 1945), p. 759.
2. For instances of this practice, turn to the accounts in the *Iliad* and *Odyssey* of individuals making pilgrimages to holy places.
3. Although Christianity sprang from the same covenant tradition, there is a different emphasis upon duty which will be discussed below.
4. See Chapter 1, p. 37.
5. Hosea 1:1–9.
6. Hosea 3:1–3.
7. Romans 7:7–11.

CHAPTER III
GOOD AND EVIL

This chapter is intended to serve as an introduction to the three that follow: "Purity," "Knowledge," and "Conduct." It is not the purpose of the writer to discuss the problem of good and evil, because no such discussion confined to a single chapter could be adequate. We will confine ourselves to a survey of how the different religions explain, combat, and overcome evil.

Many books treat only the problem of evil, but they seem to confuse more than they clarify the subject because there is no general agreement on the definition of evil. An arbitrary definition would be that evil is the absence of good. Yet that leaves one the task of defining good, which task can be avoided by completing the circle and saying that good is the absence of evil.

Good and evil are presented in their relation to three fundamental concepts of religion in the following chapters. The brief account of evil given here has the purpose of outlining the various attitudes of great religious leaders toward the problem, as shown in the practices of various religious groups. One observation may be of value at this point. Natural evil, which has given our more recent writers so much concern, was seldom considered evil by the earlier religious leaders. Famine, pestilence, flood, and earthquake were accepted by them rather as punishment. The evil lay in the sinfulness on the part of man which brought down catastrophe upon the people.

The primitive attitude toward evil was the basis for the attitudes found in the historic living religions. We shall therefore begin our survey with a glimpse of the primitive efforts to control and direct man's destiny. According to primitive man evil was present everywhere. He felt that he was responsible for it but did not always know just how to avoid the actions which brought on trouble. Evil was everything that he could not understand or explain, and the explanation of calamity and salvation from evil rested primarily on the shoulders of the shaman or priest.

Primitive man observed numerous taboos as a protection from evil, strict rules of conduct that described the limits of his activity and defined his responsibility, and which must be obeyed exactly. If he remained within the limits of the tribal taboos, he had some hope of influencing, within the spirit world, the mana that was the essence or driving force, the motivating energy of the spirits or gods, and could bring good or evil to man.

Disease, famine, or any form of disaster was thought to come either from the unexplained action of a demon, or from the violation of a taboo. Regarding the action of demons, Wilhelm Wundt writes:

> The more suddenly [disease and Death] arrived, the more they demanded an answer to the question of their origin. But how could primitive man conceive this origin otherwise than in the form of his own decision and acts? . . . The demon which appears in a dream or in the hallucinations resulting from high fever is the bringer of disease and death. But even where the demon does not appear, the coming and going of these chimeric images shows clearly that for them there is hardly any limitation of time and space. So originates the notion that the will may be active even where the one who wills is not present, and that he may produce effects from a distance through magical

means—which, in the last analysis always go back to an action of a soul on another. The evil eye, as also sympathetic magical rites and formulas are the most widespread of these means.[1]

In some cases, when a taboo was violated, the spirit entered into a man and made him ill, the violation of the taboo being the explanation of the action. Such a condition called for concentrated efforts to drive or scare the spirit away again, or the employment of bribery or enticement by means of elaborate promises or a plate of special food.

The system of sacrifice was founded, at least in part, upon the idea of payment for evil done, or advance payment to protect man from evil which might be done in the future through ignorance. As an example of this last condition, an Arab might kill a Djinn by the simple act of tossing a date pit to the sand while he was eating. Offerings to the spirits or gods and regular penance in a holy place were preventive measures among the primitives.

The full consequences of evil acts or thought could be avoided through public confession of faults. The wearing of amulets or medals was a preventive practice that appears to be almost universal among primitive and illiterate people of the earlier civilizations. These practices are familiar to us in the twentieth century of the Christian era. The primitive also tried the practice of changing his name, thinking that by such an act he would change his identity and escape the evil that might be allied to his former self.

With this brief account as a background let us turn our attention to the living religions of the world.[2]

Some religions in the world do not recognize the presence of evil, while others regard all existence as evil. Dualistic systems conclude that the world is half good and half evil. Yet even those who treat evil as though it did not exist, by their ethical position admit that man can wander from the path of virtue.

There is little or no consciousness of evil as a tangible force in the teachings of four of the eleven living religions; Shinto, Confucianism, and Taoism in the Far East and Hinduism in India. The religions of India which grew out of Hinduism did not accept the Hindu position in this regard.

There is no obvious consciousness of evil in Shinto because the belief is that the Japanese are all "god-people" and need no moral code to save them, since they possess that essential divinity. What evil there may be is accidental and nobody is responsible for it. The two types of offenses listed in Shinto are the closest to a definition of evil that the religion provides. There are five heavenly offenses and three earthly offenses listed by Archer. Heavenly offenses: 1. Skinning alive. 2. Breaking down the divisions between rice fields. 3. Filling up the irrigation ditches. 4. Marriage between unequals. 5. Human intercourse with beasts. Earthly offenses: 1. The cutting of living or dead bodies. 2. Killing of animals. 3. Intercourse of a man with his mother, daughter, mother-in-law, or stepdaughter.[3]

Salvation for the individual is through ritual purification: "Revere the gods, keep the heart pure, and follow its dictates."[4] For the whole nation the purification comes during the period of the great purification ceremony at the close of each half year. This is called the *Oho-harahi* (Great Purification) and includes a preliminary lustration, expiatory offerings, and the recitation of a formula by the Mikado which declares to all his subjects the absolution of their sins and impurities. The ceremony is held on the last days of the sixth and twelfth months.[5]

The native religions of China are almost equally lacking in evidence of a consciousness of evil. The great sage,

Confucius, saw man as inherently good, and taught that there was no evil as an active force in the world. "Man is born for uprightness. If a man loses his uprightness and yet live, his escape from death is a mere accident."[6] The implied evil, as we should call it, came through the failure of responsible men to fulfill their appointed tasks. The leader must lead and the follower must follow, and lack of proper leadership or of obedient subordination was charged to the individual who was responsible for the breach.

The fundamental sin[7] was any form of social or political impropriety. Any offense against the state was an ignoble act that would bring shame upon the man and his ancestors. Salvation was open to all who observed the rules of social correctness and political propriety; "Loyalty and good faith marked every man, and chastity and submissiveness graced every woman."[8] The same applied to national salvation: correct behavior at all times, the setting of a correct pattern or conduct for those who looked up for guidance, perfect form in government. "Order is Heaven's only law."[9]

The teachings of Lao-tze are more difficult to bring into focus on the problems of evil. There is so much of the quality of mystical escapism in Taoism that one is never sure of catching the correct meaning in the writings. The amount of evil in the world seems to vary in proportion to the ability of the individual Taoist to escape the world. For the holy man there is very little evil, but for the novice there is much. When man has withdrawn, he is not responsible for what evil remains in the world. Yet the individual is primarily responsible for the evil that results from his own actions. "Those who do evil in the open light of day, men will punish them. Those who do evil in secret, God will punish them."[10]

The Taoist saint has no idea of evil. Yet Moore[11] mentions the evils of Taoism as: Force,[12] Overgovernment,[13] and "Drought and fire, and evil doings by individuals; punished in the ten regions of hell."[14] Salvation from these evils is by the faithful adherence to Tao (The Way), which includes mastery over self and refusal to rule over others or to use force at any time. There is no national program of salvation because the nation cannot withdraw all at one time. Withdrawal can only come from the individual efforts of men. The empire must not be ruled because it exists as a divine trust. Since one of the chief evils is over-government, the best government is that which governs least and the perfect state is that in which no government is observable, which follows the course of nature.

Mysticism in India makes the definition of evil difficult and early Hinduism is quite vague on the whole subject. However, in later Indian religions there is a definiteness which allows clearer treatment of the idea of evil.

There is no distinct consciousness of evil in the Hindu faith. The existing misery which pervades all life seems to be the direct momentary result of man's error, rather than to come from the presence of sustained evil in the world. Since there is no consciousness of evil, no one can be held responsible; yet there is that temporary mistaking, due to individual error.

Hume says that neither the individual nor the eternal Brahma is responsible because of the fact that illusion is inherent in existence. Yet Widgery brings out the point that individual error in conduct or in worship would make the god angry with the individual, and unwilling to protect him or allow him to prosper.

So we have a vague position in Hinduism concerning the problem of evil in the world. On the one hand, it is the temporary illusion of apparent individuality that is due to ignorance of man's relationship to his environment, and, on the other, "Evil is an invisible and highly contagious substance,"[15] which is responsible in some way for such conditions as disease and pollution or guilt.

The result of the vague concept of evil among the Hindus is a mystical position in regard to salvation. There is no plan of salvation for society as a whole, because the caste system is rigid and continuous. However, the individual may secure salvation through certain paths of activity and attitude, concentrating on his religious devotion and paying special heed to ceremonial obligations. The individual needs to acquire knowledge of the Brahma, and must encourage the state of rapture which will bring him into contact with the mystery of life. There are suggestions of what amounts to the use of magic in early Hinduism. The transference of guilt to an enemy is an accepted practice, as is the use of the scapegoat. There is strong emphasis upon the need for purification, showing a worthy moral idea inherent in the faith: "No purification is indeed ultimate if, when it has been done, the mind walks again in the evil path."[16]

Buddhism presents a strong contrast to Hinduism; to the Buddhist the misery pervading all life becomes so real and so overpowering that all existence is regarded as evil. The whole attention is directed toward overcoming such condition, and the consciousness of evil has tremendous influence upon, in fact determines, the entire structure of Buddhist thought. Man is not responsible for the existence of so much evil in the world, but the "desires and lusts of men are responsible for the misery of existence."[17]

The reality and essence of evil lies in the insatiability of desires and lusts that are inherent in man's nature. Individuality and activity in themselves produce sad results for man. Unrighteous actions are the expression of evil,

61

and the three cardinal sins of Buddhism become sensuality, ill will, and stupidity.

Salvation from this evil existence for the individual depends on the destruction of these three cardinal sins, by the suppression of all desires and lusts, by complete escape from individuality and from all activity, thereby overcoming the necessity of further rounds of rebirth. Social salvation is obtained through the eradication of all caste divisions, the establishment of the monastic community, or the fleeing from all society into solitude, "One's own peace could be found only in seeking peace for all humanity."[18]

Jainism seems to strike the middle position between Hinduism and Buddhism with a dualistic idea of the world in which half of all existence is evil and half is good. And since the world itself is inherently dualistic, there can be no individual responsibility for the existence of evil. Yet the individual can create evil within himself through lack of self-control.

Evil, to the Jains, is the vile material body which hampers the eternal spirit of the individual. There are seven vices the Jains must avoid: prostitution, adultery, drinking any intoxicant, meat eating, gambling, thieving, inflicting injury on any living creature.

The avoidance of these evils or vices and the rigid control of the desires of the flesh through self-mastery will free the spirit of the individual and bring him salvation. He is urged to center his attention upon the virtues of spiritual life. "To salvation three things are necessary, right faith, right knowledge, right living—the so-called Three Jewels."[19]

Salvation is an individual matter to the Jains, and there is no interest in the question of social salvation. The religious man is an ascetic, and asceticism is conceived as an individual rather than a collective practice. The ascetic practices unusual self-denial and devotion as a religious discipline, and is rigorously abstinent, a position which would be difficult to maintain on a community basis or on a national scale.

While it must be remembered that Sikhism is not exclusively Indian in its religious assumptions, still it is native to India in its origin and practice. Thus the interpretation of the religious position of Sikhism is Indian even though Islam was one of its parents.

The Sikhs look upon present existence as an evil age and, for them, evil is everywhere. The individual is responsible for the evil that exists: "I have suffered the consequences of my acts: I may blame no one else."[20] This attitude is similar to the position of the Buddhists, although there is a more definite plan of salvation.

Evil, to the Sikh, is the alienation from God which results in the suffering of continued deaths and rebirths. Evil is sin, and there are five deadly sins which keep man from God: falsehood, fraud, theft, slander, and fornication. Salvation for the individual is impossible through his own efforts, and the round of rebirths is continued as long as man is guilty of any of these sins.

The saving grace of God is the only means by which man can be released from the round of deaths and births. Thus salvation for the individual depends upon a moral life and devotion to God: "My soul, turning away from sin, is absorbed in the Universal Soul."[21] This attitude brings to mind a brief statement that Jesus made: "With men it is impossible, but not with God: for all things are possible with God."[22]

In Sikhism, social salvation is based upon two principles: first, society must accept the ethical precepts of the Sikh teachers; second, all distinctions of race and caste must be eliminated. These principles bring the community into the scope of moral life and give opportunity for all to show their devotion to God. In Sikhism, rites and ceremonies are not the final tests of true religion and contain no intrinsic value.

The Zoroastrians and the Jains differ in their systems of dualism, but the position regarding the existence of evil is very similar. To the Zoroastrian, half of all existence is evil. The realm of darkness is in opposition to the realm of light, or the excellent kingdom. The dualism is so clear cut that the forces of evil are blamed for all that is wrong in the world. Angra Mainyu is the leader of the realm of darkness, in opposition to Ahura Mazda and the realm of light.

According to this dualistic position the very opposition between the forces of good and the forces of evil is virtually bad. That natural opposition, inherent in any dualistic concept, produces the dangers to which man is exposed, because having free choice he can choose the evil and, thereby, bring it into active relationship to his own life.

To avoid evil and to escape Angra Mainyu, man must obey Ahura Mazda. This obedience is guided by the three positive principles: good thoughts, good words, good deeds. The emphasis is upon the last principle, that of good deeds. "It was not prayer but work that was demanded of the worshippers of Ahura Mazda."[23]

The plan of social salvation is rather indefinite in Zoroastrianism, although there is the suggestion of a plan in the idea of agricultural improvement promoted by Zoroaster. Efforts toward the maintenance of stable order were encouraged with the promise that Good would be triumphant in the last days. "Ahura Mazda was in essence the spirit of civilization, and the only worship acceptable to him was the spreading of order and stability."[24]

According to the teaching of Judaism evil is widespread and dominant. Whenever Jehovah turns his face away from man, the time becomes an evil time and things go against the people. Man by his actions causes Jehovah to turn his face away, and therefore man is primarily responsible for calamity and suffering.

Causative evil, which brought the judgment of God into operation, includes all moral offenses, laxity, ritual impurity and impropriety, and impurity of soul. The resultant evils, seen by man as evil, are calamities, either natural or personal, which affect the national or individual life. National calamities would be flood, earthquake, military reverses, and epidemics, while individual calamities would include death in the family, personal disease, loss of property, et cetera.

Evil, then, is both national and personal calamity, such as flood, famine, defeat in battle, disease, death, sin, and suffering. Evil includes ritual violations and moral offenses: "We have in some of the Psalms a true spiritual conception of sin as an impurity of soul which makes a barrier between it and God."[25]

"Salvation from sin both for the nation and for the individual is by repentance and divine forgiveness."[26] This idea of salvation gains strength as the religious forms and theology of Judaism develop. Salvation for the ancient Hebrews meant deliverance by God, in battle or otherwise. Later came the reciprocal idea of repentance and forgiveness that carried over into Christianity.

Christianity represents evil as terrible and widespread. Even though man is potentially good, error is expected in human life and all men actually do fall short of the ideal. In falling short, they fail to complete their duty to God or their neighbor.

By and large, within the Christian systems, man is

responsible for evil because he chooses evil rather than good through the exercise of his free will.[27] God, then, becomes responsible for the possibility of evil because he gave free will to man. The evil itself is the misuse of free will and any injury resulting from that misuse.

Salvation for the individual is through the correct use of free will; through love to God and love toward neighbor; through selfless service; and finally through the grace of God. That is the simple definition of salvation which Jesus taught the people of his day. It would not hold true as an accurate definition in orthodox Christianity today.[28]

World salvation is stressed more in Christianity than in any other religion because Jesus wished to redeem all of mankind and his teachings applied to society as a whole even more than it did to individuals. In fact, the social consciousness of the individual was a requisite for his personal salvation according to the teaching of Jesus. The individual and society, of which he was an essential member, were to bring about the kingdom of God on earth and this would be the salvation of the world.

Within Islam there can, on the whole, be no evil: *Islam* means submission. The evil is outside Islam and will be found among the unbelievers. Responsibility for evil rests upon those who refuse to believe and their unbelief brings the judgment of God upon them. When a believer becomes insubordinate to God's will he becomes an unbeliever and is under the judgment. Thus the evil that exists in the world is the lack of complete submissiveness to God and His prophet. Pride and disloyalty are offenses of high degree and *Shirk,* or associating other forces with God, is unpardonable.

Individual salvation comes through submission to God's will, or "Islam." Faithful adherence to prayer, the giving of alms, fasting in the month of Ramadhan, and obedience to all the teachings of the revealed word of God is expected of all the faithful. There is no definite social salvation except that the body of the faithful is joined together in the holy quest. Islam is a God-directed group with responsibility placed upon each individual within the group.

SUMMARY

Obviously, good and evil are mere abstract concepts until they are applied to events and attitudes. They remain in the realm of speculation until defined by rules and prohibitions in relation to man and his activity, religious and social. The existence of good and evil is, in most instances, a relative matter rather than an absolute. At least the relative existence is the only one considered in the practical field of conduct.

The extent of evil is determined by the manner in which a given religion approaches the problem of human life. The concept of God, and of man's relationship to God, enters into this approach. Where the idea of God is mystical and hazy, the problem of evil is shadowy and almost unreal. Where the idea of God is clear cut, the problem of evil is well defined and directly treated.

If human life is considered to be of great value, the sense of evil is acute. If human life is considered as a necessary but painful step in the ascent of the soul, the sense of evil is dulled. The low expectation from human life leads man to expect evil as an ordinary part of the picture, and to accept its presence without alarm.

The application of the idea of evil to actions and attitudes in the process of living gives us an experiential pattern through which we may make definitions. Yet when we have the pattern of experience we need little definition because of the illustration already drawn.

We have presented the treatment of evil in outline form. Now we will apply the idea of good and evil in concrete instances in the following three chapters on purity, knowledge, and conduct. We would call the attention of the reader again to the fact that we are dealing with the consciousness of the existence of evil in the world, not with the problem of evil from a philosophical point of view. The consciousness of evil can be overcome by the greater consciousness of good, but the problem of evil should be solved or explained and does not come within the scope of this writing.

NOTES

1. Wilhelm Wundt, *Allgemeine Geschichte der Philosophie, Die Kulture der Gegenwart*, I,v. (Berlin: B. G. Teubner, 1909), p. 19.
2. In this the writer uses the method and some of the material found in R. E. Hume, *The World's Living Religions* (New York: Scribner's, 1924, 1944), pp. 254–6.
3. J. C. Archer, *Faiths Men Live By* (New York: Nelson, 1934), p. 151.
4. H. G. Underwood, *Religions of Eastern Asia* (New York: Macmillan, 1910), p. 77.
5. W. G. Ashton, *Shinto (The Way of the Gods)* (London: Longmans, Green, & Co., 1905), pp. 294–5.
6. W. C. T. Tisdall, *Christianity and Other Faiths* (New York: Revell, 1912), Analects VI:7, p. 179.
7. The word here is used in the Greek sense of *hamartano*, meaning "to miss the mark."
8. Lewis Browne, *This Believing World*, (New York: Macmillan, 1928), p. 176.
9. Ibid., p. 181.
10. R. E. Hume, *Treasurehouse of Living Religions* (New York: Scribner's, 1932), p. 46.
11. G. F. Moore, *History of Religion*, 2 vols. (New York: Scribner's, 1919, 1946).
12. Ibid., p. 53.
13. Ibid., p. 54.
14. Ibid., p. 63.

15. Ibid., p. 265.
16. Hume, *Treasurehouse*, p. 44.
17. H. G. Underwood, *Religions of Eastern Asia* (New York: Macmillan, 1910), p. 187.
18. Browne, *This Believing World*, p. 141.
19. Moore, *History of Religion*, p. 281.
20. A. G. Widgery, *Comparative Study of Religions* (London: Williams & Norgate, 1923), p. 251.
21. Hume, *Treasurehouse*, p. 46.
22. Mark 10:27.
23. Browne, *This Believing World*, p. 204.
24. Ibid., p. 204.
25. C. H. Toy, *Judaism and Christianity* (Boston: Ginn & Co., 1913), p. 187.
26. Widgery, *Comparative Study of Religions*, p. 244.
27. Two exceptions: Adam's choice introduced evil into the world, and the philosophic explanation, such as Augustine's *creatio ex nihilo*.
28. Again, we would remind the reader that the comparisons used here are the teachings of the founders as nearly as possible and not the tradition that grew up later among their followers.

CHAPTER IV
PURITY

The sense of purity is universal to religion. In every higher form of religious expression there are definite injunctions to purity in one form or another. Those living in the United States today remember the epigram that comes down from eighteenth-century New England, "Cleanliness is next to godliness." The relationship of cleanliness to godliness was recognized many centuries before the Christian era and in many different sections of the world. The Buddhists and Jains of the sixth century before the Christian era had a definite consciousness of purity which they had inherited from their parent religion, Hinduism.

There are many different aspects of purity which become dominant in the various religions. Some groups stress ceremonial purification, an approach which can only cleanse the outside of the cup, as Jesus accused the Pharisees of doing. The emphasis is placed upon the washing of the body or of special parts of the body to bring about physical purification. And the liturgical purification concentrates on the condition of the altar vessels and temple cloths, on purification of the air by incense, and on the cleansing of the sacrifice by the consuming fire upon the altar.

Other religious groups adopt purity in an entirely different sense. To them there is individual responsibility for mental and physical conditioning. The purity they stress is not ceremonial but personal. Their religious teachings strive to establish the purity of thought, word, and deed. In this sense purity becomes much more than the rite of purification. It is an earnest endeavor to bring about an attitude of mind and heart that is clear and discerning.

Some religious groups use both approaches to purity. They teach the purity of the individual mind and heart and then provide ceremonial purification so that the individual may affirm his inner cleansing through participation in some public avowal of his position.

The emphasis in this chapter will be primarily upon the sense of purity that is personal, because the majority of the world's living religions have the individual position in their laws and teachings. In fact, only one of the living religions places primary emphasis upon ceremonial purification and that one is Shinto.

Judaism has a mixture of the two positions, but individual responsibility is paramount. In the Decalogue there are two injunctions which bring out the necessity of purity of word. In addition to these there are laws which bring out the idea of purity through the description of clean and unclean food, as well as laws which define the steps of ceremonial purification.

The first injunction that commands purity of word is the prohibition of blasphemy: The name of God must not be taken in vain.[1] Just what such a statement implies is open to a wide range of interpretation, and has been given many meanings within the scope of the Jewish Scripture. The narrower sense of this injunction would be the prohibition of oaths used for the purpose of misleading others. Such an interpretation would include perjury as well as false swearing or an oath that was not sincerely taken.[2]

The wider interpretation would include any unworthy use of the name of God by an individual. A glib and formal

71

prayer, repeated from memory and without conscious thought, could be blasphemy. A profession of devotion to God made without sincerity, a calling upon God to do things that would be unworthy acts even on the part of human beings, any confession that did not affect the conscience, all these could be a blasphemy and an example of impure speech.

The second injunction urges purity of word between men through the prohibition of false witness.[3] The strict construction of this commandment would make it apply only to testimony in a court or before some official. Just as a man should not perjure himself before his God, so he should not bring a fellow human into jeopardy through false statements.

The broader interpretation of this prohibition includes calumny and abuse, which is defined in modern times as slander and gossip. One can bear false witness without being in a court under oath. All lies, including misleading half-truths, come under the broader definition of false witness. And just so do all lies or half-truths, whether uttered under oath or in the course of casual conversation, violate the idea of purity of word which Judaism upholds.

The pure food laws of Judaism[4] bring out a different sense of purity, one more applicable to health of the body than of the mind. That there is a definite connection between the condition of the body and that of the mind has been demonstrated by the medical profession in all its branches. However, it is reasonable to assume that the dietary laws of Judaism would be a part of the secular code rather than the religious laws if Judaism had not been a theocratic state.

Yet the dietary laws are worth consideration in the discussion of purity because they bring out the idea that pure food as well as pure thoughts are essential to the health of the whole man. The Jews were among the first to recognize a relationship between the regulation of the diet and the effective functioning of the mind. Many prohibitions had moral implication, such as the injunction against the use of newly fermented wine.

Ceremonial purification played a highly significant part in the religious life of Judaism. One must never eat or offer a sacrifice with unwashed hands. There were laws which protected the sacrifice from defilement and there were instructions to the priests and people alike which showed them how to remove any defilement that might exist. Jesus was concerned about the great emphasis placed upon this aspect of purity during his time because he felt that the priests had grown lax about the moral refinement which was so much more important in his eyes. Jesus saw purity as a personal virtue and he developed his teachings from the purity of word which Judaism had established.

Turning aside from the consideration of living religions for a moment we can trace, in the mythological concepts of Greece, an indirect influence on later Christian morality. The Greeks placed man midway between Zeus and the animal world around him, and this position made it possible to ascribe both spiritual and physical elements to man. Aristotle maintained that man is more than beast. Man's nature was higher than that of the beasts, although it was not on the same plane with the nature of the gods. Since man is higher than the beasts, he must act his part and show himself worthy to be considered a higher being. The beast could not evaluate his actions, but man is able to choose between worthy and unworthy acts. Instinct is purified by reason, and man is able to choose the golden mean because of that purification which has freed him from the bonds of earthly appetites.

Before we take up the position of Christianity regarding purity, we should consider the place which the sense of purity held, and still holds, in the other living religions. Through this comprehensive survey we can determine the fundamental value of purity in religion as well as the fact of its necessity in the opinion of the religious leaders of the world.

Zoroaster made a contribution to the total idea of purity by making it synonymous with piety. The fourth of his undying holy precepts is "Piety, or Holy Character." This, in addition to his first precept, "Good thought," indicates that he believed man capable of making himself good through the process of self-purification.

Purity was a part of the divine order of existence in the opinion of Zoroaster, who showed his followers how to escape the realm of Angra Mainyu through clean thought and through living above reproach. Holy character was attained by the elimination of all evil from the heart and the mind. The best method of eliminating this evil was to concentrate upon the virtues of the excellent kingdom and upon the guidance of Ahura Mazda. Man could achieve divinity through purification.

A different approach to purity is seen in India, due to its mystical approach to religion. Purity here is the way of life of the ascetic, a withdrawal from the usual temptations of earthly existence which removes the chance for contamination and produces an asepsis which is a kind of purity. The passive nature of such purity leads one to suspect its vitality.

In Hinduism it is said that there is no limit to purity and there is no beginning to impurity. During the Vedic period there are references to Deity as the Purifier who can cleanse the people for wisdom and power and life. Later, in the period of the Bhagavad Gita, wisdom is the

74

purifying agent which is more effective than anything else in the world.

Man should take pleasure in truth, justice, and purity at all times, and those who lead pure lives are the only ones who will see the Lord because His form cannot be seen by the eyes of man. The goal of life is reached through purity and understanding. Purity of heart is attained by constant meditation.

Jainism holds that purity is the goal of life for the ascetic and one can reach purity through the practice of austerities. Purity is obtained by the pious who are continually faithful to the Law. Purity brings happiness of mind and a kind disposition, which, in turn, bring purity of character and freedom from fear.

The subjective attitude toward purity is clear in this position although it may take more than one reading to acclimate occidental thinking. We are accustomed to definite rules which outline purity and impurity. By our ethical or sociological yardsticks we can say whether a thing is pure or not; yet we are apt to overlook the fundamental value of purity itself. The Jains visualized purity as an essence to be absorbed into the mind and heart, a cleansing element which must be sought and cherished.

Buddhism expresses the meaning and worth of purity in the same way that the Jains have done. For them purity resides in the individual and is essential in action, speech, and thought. One contribution Buddhism in its early stages made to the thinking of India was sanitation. One could not reach the full meaning of purity amidst dirty surroundings, so the Buddhist was urged to clean up his abode if it was possible to do so. That injunction applied to campsite and temporary abode as well as to the permanent place of residence.

The Buddhist is urged to sustain his life by pure means

so that he will avoid contamination by the impurities of the world. The Samyutta Nikaya gives a poetic illustration of that thought: "Brethren! Just as a dark blue lotus or a white lotus, born in the water, come to full growth in the water, rises to the surface, stands unspotted by the water—even so, brethren, the blessed one, having been born in the world, come to full growth in the world, passing beyond, abides unspotted by the world."[5] Such purity must be within the individual and must be nurtured by faith and by meditation. No external act could be expected to bring about the purification of the individual, neither ceremonies nor any of the self-inflicted discomforts.

The sixth step of the noble eight-fold path is "Right Effort." This idea substantiates the Buddhist position as contrasted with the practices of the fakirs and holy men of India. The principle of right effort means correct self-training and full self-control. The path of purity must be followed inwardly because the only immunity from the evils of the world is the selfless approach to the task of living.

The third of the eight undying holy precepts is in support of pure speech or good words: "One should not tell lies." False witness and perjury are condemned by the Buddhists just as such evils are forbidden by all other religious groups. Purity of word is a worldwide requirement for the religious man, and is believed to mark the existence of a pure mind. Impurity of speech, however, is the mark of the holder of impure thoughts and the doer of questionable deeds.

The strict monotheistic position of Sikhism gives purity the clear position of importance which it holds also in Christianity. If a man knows God, he cannot become contaminated; and if God dwells in his heart, he is pure. The mind is cleansed from sin by the love of God just as polluted clothing is made clean by the application of soap.

76

Guru Nanak, founder of Sikhism, taught purity of mind and body because he believed that purity protected the faithful from defilement. "Impurity of the heart is greed. Impurity of the tongue is falsehood. Impurity of the eyes is gazing on another's wealth, his wife and her beauty. Impurity of the ears is listening to slander. The pious persons who know God, have no impurity."[6]

Shinto emphasizes primarily the purity of body and clothing and ceremonial cleansing. This emphasis was made in the earlier forms of Shinto, before the influence of the Chinese philosophy and religion became noticeable. Today ceremonial purification is of great importance, and one cannot commit suicide in the approved manner without an elaborate ritual of purification in preparation for the act.

The Japanese would not think of going to a shrine or temple without first purifying themselves according to the custom outlined in the teachings of Shinto. They must make their regular trips to the shrines prepared through pure bodies and pure hearts. They must purify themselves before worship, even though the ceremony of purification be performed the previous day. Purification consists of washing the body carefully and making a complete change of clothing. For some ceremonies a special robe is worn.

Shinto absorbed much from the other religions that were introduced into Japan, especially Confucianism and Buddhism. The latter seems to have made the greater degree of change in the idea of purity. Before Buddhism there was almost total emphasis upon the ceremonial purification in Shinto.

After Buddhism had established itself in the islands, there came a change in the idea concerning purity. The purity of the body was still stressed but the need for a pure heart appeared in the statements of the Shinto oracles. The worshiper must pray with heart purified from falsehood so that he is clean within as well as without. The human heart must be kept unperverted, and those who have upright hearts are as flowers which unfold their pure beauty under the warmth of the sun. This last reference is strikingly similar to the quotation from the Samyutta Nikaya.

An ancient Chinese proverb states that there is no pure knowledge without pure men. Both Confucius and Lao-Tse were interested in man's purity, yet each had his particular trend of application of purity within the individual.

Taoism makes essential purity a prize to which the sage aspires. Thus purity becomes an end, the aim of life and the promise of wisdom and contentment. Since the purpose of Taoism is withdrawal, the man who is able to withdraw most completely is he who has purified himself from anything which might hold him to the life around him.

Confucianism, on the other hand, maintains that the head of the household must be pure so that his wife and children may have the advantage of his good example. If the head of the family strays from the right path of life, he may be held responsible for the error of any of his family. The same position is taken in regard to those in authority at each level of society, up to and including the emperor. Purity of thought, word, and action is essential to good government on every level.

In the teaching of Muhammad, individual responsibility for purity is central. "Thy raiment—purify it" is the law of the Koran, but that alone does not express the attitude of Islam toward purity. Muhammad advised his followers to keep themselves free from contaminating influences and used clean robes as an illustration of what he meant. He realized that a man was influenced by the condition of his body and clothing. If he was immaculate in dress, his attitude toward life and toward his fellow men was good. If he was unclean and ragged, his attitude was bad.

Muhammad used the symbol of outward cleanliness as a constant reminder to his followers of all the laws concerning purity. the discipline which he brought to the Arabs was a part of this same idea, a singleness of purpose and of interest which was not to be contaminated by impurity of thought or slothfulness. Happiness comes to the man who purifies himself because God loves those who seek to be clean. God purifies man, and it is only through His grace and mercy that man can attain purity. Yet man must show his willingness to be pure through his efforts and by his prayers. This is the effort which clean raiment reminds man to make every day.

Jesus was the champion of inner purity and the outspoken foe of ceremonial purification, which cleansed only the outside of the cup. He often referred to those who made much of ritual cleansing and the wearing of proper robes in terms of derision. To him they were wolves in sheep's clothing, outwardly pious but inwardly ravening. The law of God must be upheld by inner compulsion rather than by outward show of assent and conformity.[7]

This included also the laws concerning the observance of the sabbath which, according to the Pharisees, Jesus violated repeatedly.

And it came to pass, that he was going on the sabbath day through the grainfields; and his disciples began, as they went, to pluck the ears. And the Pharisees said unto him, "Behold, why do they on the sabbath day that which is not lawful?" And he said unto them, "Did ye never read what David did, when he had need, and was hungry, he, and they that were with him? How he entered into the house of God when Abiathar was high priest, and ate the show-bread, which it is not lawful to eat save for the priests, and gave also to them that were with him?" And he said unto them, "The sabbath was made for man, and not man for the sabbath: so that the Son of man is lord even of the sabbath."[8]

Jesus called the pure in heart blessed and said that they should see God. He did not reprove his disciples when they broke some of the laws of the Jewish church. He did reprove them sternly when they showed any evidence of corrupt thought or selfish desire. He looked continually for elements of goodness which were not obvious to the casual observer. He listened more to the hearts of men than to their words. He judged prince and pauper by the same measure, the purity of their intent.

The Christian position places man only a little lower than the angels and visits man with comparable responsibility for his thoughts, words, and deeds. The Christian is to be judged by his fruits, by everything that proceeds from him. He must keep himself pure, and unspotted from the world.

SUMMARY

A definite sense of purity is universal to religion as an essential part of man's approach to God and to his fellow men. In the later development of the religions there is a tendency to hide the direct responsibility of the individual under layers of interpretation and evasion.

The substitution of ceremonial purification for real purity is rather general in some of the religions, including some sections of the Christian body. Some groups restrict the application of purity of thought, word, and deed to their own cult or nation. Thus false witness is wrong if directed against one of the same religious belief, but excusable or even laudable if used to bring difficulties in the way of a foreigner.

However, there is ample evidence that upright or holy character, nourished by purity of thought, word, and deed, is essential to vital religious life and practice. The value of purity is attested by every religious leader, and the relationship of purity to the attainment of the highest good is outlined in every living religion.

NOTES

1. Exodus 20:7.
2. The Society of Friends (Quakers) maintain that truth is inherent. Integrity and honesty under all conditions require no oaths. The oath imputes a double standard which is degrading to human status as a child of God.
3. Exodus 20:16.
4. See Deuteronomy 14:4–21.
5. R. E. Hume, *Treasurehouse of Living Religions* (New York: Scribner's, 1932), p. 125.
6. Ibid., p. 129.
7. See Mark 7:1–23.
8. Mark 2:23–8.

CHAPTER V
KNOWLEDGE

Knowledge of their traditions and history is a basic element in all historic religions. It is necessary to know God in order to do his will and to know the law that it may be obeyed. The founders of every living religion in the world have stressed the importance of knowing and have urged their followers to learn well the sacred principles of their faith.

The fundamental importance of knowledge is shown in the emphasis placed upon oral instruction by the founder of his disciples and later by the establishment of schools and colleges by the religious groups for the instruction of the leaders of the people, if not for the teaching of the people as a whole. In the development of some cults this instruction has been carried on through the monastic system, which provides opportunity for study and meditation without the interruption of other tasks or responsibilities. Other religious groups depend rather upon the policy of individual tutorial apprenticeship for the dissemination of knowledge. Many groups started originally with this second method but later formed schools where many students were taught by instructors who were selected for their ability to teach the principles of their religious beliefs. Followers of the monastic system expanded their program beyond the education of the priesthood by setting up a school within the monastery for the teaching of those who wished to learn but who had no intention of entering the order. Illustrations of both methods are found within the Christian tradition and history.

On the negative side, and stemming from the realization of the importance of learning, knowledge was covered up by the followers of the founders in many religious groups, including the Christian church. These had discovered that the people were more easily controlled through superstition and fear than they could be through knowledge and understanding. Knowledge meant individual responsibility and individual interpretation. This element of personal participation in all decisions and evaluations regarding religious principle made it difficult to maintain strict discipline.

Knowledge is power. This truism has been recognized by religious and political leaders throughout history, and they have been able to maintain their leadership in most instances through their control over the spread of knowledge. Religious history shows that such control has been used to debase and distort the principles and ideals of the prophets and teachers who founded the various religious movements.

The lengths to which some religious leaders went to suppress or control the spread of knowledge illustrates the fundamental importance of that element to religious life. The civil wars in Islam and the inquisitions in Christianity are two indications of methods used to nullify the purposes of the founders. Defenders of such actions claim that the purpose was to destroy false interpretations and to uphold the truth, rather than to hamper the spread of knowledge. However, the two questions that remain unanswered are whether might proves anything beyond relative physical strength, and whether the power of knowledge is physical or spiritual.

Leaving controversy aside and turning to the field of

historical fact, we see that knowledge was a major factor in the rise and spread of all religions. Sources of that knowledge may have varied, but the need for it was recognized throughout the world.

The parents were the source of knowledge and of religious teaching in three of the historic religions. Judaism, Confucianism, and Hinduism hold to a similar idea concerning the proper source of knowledge: All three religions accept the family rather than the individual as the primary unit, although there is consideration for the individual within the family.

In Judaism the law says: "Honor thy father and thy mother . . ." and thus places children under direct control of their parents in every phase of their activity or development. Jesus, the founder of Christianity, learned not only carpentry and methods of behavior from his parents but also the religious principles upon which his people based their belief. He was subject to his parents until he became a man, as were all children of his race. Though it is natural to assume that environment also gave the children some knowledge beyond that imparted to them by their parents, the primary source of information and training remains within the family group.

The parents, then, acted merely as a conserving element in the knowledge of the race because of their own limitations. Such a restriction on the scope and progress of learning was detrimental but unavoidable unless the responsibilities of the parents were assumed by some other agency. Instruction at the temple by the leading scholars of the time was one of the first steps in the advancement of knowledge among the Jewish people. This instruction was available to only a few students in relation to the whole population.

For the great majority, knowledge was limited to a

transmission of the traditions as the earlier generation knew them. The attempt to change this situation was one of the reforms Jesus of Nazareth tried to introduce, without much success. He himself had broken away from the rigid legalism of his race and had found observation and experience to be worthy teachers toward a fuller and more meaningful life. Yet he could find only a handful of discontented or adventurous spirits who would break with tradition and follow him.

Confucius accepted a source of knowledge, similar to that of the Jews, when he taught his followers to honor "thy father and his father." The mother had no place in the Chinese family except as drudge and producer of children, male children if possible. This made the father responsible for the education of the son, and the son must regard the father as authority in every respect. The father was equally responsible to his father if living, to his memory if dead. The father could impart only the knowledge he had received from his father.

Thus although knowledge was the foundation of Confucianism, it was the knowledge of the past that was of the supreme importance rather than knowledge of the present or of the future. In fact, there was no encouragement given to the acquiring of further knowledge, and any ideas that differed from the teachings of the past were considered evil. Knowledge itself was essential so that there would be no danger of departing from the ancestral pattern.

Knowledge of the past was the foundation upon which ancestor worship was based. With ancestor worship established there was no incentive for progress and the whole nation went to sleep. An educated man was one who could recite the classics without error, and civil service examinations were made up largely of such recitations. China, they believed, had passed through a golden age, and that period could be revived if the knowledge of it were in the mind of every man.

The family as a source of knowledge is used in a different way by the Hindus, who believe that the place of every child is fixed by its parentage and that whatever knowledge the child received shall be within the limits of family position. Instruction is limited to the boundaries of the caste into which the child is born. No child can rise above his parents, nor can he choose a different occupation unless there is a choice within the caste. In early Hinduism there were three castes and an outcaste group. Within the castes at that time there was some opportunity to exercise choice of occupation or profession. In more recent times the castes have been subdivided so that freedom of choice has been virtually eliminated.[1]

There is no opportunity to overstep the boundaries of caste. Any lack of conformity may cause an individual to drop from a higher group to a lower, while violation of caste rules, such as marriage between castes, may cause the guilty parties to be placed in the outcaste category. So it is very important that the children be taught all the rules pertaining to their caste. This knowledge protects them from making unfortunate mistakes and makes them good Hindus in that respect.

Knowledge is the foundation of the caste system and of the Hindu religion. Such knowledge is limited by the strict regimentation of Indian society, but it is essential to the functioning of that society and of the religion, which is the guiding factor within the society. The Bhagavad Gita states that "he who is without affection on all sides, whatever good or bad fortune is his lot, and who is neither glad nor hates—the knowledge of that man is fixed."[2]

Shinto could be included in the same category with the three religions just mentioned because it contains elements similar to those in each of the other three. However, the superficial nature of these factors make it necessary to separate it from the three positive positions just discussed. It has a caste system, although not as rigid as that of Hinduism, and a family unit of worship similar to that of Confucianism. The parents have the same standing in the home as those within the sphere of Judaism. Knowledge is essential for the proper observance of the religious rites and customs and it is passed on from parent to child in the home. However, Shinto contributes little to the position already outlined and is mentioned only to give it place in the development of the idea of knowledge.

In contrast to this limited idea of knowledge in which the family determines the extent of learning, there is the picture of knowledge as the highest goal in life which is illustrated most clearly by the Greek philosophers. Socrates said that to understand clearly was to be good, which placed knowledge and virtue in equation: virtue is knowledge, knowledge is virtue. The Greeks became so completely obsessed by the desire to know that they exceeded the bounds of reasonableness and entered the field of sophistry.

During the period of greatness in Greece[3] there was a great stress upon the idea of knowledge. One must know and there was no excuse for one who did not know, because there were teachers in every town or city who would discuss and instruct. "Know thyself" was the key to the Greek idea, an attitude that placed the responsibility for knowledge upon the individual. The great philosophers and investigators encouraged the young men to discuss and examine problems of all kinds, one of the major problems being that of man's relation to the universe, which leads to the religious question.

The problem of good and evil interested thoughtful

Greeks, who thought the solution of that problem was sought through knowledge. Since good and evil were both present in the world, and since every action held the possibility of strengthening or destroying virtue, man was presented with an eternal choice. He must know himself, his responsibility to the gods and his duty to his fellow men so that he could choose between good and evil in every case.

The Stoics believed that man should choose virtue and devote himself to it without regard to the results of such a choice. Virtue should be selected simply for the sake of virtue and not for any good which might come from choosing. An ulterior motive would defeat the end which man was seeking to achieve through his devotion to virtue. This position made selfishness, or any choice influenced by self-interest, evil.

The logical climax of this was to place man beyond the reach of emotional appeals and to base every choice upon the decisions reached through the application of pure reason. Since the position of reason could not be maintained without thorough knowledge, pure knowledge became the greatest good known to the Greek thinkers. The influence of this position has been felt through the centuries, and the teachings of the great minds of Greece are used in many lands at the present time. Methods tried and proved by Greek scholars more than two thousand years ago are patterns for research and study today.

On the intellectual level, and on the theological level, the research of the Greeks has been a major contribution to universal knowledge and a convincing example of the way in which knowledge should be used. However, the ordinary man responds more to emotional stimuli than to the cold light of reason; and he looks for warmth as well as light. When religion supplies the warmth of understanding as well as the light of knowledge, it serves the greater number of people. Thus Greek philosophy could never become a satisfying popular religion, for its intellectual systems were too austere for common acceptance.

Knowledge is no less important in other religions or cultures than it was to the Greeks, but it is urged upon the people rather than being demanded of them. Jainism upholds knowledge as the possession which will lift man above the distracting influence of bodily pleasure or pain. By having right knowledge man will know the right things, and, if he has faith, he will do the right things and perform the penance necessary to give him purity.

The Sikhs are urged to know in truth and are warned against saying that they know, in as much as one who says he knows is suspected of knowing nothing, while one who really knows is recognized by others as a knowing person. The injunction is to, "make divine knowledge thy food, compassion thy storekeeper, and the voice which is in every heart the pipe to call to repast."[4]

The same attitude toward knowledge was expressed by Lao-tze when he said that those who speak do not know and those who know do not speak. He believed that a little knowledge was a dangerous thing but that full understanding made man the highest of all creatures under heaven. The importance that Taoism attached to knowledge was the same as that maintained by the Greek scholars, but the goal was other. While the Greeks sought complete knowledge so that they could be fully informed, Lao-tze believed that the best knowledge was attained at the level of no knowledge and that when the highest level of understanding was reached, there would be nothing to keep man from the blessed state of oblivion.

Knowledge is a great virtue, but awareness of the point at which one does not know is the greatest blessing. Conversely, if you think that you know when you do not know, then you are in an evil state. False knowledge is a dread disease which can be cured only when you recognize it as a disease and, from the recognition, cure yourself by knowledge. Knowing others brings discernment but knowing yourself brings intelligence. These ideas are discussed in the Tao-Teh-King, which was written almost six hundred years before the Christian era.

Geographical location and racial characteristics seem to have little effect on the acceptance of knowledge or upon its relative importance in the minds of the great religious leaders. Confucius and Lao-tze were founders of Chinese thought who lived within fifty years of each other, yet their acceptance of knowledge as to both source and goal was entirely different. The only true similarity lies in the importance which they attached to information and understanding.

Differences in the use of knowledge are even more marked in India, where Jainism and Buddhism are children of the parent Hinduism. Jainism shows a distinctly different emphasis on knowledge from that of the parent, without direct opposition, while Buddhism propagates an idea which stands in conscious contrast to the position of Hinduism. Three steps of the noble eight-fold path which Gautama constructed are based upon the worth of knowledge, the first of which runs counter to the Hindu idea.

Right views is the first step in the path; they will emancipate man from all bonds of superstition, fear or caste consciousness. When man has freed himself from superstition, he finds that caste is not the way of life and that man can rise as high as his understanding will permit. There is no chance for delusion when a man sees clearly, nor can he become a victim of mass suggestion. Clear vision brings freedom.

Right speech is the third step of the path and gives man freedom from hypocrisy. When man knows and understands, he has no reason to be untruthful or unkind. He speaks in terms that all may understand, simply and clearly, and never resorts to any kind of double-talk which means different things to different listeners. Such veiled speech is evil and shows a lack of understanding in the speaker or a desire to cause a similar lack in the mind of the auditor.

Right speech is truthful speech, and man must speak in full knowledge or remain silent. Gautama followed this rule himself in teaching his disciples. If he did not know, he kept silent; this is the reason for the lack of any specific mention of God or of the life hereafter in Buddhism. He was waiting until he knew before he made any statement.

The seventh step of the path is rightmindfulness, which indicates the analytical factor in knowledge. The mind must be active at all times, never sluggish or dormant. It must search out the truth and facts which indicate right views. And it must pursue this search with eagerness and with willingness to change ideas and interpretation as new truth is discovered.

But the mind must be watchful of itself so that it will not accept untruth for truth or a false idea for reality. It must be as cautious in transmitting what it receives as it is in receiving it. Finally, the mind must be selective to avoid delusion and to screen out superstition.

Zoroaster supported the importance of knowledge by inference in his instructions to his followers. Three statements which illustrate this method are found among his teachings. Man should think nothing but the truth, speak nothing but the truth and do nothing but what is proper. This was the code of behavior for those who would follow Ahura Mazda and have a part in the excellent kingdom.

91

The statements made are the core of Zoroastrian teaching and are based entirely upon knowledge, although there is no specific mention of the word.

All three are dependent upon knowing the truth and what is proper. One cannot speak or think the truth unless one knows what the truth is. Neither can anyone behave according to a certain standard unless the standard is known to the individual involved. The remaining precepts of Zoroaster depend on the three statements, consequently the knowledge of truth in thought and speech and acquaintance with proper action become the basis for Zoroastrian behavior.

There are many sacred scriptures in the world. No living religion is devoid of written testimony from the pen of its founder or of his followers. Yet in Islam, as in only a few other religious groups, the sacred book acted as instructor to the people. While Muhammad lived, he was the teacher; but after he died, the teacher was the Koran. Muhammad instructed his followers to "arise and warn," but all of the warnings were inscribed in their holy book, which was the revelation of God.

All men must be given the opportunity to know the Koran and to accept it or reject it. If they knew and did not accept, they were infidels; if they knew and did accept, they were true believers and their future lot would be a happy one. But if they did not know and had no chance to learn, they could not be called unbelievers. It was the responsibility of the faithful for all to have a chance to learn from the one true teacher, the Koran.

The warning principle which Muhammad instilled in his followers made Islam one of the great missionary religions of the world. The spread of the knowledge and influence of Islam today is second only to that of Christianity, and in many areas it is accepted in preference to the Christian teachings. The book is priest and prophet, and its pages contain all that man needs to make his knowledge complete.

Christianity also has its sacred book which contains all truth, but it also supports priesthood to interpret the book to the people, whereas in Islam each believer is his own interpreter. Although knowledge is basic in Christianity, there is no particular value placed upon abstract knowledge. Since the source of knowledge is the clergy rather than the sacred book, there is much difference between the sects which make up the whole body of believers. Of course the primary source is the book, but the majority of Christians do not go to the primary source for their knowledge.

The only sacred book to which Jesus had access was the scripture of Judaism. He wrote nothing, nor can any indication be found that he urged his disciples to make a record of his teachings or of his activities. He taught his followers through parables, nature stories, by precept and example, sermon and private conference. He ministered in every way that he knew so that his followers would know how to live and how to worship God.

Jesus said that those who hungered and thirsted for righteousness would be filled. The people knew what hunger and thirst meant and they could understand that Jesus was urging them to fill their minds with truth. He was also goading them towards an eagerness for learning, which would assure the acceptance of his teachings in spite of opposition. He wanted the people to realize that knowledge of the right way of life was just as important to them as their daily meat and drink.

So Christianity began its development with a thirst for knowledge that was similar to that of the Greek philosophers and in later centuries may have been stimulated by their influence. Jesus wanted to know, and he wanted his followers to know, the whole truth about every vital point in life. He questioned the spirit of legal prohibitions, tried to make religious life reasonable and natural, attacked any attempt to conceal the true meaning of the religious observances.

Jesus insisted that man know before he attempted to lead others; the teachings that have come down to us indicate that fact. His warnings that the blind could not lead the blind, that one must be without sin to judge a sinner, that one's own eye must be clear before he could remove an obstruction from the eye of another, show that Jesus wanted his followers to know the truth before they attempted to teach it to others.

God knows, and he alone is capable of making the final judgment on man's acts and value. Man must attain the level of intelligence whereby he knows that his own judgment is influenced by the limitation of his knowledge. Jesus would not allow his most faithful disciples to judge the actions or teachings of others and rebuked them for attempting to silence some who were active in Palestine at the time.

Jesus was not specific in his definitions of the limits to human knowledge, and his failure to clarify his warnings on this point weakened the Christian movement. He left too much room for interpretation, which could be made to favor one sect or another within the Christian body. The interpretations have caused unceasing controversy among Christian groups and have been the chief cause of sectarianism.

Some church leaders have availed themselves of that failure and have placed a narrow interpretation upon the need for knowledge. If the clergy is fully informed, the people have only to follow their leadership and accept without question the instruction given them by those who hold the keys to heaven. Under this interpretation the less knowledge the majority of the people have the better.

Such a position allowed the Christian church to cripple and condemn secular learning and to make such learning unavailable to the people in their charge. Thus an important part of the whole body of knowledge was denied to many people. Knowledge became particularized to the point where most of the faithful within the Christian body knew little beyond the Credo and the Pater Noster.

Yet Jesus insisted that all should know the how and why of living without restriction and without preference. He did not allow his disciples, who were with him throughout his ministry, to set themselves above those who had not the same advantages. One of his last acts on earth was to demonstrate to his disciples, through the washing of their feet, that they must be servants and not masters and that their knowledge was a responsibility rather than a privilege.

SUMMARY

Knowledge is life and ignorance is death. Partial knowledge is a dread disease as contagious and as deadly as the plague. The light of reason guides man's feet along the path of progress to the goal of understanding and distinguishes man from the lower animals. When one knows, and only then, can one think accurately, see clearly, speak truthfully.

The importance of knowledge at the present time is illustrated by the principle of enlightened reason that is accepted by scholars as essential to the full expression of life. We define enlightened reason the acceptance of all that is knowable, plus the acceptance of the unknowable whose existence is indicated by reasonable manifestations within the knowable. What we know determines what we are, unless we refuse to apply our knowledge to life. What we learn from day to day determines what we shall be. "And ye shall know the truth, and the truth shall make you free."[5]

"Be not proud because of thy learning. Take counsel with the unlearned as with the learned, for the limit of a craft is not fixed and there is no craftsman whose worth is perfect. Worthy speech is more hidden then greenstone, being found even among slave-women at the mill-stone."[6]

NOTES

1. American newspapers carried stories in 1947 of efforts in India to eliminate the outcaste category entirely, thus removing that stigma from the low-born of the nation. Present outcastes would become members of the lowest caste.
2. S. G. Champion, *The Eleven Religions* (New York: Dutton, 1945), p. 159.
3. Fifth and early fourth centuries, B.C.
4. Champion, *The Eleven Religions*, p. 263.
5. John 8:32.
6. J. H. Breasted, *The Dawn of Conscience*, p. 130, quoting from the Maxims of Ptahhotep, 2800–2700 B.C.

CHAPTER VI
CONDUCT

Conduct receives more attention in most historic expressions of religion than any other basic principle except belief. Conduct is defined by the law of the group and is, in fact, the concrete application of an abstract principle which is established by law. The control of man's actions is something which is not confined to the religious group. In fact, there was law and control over conduct as soon as men came together into a community and established a social life.

McDougall states that the moral code, which forms a large portion of any body of law, was established because of the strength of the parental instinct and the desire to protect the family relationship. Altruistic conduct of every kind can be traced to parental tenderness as its emotional source.

The important contribution of religion in the field of conduct was the closing of the gap between the ideal and the actual condition of man. Breasted points out that it took two thousand years for the wise men of Egypt to realize the extremity of the contrast between their inherited ideals of worthy character and the appalling realities in their present society. The hopelessness of this contrast persisted until optimistic social thinkers began preaching the values of righteousness and social justice. A positive effort to better the condition of society brought hope.

The founders and leaders of all great religious movements were primarily social reformers. They realized that man's conscience must be awakened because, as Morgan points out, unless the conscience is active, no religion worthy of the name is possible. They studied the law as it was and changed it to fit more accurately the needs of the people, supplying new sections to eliminate the weaknesses that existed.

We shall discuss the development of law in a later chapter, but it is interesting to trace the development of law in relation to conduct here through one illustration. The people of ancient Sumer in the Mesopotamian valley had a highly developed social structure and a definite code of law which governed their conduct within that society. Theirs was a democratic state and their law reflected that democracy.

The Babylonians became strong in that area as a kingdom, and Hammurabi adapted the Sumerian code to fit his own needs in governing his people. Some laws were changed and others eliminated, while punishments for infractions were generally made much more severe. If a surgical operation failed in Sumer, the physician lost his hand; while under Hammurabi, he lost his life. The code of conduct was expanded and given divine sanction by being attributed to Marduk.

This same code was adapted for the Jewish people by Moses after their release from Egypt. His code and those which followed are developments of the law that once governed ancient Sumer. Moses gave his code the force of divine law by declaring it a revelation to him from Jehovah, but his rules of conduct bear an interesting resemblance to those in the codes of the Mesopotamian area, all of which can be traced back to the Sumerian code. This does not mean that the rules of conduct are any the less effective or binding because they have been found effective through many centuries and in many different societies.

Three of the ten commandments of Moses are directed at individual conduct, although others help to clarify the social behavior of Israel. These are definite prohibitions and are taken directly from the earlier codes, or take the form of the same prohibitions which appear in earlier times. It may be a mistake to assume that any laws governing conduct were transmitted from one civilization to another because the same laws appear in every religious code, as well as in almost every secular code.

Moses said, "Thou shalt not kill." In the original statement there was no qualification of that comandment, and its strict construction would mean that no life can be destroyed. Yet the Israelites believed in sacrifices and burnt offerings at that time, and they were meat eaters as well. Consequently, the law could not have included animal life within the prohibited category. However, it did make human life sacred and made the killing of a human being a crime against Jehovah and against society.

The unqualified prohibition was later modified to include only the members of the Jewish nation within the scope of the prohibited category. When the law was made, the Jewish people were isolated from others and were a complete social unit within themselves. Later they found it necessary to fight other social units so that they could gain and hold the land upon which they had settled. Killing became a necessary part of conquest, and such conduct must be justified through the interpretation of the law in such a manner that the killing of an enemy would not violate it. Weakened by this method, the commandment lost much of its value as a guiding principle of conduct.

Moses said, "Thou shalt not commit adultery." Again the original law was without qualification and was an absolute curb on any form of illicit sexual intercourse. Husband and wife must be faithful to each other and no extramarital relationships were allowed. Then the question of sterility came up and a man was allowed another wife if the first did not give him children.

Once the original law was changed by interpretation, there was continued modification; and the prohibited categories were changed and clouded to suit the taste. The limit on wives became one of economic rather than moral concern and concubines appeared in the establishments of the wealthy and powerful. According to tradition the climax was reached by Solomon during his reign when he acquired a thousand wives and concubines. The original law governing conduct had been interpreted almost out of existence by this time.

Moses said, "Thou shalt not steal." No qualifying interpretation marred the simple law, and there was no escape from its meaning, since everyone in the days of tribal life knew just what stealing meant. It implied the taking of something which was not yours by inheritance, by right of conquest, by purchase, or by personal creation through labor. Stealing was listed as a capital crime in tribal law because nobody had enough to spare, and any serious deprivation could well mean death for the thief.

All laws of conduct have economic and social, as well as moral or religious, bases and are necessary for the control of a nonreligious society if that society is to survive for any great length of time. At the time of Moses the Israelites had very little in the way of possessions. If a cow or a sheep were lost or stolen, it meant a serious loss of food or of the raw material for clothing, which was felt immediately. If the seed for planting were stolen, that meant the loss of the next year's food and forage.

The unqualified statement of Moses was later changed so that the only prohibition was against stealing from a fellow tribesman. Anyone outside the tribe was an enemy and his property was classified as legitimate plunder. That convenient interpretation has come down through the centuries to the present time, so that a nation may be plundered of its resources by another nation, or by business organizations under the protection of a foreign power, without recourse.

Conduct does not need a theological background to support its specific influence upon the life of man. There has not been much evidence of a theological position in the development of Buddhism, but the emphasis on conduct is so strong that five of the eight undying holy precepts are devoted to it. In this, as in any religion which makes a virtue of asceticism, man's behavior is of paramount importance and the stressing of rules of personal conduct is to be expected. Yet the fact of asceticism does not discredit the importance of good conduct for the non-ascetic peoples of the world. On the contrary, this position enhances the value of the evidence which the mystical religions provide in support of correct behavior.

"Right Conduct" is the fourth step in the noble eight-fold path of Buddhism; the great teacher left little to the imagination of his followers in his discussion of the meaning that was implicit in that step. Gautama maintained that man must be honest with himself and with everyone around him. Any pretense or sham was an evil action which sullied the purity of the mind and soul and which would bring grief, shame, and bodily pain as a consequence.

Man shall be peaceful in all his dealings and in every relationship with other men, if he wishes to be considered a true follower of the Buddha. Hatred, violence in thought, word or deed, even the possession of uncharitable thoughts, is destructive of good and does not become a man who seeks to maintain right conduct.

Purity of action or behavior is the outward manifestation of that inner purity without which man cannot attain nirvana; that spotless behavior is a part of man's responsibility to himself. Gautama expected every one of his followers to follow every step of the noble eight-fold path whether that follower happened to be devoting his entire time to the pursuit of the truth as a monk or whether he was engaged in some other vocation, trade, or profession.

For the religious community of monks there were more strict and specific rules of conduct as outlined in the eight undying holy precepts. The avowed ascetic is not allowed to drink any intoxicating liquor because he must have full control of his faculties at all times. He must refrain from sexual intercourse because unchastity is unlawful for the members of the order and any indulgence of physical desires is an ignoble thing.

The ascetic must eat temperately at all times and should refrain from eating after noon. It is a serious breach of conduct to eat anything late in the evening or at night because such action is liable to disrupt or disturb rest, which is necessary for the maintenance of equanimity. No garlands may be worn, nor shall a monk use perfume, because it is a concession to personal vanity unworthy of a member of the order. One must even ignore the comfort of a high or luxurious bed and should sleep on a mat spread on the ground in order to maintain the proper humility and austerity.

The other religions of the East have their codes of conduct that are written into the law of the religious group as commandments or prohibitions. The specific rules will be discussed later, but their emphasis upon the conduct of the individual should be mentioned briefly here. Confucianism and Shinto are state religions, and their teachings are influenced by the desire to make the individual a good citizen of the state. Hinduism, Jainism, Sikhism, and Taoism have no direct connection with the state, and they strive to bring man into closer association with the Supreme by guiding and controlling his behavior. With either motive the driving force, the principles of conduct which are taught are the same, and the only difference that can be seen is one of emphasis and application. The state religions place primary value upon observance of commands and instruction, laws and ordinances, whereas the other faiths stress self-control, charity, and mercy.

Confucius said that man should be tolerant, mild, complacent, incisive, docile, straightforward, magnanimous, resolute, courageous, yet he should also be stern, firm, reverential, considerate, daring, meek, discerning, sincere, and just. Three qualities are essential for the superior man: virtue that will free him from all anxieties, wisdom which will banish perplexity, and boldness that will free him from fear. With all of these guideposts to lead man on the path of right conduct there is no doubt that he will attain leadership among his fellows if he does not enjoy idleness nor find excess pleasure tempting.

Self-control, giving, and compassion are the three principal guides to conduct that are found in the teachings of Hinduism, Jainism and Sikhism. The approach of the Indian mind to these qualities is outlined in the sacred writings of the Jains: "If he is always humble, steady, free from deceit; if he abuses nobody; does not persevere in his wrath; if, not proud of his learning, he listens to friendly advice; if he speaks well even of a bad friend behind his back; if he abstains from quarrels and rows; if he is enlightened, polite, decent and quiet: then he is called well-behaved."[1]

One must abandon the society of the evil and associate only with the good, yet one should be compassionate toward the outcaste and the wanderer. Sincerity, honesty and charity are the marks of holiness in man; justice, truth and consideration for the good of others guide his actions.

These guides to behavior are presented to help man live correctly, and there is little indication of strict law about them. Threats of dire consequence which will follow any violation are absent from the texts, and it seems to be the general assumption that man will behave if he knows how to do so. Man wishes to be free from anxiety, perplexity, and fear, just as he wishes to be well behaved, respected, and regarded as a leader among his fellow men. The path by which he may obtain the fulfillment of these wishes is outlined for him in the sacred writings, and he will walk along that path because he knows that it is right.

To the follower of Zoroaster, health is an undying holy precept, and the maintenance of health is the principal rule of conduct, upon which all others depend. Man must guard his health with the utmost care, and his mental health is just as important as that of his physical body. Most of Zoroaster's agricultural reforms were instituted to assure an adequate supply of nourishing food. He saw that a sick body seldom supported a healthy mind, and that a return to physical health would usually bring about the return of healthy thoughts and noble impulses.

As a consequence of observations regarding the relationship between bodily and mental health, Zoroaster prohibited any course of living which would bring about any bad mental or physical condition. Anything detrimental to health was evil; man's conduct must portray only the good. Healing could be had from different sources, according to the sacred writings, but the holy word was the best remedy of all. A man could be healed by holiness, by the law, or by surgery or medicine, but he should turn to the sacred scripture. And the scripture upheld health as a holy thing.

There is a temptation to over-stress this feature of Zoroastrianism because it is different from any found elsewhere in religion; yet the importance of health is emphasized by all modern psychologists and sociologists in much the same way that Zoroaster stated it in his teachings. Here, at any rate, is a definite contribution to the whole idea of conduct which opens up an entirely different aspect of it. In most religions the goal of conduct is goodness and the elimination of evil. In Zoroastrianism the goal of conduct is health and the elimination of disease and weakness. There is a tendency in religion, especially of the ascetic and mystical types, to ignore or to deprecate robust health as something which is not essential to saintliness or to wisdom. Zoroaster showed health to be the secure foundation upon which goodness can be built, and without which goodness has little chance to survive.

Islam has expressed the rule of conduct in the negative through the Koranic injunction: "The abomination—flee it." The believer must keep away from evil and from any temptation to evil actions because the gates of hell swing wide to receive him if he violates the code of conduct adopted by the faithful. The positive generalizations which outline Islamic behavior are unquestioning belief in the Koran as the revealed word of God, doing good deeds, being steadfast in prayer, and giving alms.

The primary urgency, however, is to avoid contact with evil persons or things so that the purified state of the believer will remain inviolate. Man must avoid the heinous things of filth and crime and be faithful in prayer. Social conduct is strict within the Muslim community, but its controls do not reach beyond the tribe. Filth and crime can exist undisturbed so long as the believers are not contaminated.

The Greeks had as much influence on the later codes

of conduct in Jewish and Christian circles as any other source because the Greek code of conduct set standards of justice and honor, which were defined in Homer's Odes. He placed Zeus as governor of the world and made his rule a righteous control which held men to exacting standards of honor and justice.

The Greek standard of conduct was typified by man's deportment in the games that were a major part of life. In fact, athletic competition was considered the best possible training for life. Physical fitness was required, although health did not carry the religious significance in Greece that it did in Persia.

Wrongdoing and hate were condemned by the Greeks as conduct unworthy of man, and if anyone chose to adopt such attitudes, he forfeited his freedom of choice and came under the condemnation of Moira, which pursued him until he was destroyed. The folly of wrongdoing and the tragic consequences of hate are portrayed in the great plays of Aeschylus, Sophocles, and Euripides.

During the period of Greek intellectualism the thesis was established that only a limited number of things are so by nature; the majority of things are so by custom. This position established man's responsibility for his actions and closed many avenues of escape which man had used to disclaim his ability to control his behavior. That man has some natural limitations and weaknesses was admitted, but that the limitations and weaknesses fostered and sanctioned by custom were beyond man's control and responsibility was denied. Man is expected to attain the high standards of conduct which are attainable through the advanced stage of his intelligence.

The moral responsibility of man for his conduct outlined in Greek thought was given specific application in the Christian movement through the teaching and example of Jesus. The Golden Rule is the best brief summary of this placement of responsibility upon each individual: "All things whatsoever ye would that men should do to you, do ye even so to them."[2] "As ye would that men should do to you, do ye also to them likewise."[3]

The principle of the Golden Rule is not exclusive with Christianity: it appears in one form or another in at least eight of the eleven living religions. Nor is its chief purpose a rule of conduct, because it introduces the principle of service which will be discussed in the following chapter. However, the attitude expresses the idea of conduct which was implicit in the teaching of Jesus throughout his ministry.

The great majority of the people who were listening to Jesus were uneducated, at least by Greek standards, and their ideas of conduct were rather elemental; so he gave them a rule of thumb by which they could judge the rightness of their behavior. Jesus himself saw the danger of this oversimplification and guarded against misunderstanding by giving specific rules of conduct, such as, "Love your enemies, do good to them that hate you, bless them that curse you, pray for them that despitefully use you."[4] Jesus wanted to make sure that his followers understood their responsibility for their actions, regardless of any attitude which might be taken against them.

The rules of conduct for the follower of Jesus are clear from his teachings and parables and can be grouped under three general headings: self-correction, self-forgetfulness and neighborliness. One must clear away his own blindness before he can show the way to another; one must be indifferent to his own position in life, losing himself in the work of building the kingdom of God; one must hold himself responsible for the welfare of his fellow man, regardless of race, creed, or color.

There is a weakness in the Christian code of conduct which does not appear to the same extent in any other religion of the present day. That is the bargaining aspect which is most clearly brought out in the beatitudes. "Blessed are the merciful, for they shall obtain mercy."[5] Here is a promise to those who follow the principles of conduct which Jesus outlined, but the promise is vague and might be redeemed either here or hereafter. The bargain element suggested in the beatitudes colors the whole field of Christian conduct and defeats the fundamental idea of self-forgetfulness which Jesus tried so hard to plant in the minds of his disciples.

Rewards for good conduct and punishment for evil are stated in many sacred scriptures in general terms, just as they are in Christianity. Specific rewards for certain types of action are the exception rather than the rule in the teaching of Jesus but the later teachings of the Christian church have made these very exceptions the primary reasons for right conduct. This has destroyed the ethical balance and has given rise to divisive dogmas which have split the followers of Jesus into opposing factions, weakening the total influence of Christianity in the world.

SUMMARY

The conduct of man shall be such that his actions will be clean, honest, just, and merciful. His body and mind shall be healthy and he shall have compassion in his heart for others. Conduct, on the highest plane, is fundamentally religious in character, but its importance is demonstrated on the economic, social, and moral levels as well.

Treatment of all men as brothers is a part of conduct on the higher levels, although brotherhood in the larger sense is a future condition of man rather than an actuality in the past or present. Equality of opportunity and of value is the basis of conduct, but that equality is limited in practice to the religious group.

The founders of the different religions saw their principles as worldwide in scope and hoped that their followers would apply those teachings to all men everywhere. The followers did not continue the broad interpretation of their religious ideals but narrowed the application of them to a single sectarian group. Consequently the great contributions of the prophets were denied to the world because of the lack of vision and understanding on the part of their disciples.

The rise and fall of the many religions can be charted by the changes made in the conduct of the worshipers. Where right conduct had general application, the cult grew and spread; but where the code of conduct had a narrow application, the cult became weak and comparatively ineffective. There can be no robust health where discrimination is the rule, since the denial of equality brings about the refusal of responsibility and creates an area of moral anarchy which weakens the whole structure of society.

NOTES

1. R. E. Hume, *Treasurehouse of Living Religions* (New York: Scribner's, 1932), p. 282.
2. Matthew 7:12.
3. Luke 6:31.
4. Luke 6:27–8.
5. Matthew 5:7.

CHAPTER VII
SERVICE

Service, as the term is used in this chapter, means: the rendering of assistance or aid, helpful activity for the advantage or welfare of others, an act of helpful work or friendly assistance to another or others. The negative definition of service is the act of consciously refraining from doing anything which will bring harm or injustice to others. In brief, service is the practical application of religious teachings.

Many believe that Jesus was the originator of the program of unselfish service, but a closer survey of the guiding principles in other living religions shows that the idea of serving others is a broad fundamental which appears in some form within the framework of each religious group. The idea of service is more graphically presented in the parables and teachings of Jesus than in the writings of the other religious founders, and the application of the idea is broader in many respects in the Christian tradition. However, consideration for one's fellow men is a fundamental necessity which has been recognized throughout the world.

Reciprocity is expressed in the sacred writings of all religions which are vital forces in the world today.[1] The Golden Rule is not only a code of conduct but also a guide to service, because it states that one must benefit others if he expects any benefits from them. The importance of this belief in reciprocity is deliberately overlooked by many because of the responsibility which it places upon each individual within the group. A careful reading of the sacred books will show that each religion considers reciprocal action necessary to the fulfillment of the good life.

Confucius developed a saying that some students have called the Silver Rule and states the idea of the Golden Rule in negative terms. He taught that you should not do anything to another if you did not like it when done to yourself. This idea was of such importance to him that he went into great detail to explain exactly what he meant. He applied the principle of reciprocity to an individual's relations with superiors and inferiors, ancestors and heirs, showing that he should not display what he dislikes in others nor should he adopt an attitude which he hates to encounter.

The Taoist is urged to pity the misfortunes of others and rejoice in their well-being even as though he were in their place and they in his. He must help all who are in want and expect no return for his help, nor should he hesitate to save another from danger even though he must encounter danger himself to perform the act. Shinto has a similar emphasis in the idea that the width of pity and charity determines the length of life. For further knowledge of the Japanese attitude we turn to the old proverbs and discover that one good deed is better than three days of fasting before a shrine. It is said in Japan that a person becomes what he does, and that evil becomes a necessity after three years.

The Hindu is advised that the proper rule for judging his action toward others is to consider the case as his own. He should do nothing to anyone else which would cause him pain if it were done to him and any man who has intelligence and a purified soul will treat others as he himself wishes to be treated. This position was accepted by the Jains and expanded in their teachings so that one could gain religious merit through his good deeds to others but he would be considered a sinner if he caused others pain. This principle is stated in the Yogashastra: "In happiness and suffering, in joy and grief, we should regard all creatures as we regard our own self, and should therefore refrain from inflicting upon others such injury as would appear undesirable to us if inflicted upon ourselves."[2]

The Buddhist is instructed to minister to others by treating them as he treats himself. At first glance this would seem to be a repetition of the preceding statements, but the whole emphasis is different because the action of others does not enter into the picture at all. The Buddhist is the originator in both instances and is to measure his actions toward others by his actions toward himself, not by his wishes concerning the actions of others toward him. Here is a new moral and ethical position which has been ignored generally. The welfare of others is as important to you as your own condition and well-being. You will do nothing for yourself that you are not ready and willing to do for another person and you cannot favor yourself over others at any time or in any way. Such an attitude is a social position which would eradicate all of the slums in the world if it were applied faithfully. It leads to the true meaning of socialism in which each individual, rather than the state, is equally responsible for the total condition of man. Sikhism adopts this same position in the teaching that one should deem others as one deems himself, but the traditional idea is also present that one should treat others as he would be treated himself.

Judaism has the negative statement that Christianity reversed into the positive Golden Rule as illustrated by, "And what thou thyself hatest, do to no man;"[3] "All things therefore whatsoever ye would that men should do unto you, even so do ye also unto them: for this is the law and the prophets."[4] Zoroastrianism has the same negative approach as Judaism in stating that one should treat others as you would be treated. In Greek philosophy both approaches are used, the negative by Isocrates (436–388 B.C.) and the positive by Aristotle (384–322 B.C.). Philo (20 B.C.–A.D. 40) states the rule in the negative.

In view of this evidence the Golden Rule is universal as a guide for human relationships; it indicates that man is expected to serve his fellow men in every way as he expects others to serve his own needs. Yet none of the religions have left the principle of service dependent upon this one general statement. Admitting the importance, in fact the esential nature, of reciprocity, the founders of the different religions expanded and explained their idea of service so that no mistake could be made by their followers as to the meaning of the teachings.

The religion of Israel holds that one must respect the rights of others to life and property in order that his own rights may be protected. The injunction in the Decalogue against covetousness is one of the fundamental rules of Judaism to the present day, just as it was to the Israelites in the time of Moses. The belief was that Jehovah assigned all things and therefore man possessed his land and animals by divine right. To take that which belonged to a neighbor, or even to desire the possession of it, was a sin against the will of God as well as against the neighbor.

This law was not wholly altruistic, either in conception or in practice, because it protected self-interest by guaranteeing the rights of others. The reciprocal implications of the law did not escape the notice of the people concerned; the necessity for it, or the recognition of the necessity for it, marked the development of community consciousness.

The Hebrew tribes were nomads and had little or no

consciousness beyond the family group. Anyone outside that group was a real or potential enemy who would not hesitate to raid and steal if the opportunity presented itself. Now the Israelites found themselves in a larger group with new problems and the necessity for different adjustments in living. Families were in close communication with other families, and many flocks and herds grazed the same hillside slopes. The fields of grain were close together and one man or one family could not prosper at the expense of another when both were in the same circumstances and locality. The condition of one affected all, and there grew up a community loyalty which transcended the family ties. Mutual assistance and mutual protection were necessary and so they must be accepted as desirable.

With the idea of possession by divine right came the development of the theory of stewardship, and almsgiving was made a religious exercise. This was a primitive profit-sharing plan in which the man who had been blessed with great increase shared his abundance with the less fortunate. In our present thinking this is a crude and undesirable form of service because it sets men apart into superior and inferior classifications. However, the existence of the idea shows that service to his neighbor was a part of the religious obligation of the Israelite.

Judaism expanded the principle of service to the point where no person could oppress the poor or turn his back on the homeless and where every true follower of God helped his neighbor, clothed the naked, and sheltered the homeless. It was this attutude that Jesus adopted and developed in his teaching.

Another interpretation of service which had much influence beyond the group to which it applied was the idea of the Greek and Roman thinkers. Their attitude was pragmatic and realistic and their acceptance of the ideal of

114

service was on that basis; they were frankly interested in bettering their own lot. The Greek approach to service is portrayed with some degree of accuracy by this statement, "I urge myself to participate most fully in the life around me because I have discovered that I reap much more from other minds than I have sown from my own."[5]

The Romans approached service in a realistic way and applied it to their family life long before they adopted it as a policy of empire. Their neighbors the Estruscans, with whom they later commingled, showed Greek influence in their religious life and in their home life as well, but it is in the area of the family that service became more important to them. The family was the center of their daily living and the father acted as priest for the household, since the foundation of their worship was in the family virtues. Later these family virtues became the guiding principles for the conduct of imperial policy when Rome became a great power.

The three outstanding family virtues were a well-ordered house, a clean hearth, and a tended fire. These were the symbols of service, and their maintenance required the combined efforts of the whole family. Order became a virtue of the city and of the empire, and it was maintained by the operation of Roman law, which has stood as a legal pattern for following generations. The clean hearth became a great system of public works which were of great value to the Roman people in the maintenance of their empire and in the spread of their civilization. The tended fire became the pattern for the provision of the needs of the growing population, just as the responsibility for the condition of the family became the pattern for the way in which the whole empire was governed. Social and political responsibility was the direct outgrowth of the early family virtues, which had great influence upon all who had any experience with them, including Christians.

Service does not require the development of a great social or political system to be effective in the lives of the people. From the writing known as the Wisdom of Amen-emope come these words, "Plow the fields that thou mayest find thy needs, and receive thy bread from thine own threshing floor. Better is a bushel which God giveth to thee, than five thousand gained by transgression."[6] Zoroaster echoed these sentiments in his teachings and demonstrations in Persia, especially in his agrarian reforms which were of such great benefit to his followers. He stressed good deeds and just dealing between men at all times. He would not permit the enlightened man to take advantage of the ignorant and directed that the men who had benefited from instruction teach and serve those who had not been so fortunate. Relief to the poor and attention to the neglected were important elements in Zoroastrian teachings.

Gautama held a similar belief as a part of his teaching of right livelihood. Man should bring hurt to no living thing and should live in such a manner that he would not endanger the life or livelihood of his fellow man. He must not take anything that is not given nor should he expect any return for his service to his neighbor. A man shall be content with whatever voluntary payment he receives in return for the service which he renders voluntarily.

This position is also established in Islam when Muhammad instructs his followers not to bestow favors in the expectation of receiving them again with interest. There are two purposes behind such a statement, and the prophet had both of them in mind as his additional words on the subject pointed out. He did not want the believers to place anyone within their debt because that factor would affect their judgment of the debtor and might cause a weakening of their faith through evil thoughts. Nor did he wish to encourage the practice of money lending because he felt that such action would endanger the welfare of the believer. Man should not encumber himself needlessly nor should he corrupt his soul by greed and desire for possessions. The true believer should give without thought of personal profit and should serve his fellow men for the glory of God. A man who seeks the well-being of others serves his own interests best by coming closer to the will of God. One should always try to win others to the true faith by doing always what is beneficial to them. The true believer delights in the good of all beings.

Service has reached its highest religious development in the teachings of Jesus and his followers; the principle is central in the Christian group to the present day. Jesus took time on the eve of his death to demonstrate the value of service to his disciples. He dressed as a menial servant and washed their feet to show them the value of humble service which would take no thought of self into consideration. The leader must be the servant of all. All men are judged by their works rather than by their words.

Jesus showed his followers that any service to a needy person was service to him and to God, and that the best service was to those who had no means to repay. The infirmities of the weak should be borne by the strong, and the sharing of goods with those in need was the mark of a true follower. The children of God must serve one another that all may benefit equally from the blessings that are freely given.

Jesus said, "Freely ye have received, freely give,"[7] and brought into his teaching the idea which was developed in Judaism that God is the source of all good which He has freely transmitted to man. Paul gave his interpretation of this statement and summarized the position which Jesus maintained throughout his ministry in these words: "In all things I gave you an example, that so laboring ye aught to help the weak, and to remember the words of the Lord Jesus, that he himself said, It is more blessed to give than to receive."[8]

Jesus knew that he and his followers would be persecuted for the position they took on the importance of selfless service, and he promised that those who were persecuted for righteousness's sake would be blessed by God for their faithfulness. He insisted that man should not falter in his efforts to serve his fellow men because of any ridicule or efforts at defamation. They must oppose injustice and discrimination regardless of attack or personal injury from the privileged classes or groups who feared such activity and would try every means to suppress it.

Jesus brought out the negative aspects of service clearly in his teachings, especially in the injunctions against causing a weaker brother to be offended or made weak. He warned his followers that they would be held strictly accountable if they should cause anyone to stumble through their actions, either a "little one" or a "brother" or any neighbor. There was only one road open for the Christian. He could not refrain from action, nor should he do anything which would be a disservice to his fellow man, but he must serve his neighbor and seek the good of his fellow man.

SUMMARY

The ordinary limit of service is reciprocity as far as most religious teachings go, and there is always some question about the unselfishness of the position described in the statement of the Golden Rule. Even though the leaders tried to bring out a different emphasis through their insistence upon altruistic actions and upon the absence of covetousness, the followers have adopted reciprocity as their guiding principle.

Reciprocity is nothing more than the opposite side of the blood revenge idea which has been practiced by men for many centuries. One says that you should do as you wish to be done by, while the other says that as you have treated me so shall I treat you. Both positions seem essentially selfish in their emphasis upon the subject rather than the object.

The Buddhist principle of treating others as you treat yourself and the Sikh equivalent of deeming others as you deem yourself place service on the higher plane that religion attempts to introduce into every phase of life. With this position as the starting point, the individual is encouraged to act for the advantage and welfare of others without any thought of the consequences of his actions to his own state of being.

This unselfish service was recognized by each religious leader but was best exemplified by Jesus, who went about doing good. Perhaps the reason for the strength of Christianity is that Jesus did not draw apart from the ordinary people but sought to serve them whenever it was possible, regardless of the cost to himself. That is the true meaning of service.

NOTES

1. Text of all statements on the Golden Rule in Appendix A.
2. S. G. Champion, *The Eleven Religions* (New York: Dutton, 1945), p. 218.

3. Tobit 4:15.
4. Matthew 7:12.
5. Professor A. D. Nock, in a class lecture at Harvard University.
6. J. H. Breasted, *The Dawn of Conscience* (New York: Scribner's, 1933), p. 322.
7. Matthew 10:8.
8. Acts 20:35.

CHAPTER VIII
ASPIRATION

Aspiration here is used in the sense of lofty or ambitious desire. When one aspires, one longs, aims, or seeks ambitiously. In religion, then, aspiration is the longing for communication with God, the yearning for better things, the upward pull generated by the desire for perfection. It is hope with additional activating force which prompts the individual to seek the better life through conscious effort rather than to remain passively expectant.

The longing for communication with God is the reason for each spire that points upward, whether that spire be a part of mosque, temple, shrine, or cathedral, and that same ambitious desire has made the heights and high places a part of religious practice since prehistoric times. It was lofty or ambitious desire that prompted men to build altars and to burn sacrifices upon them so that the smoke of the sacrifice could ascend heavenward and carry man's message to God.

Aspiration is the root of the mysticism found in all humanity, the quest for something more than food and shelter and the material things of earth. Perhaps this urge is the creative factor in religion which has caused man to create God, as George Foot Moore has suggested. On the other hand, it may be the instinct in man which directs his attention to the relationship between himself and his creator and prompts man to recognize the eternal presence of God.

The fact of the presence of aspiration in the life and experience of man, not the theological implications of the fact, is of primary interest to us here. Manifestations of the act of seeking are present in the life of primitive peoples, and legends indicate such presence before the dawn of history. The evolutionary development of man shows a yearning for better things, an upward pull which cannot be explained entirely by the theory of the survival of the fittest physical specimens.

The earliest recorded religious activity on the part of man shows a yearning for better things and an effort to gain an understanding of the meaning of life. The savage reached out for strength that was beyond human experience, at least beyond his personal experience, when he consulted the shaman or medicine man on problems which he could not solve by his own efforts and understanding. The American Indian was not content with the fact of sickness or of the scarcity of game; he wanted to know why sickness had struck his family, or why the game was not plentiful.

The urge to know the "why" of life led to a desire to communicate with the originator of life so that the course of human events could be discussed and, perhaps, altered. If the Great Spirit was angry, there should be some way of appeasing that anger. There should be also an opportunity for man to seek help in the everyday problems of living so that his welfare would be more fully guarded from misfortune.

The desire to communicate with God, and the deep yearning for better things, has been one of the chief growth factors in religion through the centuries. The attempts of the primitives seem awkward and ineffectual to the student in the twentieth century, yet these groping efforts are the introduction to a stream of thought which has grown more powerful as it has advanced. Aspiration has an important place in the flow of this stream, as Immanuel Kant, William James, and others illustrate through their writings.

Kant points out that

> The proof of religion is not afforded by historical facts (miracles, revelation) but by the moral law, the will in ourselves that is directed towards the highest good. . . . The essence of religion is not belief in supernatural beings (demons, demiurges) that occasionally influence the course of nature and man's destiny, but a belief in God, in a will that directs everything for good, and that realized itself in nature and in history. . . . The function of religion is not to subject the will or the understanding to any powers of this world or the other, but only to strengthen it as the power to will the good."[1]

James also pays tribute to the value of aspiration when he defines religion as "the feelings, acts, and experiences of individual men in their solitude, so far as they apprehend themselves to stand in relation to whatever they may consider the divine."[2] "For religion, in its strong and fully developed manifestations, the service of the highest never is felt as a yoke. Dull submission is left far behind, and a mood of welcome, which may fill any place on the scale between cheerful serenity and enthusiastic gladness, has taken its place."[3] "Religion thus makes easy and felicitous what in any case is necessary."[4]

There is a tremendous gap between the thought of the naked savage and that of Kant or James, but the same ambitious desire is present in both because both are yearning for better things, longing for a fuller understanding of the meaning of life, desiring to establish communication with the source of all truth. This gap is filled by the teachings and practices of the world's great religious leaders who have added their aspirations to the total of human experience.

Aspiration appears to be instinctive rather than deliberate in Judaism. The prophets were reaching out continually in an effort to bring themselves and their people into close communion with God, but there is no clear statement concerning the nature of salvation that we can discover in the prophetic records. Since there was no real idea, no clear picturization, of the road into eternity, the efforts of the Jews were directed to living righteous lives and entrusting the future to the hands of God.

The outreaching of Judaism is reminiscent of the construction of a bridge over a chasm when the opposite bank is out of reach. The bridge must be built, so the builders begin at the edge of the bank on their side and carefully build toward the opposite bank. They are not sure when or just how they will reach their goal, but they build as securely as their knowledge permits and hope that their efforts will bridge the chasm and permit them to cross in safety. The point in this illustration for us is that the builders were active in their attempt to cross the chasm, rather than waiting for an earthquake to close the rent in the earth and permit their onward progress.

Aspiration was much more real to the Greek than to the follower of Judaism because the Greek popular religion makes it a part of man's fundamental nature. As we have pointed out elsewhere, Aristotle believed that man was half spiritual and that he was directly connected with Zeus by spiritual ties. The Orphic Brotherhood taught that man was half divine and that he belonged to the kindred of the gods.

Both the Orphic Brotherhood and the Pythagoreans maintained that man might have communion with the gods in this life, as well as in the next, if he conducted his life in the proper manner. The Greeks aspired to an ever-closer communion with the gods, reaching toward direct fellowship through self-purification. This direct fellowship was on a mystical plane and could be fully established only following death, yet man's nature was essentially different from that of the beasts and the fact that he could seek God was a part of that difference. Much of the outreaching quality of the Christian religion has come from this Greek idea.

An entirely different attitude toward aspiration is displayed in Zoroastrianism, although it is comparable in some respects to the position of Judaism. Here it is the responsibility of each individual to reach out toward God and the better things of life. Zoroaster taught his followers to rely on their own thought, words, and actions to get them into right relationship with God.

Individual responsibility is carried to greater lengths in Zoroastrianism than in any other of the eleven living religions; in fact, man cannot expect any help from either God or man in the development of his contact with better things. The individual must lift himself to higher plane of living by his own efforts: nobody can intercede for him at any time. The austerity of this position has contributed greatly to the decline of the religious body founded by Zoroaster, whose followers constitute the smallest group among the eleven living religions of the twentieth century.

Buddhism advocates individual responsibility for the attainment of perfection, but the austerity of Zoroastrianism is lacking: man must help his fellow men in the endless struggle. The second step of the noble eight-fold path is "Right Aspirations," and this path must be taken by all who would be worthy followers of the Buddha. From his sayings we learn that a man is unfit to reach supreme enlightenment if he is indolent and idle, or shameless and disrespectful. However, if a man is thoughtful, prudent, reflective, fervent, and earnest, he may attain supreme enlightenment.

Aspiration, then, must be high and worthy of the intelligent, earnest man in order to be right. It must be a power that will bring emancipation of the heart and produce an undefiled mind that is firm and immovable. God and eternity are mysteries to the Buddhist. Both may be very real and neither is denied, but they are shrouded in mists too deep for man's eyes to penetrate. So a man must attain the highest that he knows and must aspire to the lofty and worthy aims of life. The beyond, which Gautama refers to as "the wholly other," will be faced when the time comes, or, if you prefer, when time ceases to be.

Mystical aspiration is fundamental to the oriental mind because contemplation is indigenous to their religious life. The Confucianist and the Shintoist wish to become a perfect part of the perfect whole, while the Taoist wants to become perfectly withdrawn and completely sufficient within himself. The Hindu has hope in the midst of hopelessness, and the Jain seeks liberation from all bonds. All of this is merely an expression of a mystical outreaching, an attempt to adjust to life and to explain the desires of the individual. An indication of this oriental attitude is given in the *Te Deum* of the Sikhs: "Thou are our universal Father. In Thine inexhaustible storehouse are all treasures. Every one reposeth his hopes in Thee. Thou abidest in every heart. All are partners in Thee; thou disownest none."[5]

The aspiration of the followers of Muhammad is quite different from any other form found in religious teachings because it is an earnest desire for communion with God which can be fulfilled only by God. "And for thy Lord wait thou patiently" is a fundamental part of the doctrine of

Islam and it indicates the direction which the longing of the people takes. The Muslim prepares for eternity through the doing of good works during his life on earth and, when he has done all that he can do, he waits patiently for the call of God.

We read in the Koran that, "Wealth and children are the adornment of this present life; but good works, which are lasting, are better in the sight of thy Lord as to recompense and better as to hope."[6] The Muslim cannot be idle as he waits for the call of his Lord; he must be occupying his time with deeds which will be acceptable to God. This is his aspiration, the earnest desire to be worthy in his life on earth so that God will not overlook him at the last judgment.

Thus far we have seen aspiration in many phases, as it has applied to the different religious cults throughout the Indo-European and Asiatic lands, but no development elsewhere can compare with the Christian use of it. Each phase that is mentioned or discussed above has its counterpart somewhere within the body of Christian teachings. Jesus practiced and preached, urged, even commanded aspiration on the part of his followers. The church which is based on his teachings has increased his use of aspiration a hundredfold until, today, some of the Christian sects base their entire belief and practice upon it.

Aspiration is evident in all the teachings of Jesus as well as in the later teachings of his followers. The whole of Jesus' life was guided by earnest aspiration, and if we take the Gospel according to Mark as our guide, we see his start in the ministry was in response to an aspirational challenge, "Make ye ready the way of the Lord, make his paths straight,"[7] His temptation story is one which shows wrong aspirations being placed before him, all of which he rejected as unworthy.[8]

The first invitation which Jesus gave to anyone to follow him as a disciple shows high purpose and earnest seeking, when he said to Simon and Andrew, "Come ye after me, and I will make you to become fishers of men."[9] Throughout his work with the disciples Jesus urged them to seek always for the best way, for the highest goal.

Jesus made many public statements which illustrate his own aspiration and his desire that all men should aspire to better things. "But seek ye first the kingdom of God"[10] and "Seek and ye shall find, knock and it shall be opened unto you"[11] are statements that are repeated in various forms in all of the gospels. This attitude is similar to the "Right Aspiration" of the Buddhist in many respects.

A similarity to the attitude of Islam is found in the words of the beatitude, "Blessed are the poor in spirit, for they shall see God."[12] The idea of patient waiting is implicit in this statement, and the whole emphasis is Godward. The spirit of this form of aspiration is that man should seek humbly, rather than to seek ambitiously, because the suggestion is that pride and ambition are detrimental to the seeker after God.

The other side of the same idea of aspiration as expressed in the beatitude is found in the admonition "Lay not up for yourselves treasures upon the earth . . . but lay up for yourselves treasures in heaven."[13] Since man is hopeful of obtaining future treasure, he should spend his life building up credits against the day of judgment, to make sure that the treasure will be waiting for him. Man should build continually for life in the kingdom of heaven and should ignore the temptations of the flesh. This position places a high valuation upon the spiritual values and a low estimate upon physical things.

The thought that one should endure present evils with patience because heavenly mansions were waiting for the elect became the weakness of Christian religion. Aspiration was divorced from reality as Jesus never intended or taught that it should be, and became a purely spiritual act which was performed best in cloister. This distortion of Jesus' teaching, when isolated and upheld as a great virtue, brings great danger to the Christian religion. It is a position of *reductio ad absurdum,* which makes of the church a fool's paradise. Such a position is a withdrawal from reality which is more complete than that of the Taoist and much less worthy because it is inconsistent with the whole practice and teaching of Jesus.

In this connection it might be well for followers of Jesus to use the same rule of thumb that Muhammad commanded his followers to use when judging the truth of traditions. The prophet told his followers to compare anything they heard or read with the Koran and with his sayings and doings. If what they were questioning was in line with his sayings, then he had said it, whether he had said it or not. If the things they were bringing into question were contrary to his sayings or doing, then they were false, no matter what their source.

So with the Christian teachings; if attitudes in the Christian group are in line with those attitudes taught or lived by Jesus, then it is as though Jesus himself had ordained them. But if the attitudes and teachings are contrary to the words and example of Jesus, then they are un-Christian, regardless of their source. Complete withdrawal from reality and aspiration which ignores life are both contrary to the preaching and practice of Jesus and, although present in some Christian sects, are un-Christian by this measurement.

SUMMARY

Aspiration is essential to man's progress as he continues to work his way onward and upward toward perfection. His yearning for better things, his desire to communicate with God, his earnest longing for an understanding of life both here and hereafter give him the dynamic, the motivating energy, to rise above the destroying hungers and frustrating limitations of physical existence. This driving force is essential to evolution as it is to religion because the upward pull is a fundamental of life. If there were no pull then there would be no advancement because movement would cease as soon as the urge to move was gone.

One of the most fascinating illustrations of aspiration to me lies in the realm of nature where the asparagus plant will send up another stalk as fast as one is cut until the plant is permitted to complete its cycle, and where the leaves of the shade trees will turn their backs to the sun to slow down the natural evaporation during a period of drought, and the lower limbs of those same trees will lengthen as the tree grows so that the leaves of each limb will get a share of the life-giving sun.

On the other hand, one of the most depressing sights is that of a human being who has lost the ability to reach out for better things. The starved and the enslaved and the persecuted or oppressed peoples of the world show us how essential aspiration is to life. To aspire, man must be free. The enslaved and the starved may hope for a time, but even that dim spark fades and dies and they become clods without life or voluntary movement.

Spiritual freedom and aspiration are synonymous insofar as the one cannot exist without the other. Religion is vital when it allows the spirit of man to course freely through earth and heaven in search of better things, because that earnest seeking gives vitality to religious life.

NOTES

1. Friedrich Paulsen, *Immanuel Kant, His Life and Doctrine* (New York: Scribner's, 1902), pp. 371–2.
2. William James, *Varieties of Religious Experience* (New York: Longmans, Green, 1903), p. 31.
3. Ibid., p. 41.
4. Ibid., p. 51.
5. R. E. Hume, *Treasurehouse of Living Religions, (New York: Scribner's 1932), p. 53.*
6. *Ibid., p. 52.*
7. *Mark 1:3*
8. *Mark 1:13, Matthew 4:1–11, Luke 4:1–13.*
9. *Mark 1:17.*
10. *Matthew 6:33.*
11. *Matthew 7:7.*
12. *Matthew 5:3.*
13. *Matthew 6:19, 20.*

CHAPTER IX
IMMORTALITY

Immortality is defined for the purpose of this chapter as the condition or quality of not being liable to death nor subject to death: unending life or existence. The idea of life-continuance is very old in the consciousness of man and it appears to us in many forms because it is approached by many paths. The question as to whether immortality is merely the projection of the ego of man, or whether it is the manifestation of the presence of an essential divinity within each person, is not germane to this discussion.

The approach to immortality follows four general paths in modern scholarship as a rule. There are other avenues, but these are variants of one or another of the four general classifications. Immortality, then, is arrived at by the employment of wish fulfillment, deductive reasoning, logical progression and growth, or the acceptance of the essential unknown.

The approach to immortality through wish fulfillment is probably the path that has been most generally used through the centuries because it is most closely allied with the instinctive reactions of the great majority of people. Wish fulfillment is the way of the primitive, true, but it is also the way of the vast group of people, both past and present, who have not had philosophic or scientific training at the higher levels of academic scholarship. This is stated, not as a criticism but by way of analysis, because man has proved his ability to discover truth by instinct as well as by laboratory test or by Socratic discussion.

The basic quality of wish fulfillment as an approach to immortality is illustrated by dreams, manifested activity of the subconscious that is little more understood today than it was centuries ago, despite the research of Freud and others. Men had dreams in which those who had died came to them with advice and admonition, dreams in which they themselves were projected into a realm beyond death or, at least, beyond their experience. These dream experiences brought about an emotional stimulation which prompted the conscious effort to explain them and convinced man that existence in some form must survive physical death.

Simply stated, wish fulfillment means that man wants to escape death and extinction and so he establishes immortality as the avenue which provides that escape and dreams become the substantiation for the immortality which he desires. Such a simplification, however, eliminates the speculative element and so presents an inadequate basis for evaluation. As we have seen in the preceding chapter, man's instinctive outreaching is not based entirely upon selfish motives. So immortality cannot be listed as the outgrowth of selfishness or of egotism, since it is the goal of man's aspiration, because belief in the immortality of others surely is not entirely selfish.

The philosophic approach to immortality uses deductive reasoning as a basis, and holds certain hypotheses which lead to the conclusion that there is continuous existence of some kind. Plato argues that day generates night and night generates day, so life generates death and death must in turn generate life. He also defines the soul as the life principle and therefore it cannot die because no such thing as a dead soul can exist. Then, also, the soul is simple and cannot be subject to dissolution because only complex things can be dissolved. The soul has its own motion and so cannot be subject to motion or lack of motion from another source, thus escaping the loss of physical motion which comes with the death of the body.[1]

The general hypothesis of the philosopher is that God is good. Assuming that quality, it follows that He will conserve value and not allow it to be destroyed along with the disintegration of the physical body. The annihilation of value establishes injustices and defeats aspiration, just as it defeats Kant's moral argument for immortality and nullifies his belief in the relevance of duty to truth.

The logician analyzes immortality as a part of the logical progression and growth in life. It is logical to assume a parallel between the continuance of spirit and the indestructibility of matter, since both elements have been established by the same creative intelligence. This, of course, is based upon the primary assumption that there is a creative intelligence, and the assumption is established by inductive reasoning from the observation of the natural laws operating in the world and in our universe.

The scientist does not go as far in his basic assumptions as does the logician, because he does not deal with the spiritual realm in conjunction with the material. However, he does not deny immortality but classifies it as the essential unknown, the presence of which is indicated by the fundamental rationality of the universe. The scientist does believe in this fundamental rationality of the world and all of his great achievements are founded upon that position. Most scientists have reached the conclusion that, in addition to rationality, there is present in the universe a fidelity to purpose, even though the purpose may not be observable. Here is the meeting ground of science and philosophy.

The four approaches to immortality outlined above illustrate the means by which man has attempted to prove that he will not die. His ideas concerning the future life or the continuation of consciousness are as varied as these paths themselves. Some of these ideas must be considered briefly as they are brought out in the religious history of mankind, so that we may understand the wide range covered by them, a range which goes from the definite objective ideas found in the West to the extremely subjective positions maintained in some Asiatic religions.

Perhaps the most objective approach to immortality is that which was made by the primitive peoples, the great majority of whom believed that life continued in spirit form after the death of the physical body. The spirit remained an inhabitant of this earth, taking up its abode in rock, tree, spring, high place, or mound or just under the surface of the earth or sea. It must be fed and cared for by the living relatives or friends in order to be contented and of kind disposition. The uncherished spirit became restless and demonstrated its displeasure through interference in the affairs of the living.

The Happy Hunting Ground of the American Indian was a much more advanced concept of immortality, although still definitely objective. The future life was a perfected version of life here on earth; all of the disagreeable aspects of mortal life were absent. On this point there is a striking similarity between the idea of the Happy Hunting Ground and that of the Islamic paradise.

When the American Indian thought about life after death, he pictured a region where he would find everything to make life pleasant. There would be a comfortable lodge waiting for him, in which a cooking fire burned brightly without smoke. His arrows would be always sharp, well fletched, and straight-shafted, and his bowstring would never break. Game would be abundant and within easy reach. The Great Spirit would be his chief and would make certain that all of his wants were supplied.

This objective idea of immortality was held by many groups who had no connection with the American Indians. The clans of ancient Germany believed in their Valhalla, where the brave and the virtuous joined the gods in feasting and revelry. The legends which have come down to us show that the Germanic people believed the hardships of mortal life to be supplanted by abundant pleasures in the life to come.

The Greeks and Romans, in the mythological period of their history, held positions that were refinements of this same idea. They believed that the just and honorable, purified of all sin, had fellowship forever with the gods in the next life. This fellowship of men and gods was ruled absolutely by Zeus, or Jupiter, who held the position of supreme judge and arbiter.

For these people the resuscitation of plant life after the death of winter was accepted as a promise, in fact as proof, that man also may conquer death and go on to newness of life. An illustration of this belief is the legend of Persephone, who was the daughter of Demeter, the goddess of soil and crops in Greek mythology. She was abducted by Pluto, who made her the queen of Hades, but Demeter refused to let the earth yield any harvest so long as her daughter was held captive. Zeus decreed that Persephone should spend two-thirds of each year with her mother, who then mourned only during the four winter months.

This legend gave rise to the Eleusinian mysteries, which included secret rites giving the initiate the true understanding of life in this world and the next. There were many other mysteries of similar character whose influence was felt at one time or another throughout the Mediterranean world, including the mysteries surrounding Dionysus and Orpheus, Cybele and Attis, Aphrodite and Adonis, Isis and Osiris, and Mithra.

Breasted points out that the conception of a celestial paradise, which later became universally accepted in the Christian world, undoubtedly had its origin in the ancient Egyptian beliefs which are preserved for us in the Pyramid Texts. "Two ancient doctrines of this celestial hereafter have been commingled in the Pyramid Texts: one represents the dead as a star, and the other depicts him as associated with the Sun-God, or even becoming the Sun-God himself."[2]

An even closer relationship between the ancient Egyptian and the occupants of the Mediterranean world at the dawn of the Christian era is highlighted by Breasted in his observation, "In the life of early man as he shifted from hunting to agriculture this feeling of dependence on the fruitfulness of the earth became the ultimate religious expression of the profound change in his manner of life. The imperishable life of the fruitful earth, which died and ever rose again many times multiplied, was personified as a dying and ever rising god."[3]

So far we have illustrated immortality in the objective sense by showing the thoughts of men who believed that life does go on, although they could picture that ongoing only in the physical sense of some sort of bodily continuation or resurrection. In the dualistic forms, and in the mystical or subjective religions of Asia, the idea of future life enters the metaphysical field.

"Immortality" is the sixth of Zoroaster's undying holy precepts, one of the Amesha Spentas, which are the attendants of Ahura Mazda and personifications of his character. In the dualistic teachings of Zoroastrianism the body is classified as mortal, while the character or soul within the body is immortal. When the follower patterned his character after that of Ahura Mazda, whose character was good thought, perfect righteousness, desired kingdom, holy harmony, saving health, and immortality, then his soul or character would transcend his mortal body and he would achieve the excellent kingdom.

The kingdom of Ahura Mazda is one of pure goodness and truth, where the soul will come into its completeness after it has been released from the mortal body. This thought finds expression also in the teachings of Plato and Aristotle, where the sincere efforts of man to improve himself bring a sure reward. The dualistic position maintains that man has a future life in any case, but his failure to merit the good will be rewarded by a future of pain and misery, unending and unalterable. As the Yasna says: "The world hereafter shall be the worst world for the wicked, but the best thought for the righteous."[4]

The dualism of Islam is more objective than that of Zoroastrianism, although equally definite. One of the most familiar texts in the Koran is that which states, "for when there shall be a trump on the trumpet, that shall be a distressful day; a day, to the infidels, devoid of ease."[5] Thus, in one statement, we have a summary of the thought of Islam regarding immortality. There is a period of waiting for the trumpet which shall announce the last judgment, the day in which the infidels will be separated from the faithful and cast into the pits of hell.

The faithful followers of Muhammad will be lifted up at the last judgment into the realm of the blessed and will live evermore with God (Allah) in paradise. Heaven, to the Muslim, is a region of the greatest delights and pleasures, a perfected version of life on earth, as we have mentioned earlier. There is no complete agreement among Muslim theologians concerning the conditions that will be found in paradise, but the most generally accepted idea is that of green meadows and shady trees. All agree that the faithful will quench their thirst at Muhammad's pool, and that there will be plenty of food and of wine that will not give the partaker a headache. There will be silken garments and rich adornment, accompanied by an abundance of rare perfumes, and the maidens will all be beautiful with complexions like pearls and rubies.

The truly subjective approach to immortality is found in the religions of India and China, none of which take the dualistic position of Zoroastrianism or Islam. The choice which the oriental makes is that between life and death, rather than between a future state of bliss and a future state of torment. If a man is worthy, he becomes immortal; if unworthy, he has no life beyond that of earth and he either returns to earthly life through the round of rebirth or he disintegrates and ceases to be.

"Right Rapture" is the last step in the noble eight-fold path of Buddhism, and that step can be attained only through deep meditation upon the realities of life. The most important reality is the world-soul, which each individual strives to attain so that he may be absorbed into the whole of life, and, in this absorption, achieve immortality. The Buddhist makes his personal adjustments by thinking right thoughts, speaking right words, and doing right acts so that he may attain learning and virtue in his lifetime. He leaves the rest until the time comes to consider it, believing that his loss of selfishness and his benefactions will bring favorable results hereafter. "Earnestness is the path of immortality; thoughtlessness, the path of death. Those who are in earnest, do not die; those who are thoughtless, are as if dead already."[6]

Immortality is inherently unavoidable, according to

the beliefs of the Jains, because everyone has an indestructible soul which goes to the highest heaven and there continues to grow until it reaches its natural form of perfection. When the goal of final perfection is reached, then there is an end to all misery and complete deliverance into the final beatitude.

Hinduism, parent of Jainism and Buddhism, holds, in the later sacred writings, a view of the future life similar to that expressed in the Jain and Buddhist writings. However, the belief in a future life developed slowly through centuries of thought and practice within the ranks of Hinduism itself. The Vedas warn the individual to gird himself for immortality, but have very little to say concerning the future life itself. The Upanishads are more specific and, at one point, liken the soul to a piece of gold in the hands of a goldsmith, which takes on a new and more beautiful form under his hammer; so the soul makes a newer and more beautiful form for itself by striking down the mortal body and eliminating ignorance. The Laws of Manu show virtue to be the one surviving element which will carry man from this world to the next, and the only helper in the other world.[7] The Bhagavad Gita promises punishment for the wicked who enjoy their lusts in the thought that this life is all there is, but places the dominant emphasis upon the survival of the good who place their faith in the supreme mystery of life.

The summary of the Hindu position is illustrated by this passage from the Agni Purana:

In the darkness of death, the terrestrial friends of a man cannot follow his departed soul. It is virtue alone that walks by his side, be it in the wilderness of death, or on the ever-glad and sunlit fields of Paradise, or where none can follow. Death waits for nobody, and never stops to consider whether a man has finished his work or not. It takes a man busy with trade or agriculture, as well as the spendthrift and the indolent. Death knows no favorite or enemy. He carries away a man, as a wolf and a deer. The good or evil deeds of a man are sure to overtake him in the next existence. As there are different stages in the life of a man, so there is a Hereafter.[8]

Immortality means the same thing to the Sikh that it does to most Christians, the main difference residing in the terms used to express the thoughts. To the Sikh, the man who knows God never dies but lives on in the company of the saints. They who do not know God die; they who die in divine knowledge live eternally. There is no transmigration for those who serve the Lord, and the fear of transmigration is burned away by the fear of God. The instructions of the founder were to "Make thy body the field, good works thy seed, irrigate with God's name. Make thy heart the cultivator; God will germinate in thy heart, and thou shalt thus obtain the dignity of Nirvana."[9]

The subjective attitude reaches its ultimate in the religions of China and immortality becomes a ghostly thing, an implication almost, undefined and approached with extreme caution of description which leaves the student somewhat bewildered and unsure. Still, there is evidence that future life is expected and, within limits, anticipated. Lao-tze believed in life-continuation of some kind, according to the passage from the Tao Teh King: "To know Eternal Law, is to be enlightened. Not to know It, is misery and calamity. He who knows the Eternal Law, is liberal-minded. Possessed of the Eternal, he endures for ever. Though his body perish, yet he suffers no harm."[10]

Nothing of such a specific nature can be found in the teachings of Confucius, whose belief in the future life seems to be of little concern to him because of his primary interest in the correctness of life here. He suggests in some of his statements that the spirit issues forth from the dying body and is displayed on high in a condition of glorious brightness, but there is a ghostly quality about the future which is not resolved by any definitely descriptive idea.[11]

Shinto incorporates heaven into the life of the people as a definite part of their being. Heaven is the father and earth is the mother of the Japanese people, according to the traditional teachings of their religion, and they are assured of continued existence by virtue of that divine heritage. The only requirement is that the individual be aware of his divine inheritance and keep it unperverted.

Judaism is vague in reference to immortality. There is no doubt in the mind of the prophets that there is a future life, but they do not go much farther than to say that the souls of the righteous are in the hands of God. The basic requirements for continued life are given in the words of Psalm 15:

> Lord, who shall abide in thy tabernacle? Who shall dwell in the holy hill? He that walketh uprightly, and worketh righteousness, and speaketh the truth in his heart. He that backbiteth not with his tongue, nor doeth evil to his neighbor, nor taketh up a reproach against his neighbor. In whose eyes a vile person is condemned; but he honoreth them that fear the Lord. He that sweareth to his own hurt, and changeth not. He that putteth not out his money to usury, nor taketh reward against the innocent. He that doeth these things shall never be moved.

The vagueness of Judaism fades out before the definiteness with which Jesus interprets the Law and the prophets when he teaches his disciples concerning the future life which they may expect if they follow his teachings.

142

The emphasis of the prophets of Judaism was upon present righteousness, and Jesus shifted that emphasis to the kingdom of God, using present righteousness only as the pathway to the entrance of the eternal kingdom. The preparation of man for the next life was the sole reason for present existence, and the present life was insignificant in comparison with the life which lay just beyond the grave.

That Jesus did not ignore the present life has been illustrated in the earlier chapters, but the main incentive for the Christian is the beatific vision and the immortality which attends it and, without that incentive, Christianity would shrivel and die. The promises that Jesus made are payable in heaven, although he indicated that his faithful followers would be recompensed for their devotion in this life as well. "Verily I say unto you, There is no man that hath left house, or wife, or brethren, or parents, or children, for the kingdom of God's sake, who shall not receive manifold more in this time, and in the world to come eternal life."[12]

The followers of Jesus established a dogma which would make the attainment of immortality easier, when they adopted the doctrine of vicarious atonement to explain the death of Jesus.[13] This dogma sets Christianity apart from the other historic religions because it imputes to the founder of the group an intrinsically different status from that of an ordinary man. This point is illustrated by a verse in the Gospel according to John which is probably the best known Bible verse among the Christian group, "For God so loved the world, that he gave his only begotten Son, that whosoever believeth in him should not perish, but have eternal life."[14]

SUMMARY

In the discussion of immortality we are in the realm of pure speculation, just as we are in the discussion of God, because none of the positions which have been taken by the religious teachers of the world can be proved or disproved this side of the grave. The evidence for immortality is primarily intuitive in nature, although philosophers and logicians bring the forces of reason to bear upon the subject insofar as they are able to do so.

Provable or not, immortality is attested by the statements of the founders and teachers in every one of the eleven living religions, and it is logical to assume that the idea of a future life is as fundamental to religion as the idea of a supreme being. Whether the belief in immortality is belief in a fact or in a dream, the great religious leaders believe that man should be prepared for any eventuality.

The preparation for eternity, as outlined in the religious teachings, is a pattern of behavior that brings out the greatest worth in any individual and creates a mode of existence in this present life that brings life to a higher level of value and accomplishment. Whether civilization would continue to improve itself without the dynamic urgency of this preparation is questionable, in the opinion of many of us. History has shown that a vital religious impulse has improved the condition of man in most instances, whereas the weakening of the religious impulse has been followed by a marked degree of deterioration in both moral and social conditions.

NOTES

1. These arguments are listed as illustrations, not as the position of the author.

2. J. H. Breasted, *The Dawn of Conscience* (New York: Scribner's, 1933), p. 73.
3. Ibid., p. 95.
4. R. E. Hume, *Treasurehouse of Living Religions* (New York: Scribner's, 1932), p. 73.
5. Robert O. Ballou, *The Bible of the World* (New York: Viking, 1939), p. 1290.
6. Hume, *Treasurehouse,* p. 65.
7. S. G. Champion, *The Eleven Religions* (New York: Dutton, 1945), p. 166.
8. Hume, *Treasurehouse,* p. 70.
9. Champion, *The Eleven Religions,* p. 265.
10. Hume, *Treasurehouse,* p. 73.
11. See article by Professor Hu Shih, Harvard Divinity School Bulletin, March 10, 1946, p. 23.
12. Luke 18:29,30.
13. For discussion of atonement theories see Ferm, *Encyclopedia of Religion,* page 44.
14. John 3:16.

CHAPTER X
LAW

In this chapter the term *Law* will be used in the general sense, the body of rules or principles, prescribed by authority or established by custom, which a state, community, society, or the like recognizes as binding on its members. Such definition excludes the great body of natural law from our field of investigation, because natural laws are not made by man and give no indication of social or religious development.

Every religion has its own code of law or table of commandments which establishes the form of worship, pattern of conduct, area of social responsibility, and comparative values for the believers. In each instance the body of rules or principles which was introduced was brief, clear and inclusive, only to be made ponderous, confusing and comparatively ineffectual by the later addition of an intricate maze of interpretations. For the purpose of comparison we must confine ourselves as closely as possible to the original codes, to the basic rules and principles which were considered essential by the founders of the religious groups.

Law, as the basis of community life, antedates our written records and appears in history as legend and tradition. Some of the first legal codes known to historians are examples of mature experience, indicating generations of development. Not all law is connected with religion, even though all organized religion is based upon law.

There were at least four legal codes in effect in the Mesopotamian area before the formulation of the Mosaic code of the ancient Israelites.[1] The earliest of these was the Sumerian code, which governed the life and conduct of the people who occupied the fertile region of Mesopotamia before the rise of the Babylonian civilization. Many portions of this code have been discovered and translated, showing that the Sumerians had a democratic form of government with courts of justice and a well-developed consciousness of individual rights and responsibilities. Yet there was little mention of religion in this code, except in the tests of innocence which should be given to those accused of certain crimes.[2]

The famous code of Hammurabi is the second of these formulations, and bears such a resemblance to the Sumerian code that the author is believed to have been familiar with the earlier work. In his introduction, Hammurabi attributes his laws to Marduk, but the code itself does not contain the hallmark of the religious rules which are found in the sacred writings of the cults. The laws, 282 of which have been discovered and translated, deal with the everyday life and conduct of the Babylonians and make only an occasional reference to the gods or to any form of worship. The "trial by water" is mentioned often, however.

The first sentence of the introduction to the code of Hammurabi is of interest to students of religion.

When the lofty Anu, king of the Anunnaki, and Enlil, lord of heaven and earth, who determines the destinies of the land, committed the rule of all mankind to Marduk, the first-born son of Ea, and made him great among the Igigi; when they pronounced the lofty name of Babylon, made it great among the quarters of the world and in its midst established for him an everlasting kingdom whose foundations were firm as heaven and earth—at that time Anu and Enlil named me, Hammurabi, the exalted prince, the worshiper of the gods, to cause righteousness to prevail in the land, to destroy the wicked and the evil, to prevent the strong from plundering the weak, to go forth like the sun over the blackheaded race, to enlighten the land and to further the welfare of the people.[3]

In this statement Hummurabi established religious or divine sanction for his code, employing the same method which later religious leaders used to insure the acceptance of their principles. Yet the reference to worship and the gods which appear in the introduction and conclusion of the code do not occur in the text of the individual law. These two general statements may have carried the same force of law that the numbered statutes did and, if such is the case, gave to the whole code the status of religious principles.

Two later codes have been discovered and translated: the Assyrian code and the Hittite. Both of these were in existence long before the Mosaic code was formulated; yet they show a stage of civilization which was much more advanced than that of the Israelites in the days of Moses. Here again is enough similarity to the preceding codes to warrant the assumption that the writers of the Assyrian and Hittite codes were familiar with that of Hammurabi, if not that of Sumer. And it was against this legal background that the first distinctly religious code of the area was developed.

The Mosaic law, or the Decalogue as it is called because of the ten divisions, was the brief constitution of the Israelite clans who left Egypt. The several codes found in the Torah are expansions and interpretations of this brief statement of law. Moses wished to bind his people together so that they could live together without misunderstanding or violence. His establishment of undivided allegiance to Jehovah provided the basis for that community life.

The codes of the Israelites were patterned after the laws of the Canaanites, which were evolved from the ancient codes mentioned above. The laws regarding slaves, personal injuries, sexual offenses, taxation, rentals, contracts, et cetera, can all be duplicated in the earlier codes, and without much doubt owe their form to that origin. The religious emphasis in the law of the Israelites is distinctive, making the moral and spiritual quality of the Hebrew law superior to all previous or contemporary law in that region.

Thus we can catch a glimpse of the development of law as it grew through the centuries in the Mesopotamian area. The Hebrew use of law demonstrates the theory that a code of rules or principles is as essential to religion as it is to orderly life in any phase of existence. This theory is also illustrated by the definite codes of law which appear in the sacred writings of the world's great religions. We proceed to the outline and the comparison of these codes.

Perhaps the oldest collection of laws that were primarily of religious character was the Mosaic Code, which we have mentioned above: certainly, this comes first to the mind of the Occidental student when religious law is discussed. Known to Christian and Jew alike as the Ten Commandments, the law of Moses is the core of Judeo-Christian law.

And God spake all these words, saying, I am Jehovah thy God, who brought thee out of the land of Egypt, out of the house of bondage. Thou shalt have no other gods before me.

Thou shalt not make unto thee a graven image, nor

any likeness of any thing that is in the heaven above, or that is in the earth beneath, or that is in the water under the earth: thou shalt not bow down thyself unto them, nor serve them: for I Jehovah thy God am a jealous God, visiting the iniquity of the fathers upon the children, upon the third and upon the fourth generation of them that hate me, and showing loving kindness unto thousands of them that love me and keep my commandments.

Thou shalt not take the name of Jehovah thy God in vain; for Jehovah will not hold him guiltless that taketh his name in vain.

Remember the sabbath day, to keep it holy. Six days shalt thou labor, and do all thy work; but the seventh day is a sabbath unto Jehovah thy God: in it thou shalt not do any work, thou, nor thy son, nor thy daughter, thy man servant, nor thy maid-servant, nor thy cattle, nor thy stranger that is within thy gates: for in six days Jehovah made heaven and earth, the sea, and all that in them is, and rested the seventh day: wherefore Jehovah blessed the sabbath day, and hallowed it.

Honor thy father and thy mother, that thy days may be long in the land which Jehovah thy God giveth thee.

Thou shalt not kill.

Thou shalt not commit adultery.

Thou shalt not steal.

Thou shalt not bear false witness against thy neighbor.

Thou shalt not covet thy neighbor's house, thou shalt not covet thy neighbor's wife, nor his man-servant, nor his maid-servant, nor his ox, nor his ass, nor anything that is thy neighbor's.[4]

We should add one more statement of law to the above, because this statement is the activating principle of the Jewish religion:

Hear, O Israel: Jehovah our God is one Jehovah: and thou shalt love Jehovah thy God with all thy heart, and with all thy soul and with all thy might. And these words, which I command thee this day, shall be upon thy heart; and thou shalt teach them diligently unto thy children, and shalt talk of them when thou sittest in thy house, and when thou walkest by the way, and when thou liest down, and when thou risest up. And thou shalt bind them for a sign upon thy hand, and they shall be for frontlets between thine eyes. And thou shalt write them upon the doorposts of thy house, and upon thy gates.[5]

Because Christianity is founded upon the religious laws of Judaism, accepting the ten commandments as the basis for Christian conduct, we shall add here a few commandments which show the general nature of Christian law.

Thou shalt love the Lord thy God with all thy heart, and with all thy soul, and with all thy mind. This is the great and first commandment. And a second like unto it is this, Thou shalt love thy neighbor as thyself. On these two commandments the whole law hangeth, and the prophets.[6]

. . . Take heed that ye do not your righteousness before men, to be seen of them: else ye have no reward with your Father who is in heaven. But when thou doest alms, let not thy left hand know what thy right hand doeth: that thine alms may be in secret: and thy Father who seeth in secret shall recompense thee.[7]

And a statement from the writing of Paul, first century missionary of the Christian faith, "Stand, therefore, having girded your loins with truth, and having put on the breastplate of righteousness, and having shod your feet with the preparation of the gospel of peace, withal taking up the shield of faith, wherewith ye shall be able to quench all the fiery darts of the evil one. And take the helmet of salvation, and the sword of the spirit, which is the word of God."[8]

151

The quotations listed in this chapter are given to show the basic law of the various religious groups in briefest outline, enabling us to draw some important comparisons. In many cases the numbering is an arbitrary device to separate the statements so that only one law or thought appears in each. There is no set number of basic laws among the different religions, although the number ten appears in several; nor do the various laws follow the same pattern or sequence. Yet the content is strikingly similar.

From the Avaiyar of Hinduism we may draw a decalogue of basic laws and principles.

1. Honor thy father and mother.
2. Forget not the favors thou hast received.
3. Seek the society of the good.
4. Live in harmony with others.
5. Remain in thy own place.
6. Speak ill of none.
7. The sweetest bread is that earned by labor.
8. Knowledge is riches, what one learns in youth is engraven on stone.
9. The wise is he who knows himself.
10. There is no tranquil sleep without a good conscience, nor any virtue without religion.[9]

To these precepts we would add the six marks of the quality of goodness, found in the Laws of Manu:

1. The study of the Vedas.
2. Knowledge.
3. Purity.
4. Control over the organs.
5. The performance of meritorious acts.
6. Meditation on the soul.[10]

and the five Brahmin vows:

1. Not to injure living beings.
2. Not to lie.
3. Not to steal.
4. To be continent.
5. To be liberal.[11]

In order to make comparison easier, it seems best to list the laws of the other Indian religions in sequence to those of Hinduism. There is a distinct relation between them, as a survey of the fundamental legal positions will show, and we can take the four Indian religions as a group when we compare them with the non-Indian groups. Islam is not included as an Indian religion because its origin is basically Judaistic, although it is one of the major religions in India today.

The familiar number in Buddhism is eight, rather than ten, and "The Noble Eight-fold Path" is the central theme of the teachings of Gautama. The "Eight Precepts" are the rules that apply especially to the Buddhist monks. Later writings show the eight precepts extended to ten, and ten negative commandments make their appearance. The only decalogue that has been attributed directly to Gautama is the group of "Ten Fetters" that the monk must break in his gradual progress along the eight-fold path:

1. Right views (free from superstition and delusion).
2. Right Aspirations (high, and worthy of the intelligent, earnest man).
3. Right Speech (kindly, open, truthful).
4. Right Conduct (peaceful, honest, pure).
5. Right Livelihood (bringing hurt or danger to no living thing).

6. Right Effort (in self-training and self-control).
7. Right Mindfulness (the active, watchful mind).
8. Right Rapture (in deep meditation on the realities of life).[12]

The "Ten Fetters" that the monk must break are:

1. Delusion of self.
2. Doubt.
3. The efficacy of good works and ceremonies.
4. Sensuality.
5. Ill-will.
6. Love of life on earth.
7. Desire for a future life in heaven.
8. Pride.
9. Self-righteousness.
10. Ignorance.[13]

The eight precepts that apply to the monks, the first five of which apply to all Buddhists, are:

1. One should not destroy life.
2. One should not take that which is not given.
3. One should not tell lies.
4. One should not become a drinker of intoxicating liquors.
5. One should refrain from unlawful sexual intercourse—an ignoble thing.
6. One should not eat unseasonable foods at night.
7. One should not wear garlands nor use perfumes.
8. One should sleep on a mat spread on the ground.[14]

The six perfections that are the goal of the monk and

the faithful follower of the Buddha are:

1. Charity or benevolence.
2. Virtue or moral goodness.
3. Patience or forbearance.
4. Fortitude.
5. Meditation.
6. Knowledge.[15]

The ten commandments that are binding upon all Buddhist monks were evolved from the eight precepts. All of the followers of Gautama are bound by the first five at all times, and keep all of the commandments except the last on fast days.

1. Not to destroy life.
2. Not to take what is not given.
3. To abstain from unchastity.
4. Not to lie or deceive.
5. To abstain from intoxicants.
6. To eat temperately, and not after noon.
7. Not to behold singing, dancing or plays.
8. Not to wear garlands, perfumes or adornments.
9. Not to use luxurious beds.
10. Not to accept gold or silver.[16]

The ten negative commandments which apply to all Buddhists are:

1. Thou shalt not kill anything.
2. Thou shalt not steal.
3. Thou shalt not commit adultery.
4. Thou shalt not be double-faced.

5. Thou shalt not curse.
6. Thou shalt not lie.
7. Thou shalt not speak vanity.
8. Thou shalt keep far from coveting.
9. Thou shalt not insult, deceive, flatter or trick.
10. Thou shalt be free from anger and heresy.[17]

The laws of Jainism are similar to those which have been outlined in the Buddhist religion, but there is a changed emphasis which marks the difference in the two groups. The Jain ascetic has five religious observances to follow:

1. Walking carefully so as not to hurt any living being.
2. Speaking reverently and without hurting anyone's feelings.
3. Taking only pure food not especially prepared for a saint.
4. Careful handling of the few things, such as water-bowl, brush, and scriptures, which ascetics may keep.
5. Great care as to where to answer the calls of nature.[18]

The Jain monks have five vows which they must take in the full strictness of their meaning and implications, while those Jains who are not monks must observe the rules as closely as their circumstances and avocations permit. These vows are:

1. To refrain from taking life.
2. To refrain from untruth.
3. To refrain from stealing.
4. To refrain from sexual intercourse.
5. To renounce all worldly possessions.[19]

The saints in the Jain cult have six essential duties in addition to the vows and religious observances, which are:

1. Repentance.
2. Renunciation.
3. Praising the worshipful Lords.
4. Obeisance to the worshipful Lords.
5. Practising equanimity.
6. Relinquishment of bodily attachment.[20]

A general statement of principles for all Jains is found in the sacred scriptures under the definitions of what right faith is. "Right faith consists in believing in the true ideal, scriptures and teacher. Such right faith is free from three follies, has eight members, and no pride. The three follies are:

1. Worshiping, with the desire of obtaining the favor of deities whose minds are full of personal likes and dislikes, is called the folly of devotion to false divinity.
2. Bathing in so-called sacred rivers and oceans, setting up heaps of sand and stones as objects of worship, immolating oneself by falling from a precipice, or by being burnt up in fire.
3. Worshiping false ascetics who have not renounced worldly goods, occupations, or causing injury to others.

The eight members are:

1. Freedom from doubt.
2. Freedom from desire for worldly comforts.
3. Freedom from aversion to or regard for the body.
4. Freedom from inclination for the wrong path.

5. Redeeming the defects of ineffective believers.
6. Sustaining souls in right conviction.
7. Loving regard for pious persons.
8. Publishing the greatness of Jaina doctrines."[21]

The Sikhs, fourth of India's great religious groups and latest in origin of all the great living religions (fifteenth century A.D.), have eight commandments which form the basis of the Sikh law. These are known as "Kabir's Commandments" and follow very closely the familiar pattern of Indian religion:

1. Not to strike anyone without just cause.
2. Not to wear religious garb to deceive the world.
3. Not to drink wine.
4. Not to steal.
5. Not to commit suicide.
6. Not to smoke tobacco.
7. Not to commit highway robbery.
8. Not to take life.[22]

Some of these commandments, especially the second and sixth, are unique among the religions of the world.

The principles of the Sikhs are pointed out clearly in a simile that is found in the sacred writings, although this statement is not in the form of law; "Make honesty thy steed, truth thy saddle, the five virtues thine arrows, and truth thy sword and shield."[23] The five virtues which are mentioned here are contentment, piety, compassion, patience, and morality.

Turning to the religions of the Far East, we find greater difficulty in cataloguing the law of the cults, with the exception of the ten negative precepts of Shinto. Yet from the philosophy and teachings of the founders we can draw certain basic statements which will give us a yardstick for the purposes of comparison with the more systematic legal forms of the other religious groups.

From one of the Shinto oracles we get the laws which bring conformity to the wishes of heaven. "That you may conform to the wishes of the heavenly spirit:

1. Attend strictly to the commands of your parents and the instructions of your teachers.
2. Serve your chief with diligence;
3. Be upright of heart;
4. Eschew falsehood;
5. And be diligent in study."[24]

The ten negative precepts of Shinto do not include the heavenly and earthly offenses, which were given in the chapter on conduct, but they do give the attitude of the religion and its position in the life of the people of Japan. They are:

1. Do not transgress the will of the gods.
2. Do not forget your obligations to ancestors.
3. Do not transgress the decrees of the state.
4. Do not forget the profound goodness of the gods, whereby misfortune is averted and sickness is healed.
5. Do not forget that the world is one great family.
6. Do not forget the limitations of your own person.
7. Even though others become angry, do not become angry yourself.
8. Do not be slothful in your business.
9. Do not be a person who brings blame to the teaching.
10. Do not be carried away by foreign teachings.[25]

The law of Taoism is summed up in sundry commands and in the description of a good man:

1. Will not tread in devious byways.
2. Will amass virtue, accumulate deeds of credit, feel kindly towards all.
3. Will be loyal, filial, loving to his younger brothers, and submissive to his elder.
4. Will make himself correct, and so transform others.
5. Will pity orphans, compassionate widows, respect the old, cherish the young.
6. Ought to put a stop to what is evil, and exalt and display what is good.[26]

Sundry commands:

1. Obey the instructions of your father and mother; never divulge the faults of your parents.
2. Never confuse right and wrong: neither reward the unrighteous nor punish the innocent.
3. Repay what you have borrowed.
4. Do not use a short foot or an unfair measure, a light balance or a small pint.[27]

For information of the law of Confucianism we turn to the Analects of Confucius to find that "the master was entirely free from four things: Prejudice, foregone conclusions, obstinacy, and egotism" (9:4). "People despotically governed and kept in order by punishments may avoid infraction of the law, but they will lose their moral sense. People virtuously governed and kept in order by the inner law of self-control will retain their moral sense and moreover become good" (2:3).

Confucius said, "At fifteen my mind was bent on learning; at thirty, I stood firm; at forty, I was free from delusions; at fifty, I understood the will of God; at sixty, my ears were receptive of the truth; at seventy, I could follow the promptings of my heart without overstepping the boundaries of right" (2:4).

From "The Great Learning" we see the progression by which the follower of Confucius can attain the highest good:

From the Son of Heaven down to the mass of the people, all must consider the cultivation of the person the root of everything besides.

The ancients who wished to illustrate illustrious virtue throughout the kingdom first ordered well their own states. Wishing to order well their states, they first regulated their families. Wishing to regulate their families, they first cultivated their persons. Wishing to cultivate their persons, they first rectified their hearts. Wishing to rectify their hearts, they first sought to be sincere in their thoughts. Wishing to be sincere in their thoughts, they first extended to the utmost their knowledge. Such extension of knowledge lay in the investigation of things.

Things being investigated, knowledge became complete. Their knowledge being complete, their thoughts were sincere. Their thoughts being sincere, their hearts were then rectified. Their hearts being rectified, their persons were cultivated. Their persons being cultivated, their families were regulated. Their families being regulated, their states were rightly governed. Their states being rightly governed, the whole kingdom was made tranquil and happy.[28]

Returning to the religions of the Near East, there are two that have not been listed so far; Islam and Zoroastrianism. Islam has a decalogue, rather a statement of law which can be divided into ten parts, in the Koran. Sura 6:152–4 reads:

Come, I will rehearse what your Lord hath made binding on you:

1. That ye assign not aught to him as partner,
2. And that ye be good to your parents,
3. And that ye slay not your children, because of poverty; for them and you we will provide.
4. And that ye come not near to pollutions, outward or inward.
5. And that ye slay not anyone whom God hath forbidden you, unless for a just cause. This hath he enjoined on you, to the intent that ye may understand.
6. And come not nigh to the substance of an orphan but to improve it, until he come of age;
7. And use a full measure, and a just balance; we will not task a soul beyond its ability.
8. And when ye give judgment observe justice, even though it be an affair of a kinsman,
9. And fulfill the covenant of God. This hath God enjoined you for your monition—And, "this is my right way". Follow it then.
10. And follow not other paths lest ye be scattered from his path. This hath he enjoined you, that ye may fear him.

The five pillars of Islam have the force of law because they are requirements upon every one of the faithful. The Muslim shall recite the Kalima or confession faithfully, "There is no God but God and Muhammad is his prophet." He must observe five daily periods of prayer. He must give alms. He must observe the fast of Ramadan. He must make the pilgrimage to Mecca at least once during his lifetime.

Zoroastrianism places the major emphasis upon the *Amesha Spenta,* the personifications of the characteristics of Ahura Mazda. There are six of these:

1. Good thought.
2. Right, or divine order.
3. Dominion, or excellent kingdom.
4. Piety, or holy character.
5. Health.
6. Immortality.[29]

Other legal statements are scattered throughout the sacred writings, and the best summary which we have found is in the description of the rich and the poor.

These are the people it is necessary to consider as rich:

1. He who is perfect in wisdom.
2. He whose body is healthy, and he lives fearlessly.
3. He who is content with that which has come.
4. He whose destiny is a helper in virtue.
5. He who is well-famed in the eyes of the sacred being, and by the tongues of the good.
6. He whose trust is on this one, pure, good religion of the Mazda—worshipers.
7. He whose wealth is from honesty.

And these are the people to be considered as poor:

1. He with whom there is no wisdom.
2. He whose body is not healthy.
3. He who lives in his fear, terror, and falsehood.
4. He who is not ruling his own body.

5. He whose destiny is no helper.
6. He who is infamous in the eyes of the sacred beings, and on the tongues of the good.
7. He who is old, and no child and kindred exist.[30]

When these codes of law and tables of principles are read consecutively there is a pattern which forms in the mind of the reader as the same injunctions are repeated in code after code. Certain laws stand out as fundamental to every religion, and these can be set down first in our comparative study as being the most important in the eyes of the religious leaders. Again we will take an arbitrary choice and use the code which is most familiar to the Western world as a pattern, since the Mosaic Law is the basis for the Judeo-Christian group. The selection of this specific formulation is not made from any idea of its superiority over other religious laws, but simply as a measure of comparison.

Here, then, are the ten commandments of religion, which form the foundation of religious life and worship throughout the world:

1. THERE IS NO GOD BUT GOD [Islam, Judaism]. THOU SHALT LOVE THE LORD THY GOD WITH ALL THY HEART, AND WITH ALL THY SOUL, AND WITH ALL THY MIND [Judaism, Christianity].

   You shall not confuse God with lesser beings [Islam]. You must maintain the highest ideals and worship God with a faith that knows no doubt [Buddhism, Jainism]. You must conform to the wishes of the heavenly spirit and believe in the true ideal [Confucianism]. Do not transgress the will of God but [Shinto], rather, meditate upon the eternal truth until your thoughts are sincere and your knowledge complete [Confucianism].

2. THOU SHALT BE LOYAL [Taoism] TO THY GOD AND TO THE TRUTH OF THY FAITH [Jainism].

You shall not take the name of God in vain [Judaism], nor shall you wear religious garb to deceive the world [Sikhism]. You shall not place yourself in an exalted position [Hinduism], nor forget the profound goodness of the holy one whereby misfortune is averted and sickness is healed [Shinto]. And do not follow other paths [Taoism], lest you be scattered from God's path [Islam], but free yourself from any inclination for the wrong path. Make yourself correct and so transform others [Taoism].

3. HONOR THY FATHER AND THY MOTHER [Judaism, Hinduism], AND THOSE RIGHTFULLY EXERCISING AUTHORITY [Shinto].

Be not obstinate [Confucianism], deceitful, nor a user of empty flattery. Remain in your own place and maintain that humility which is the sole defense against pride and arrogance [Buddhism].

Be considerate and loving to those who look to you for leadership, respectful and submissive to those who are your leaders [Jainism]. Attend strictly to the commands of your parents and the instructions of your teachers [Shinto].

4. THOU SHALT LOVE THY NEIGHBOR AS THYSELF [Christianity].

You shall not kill, nor be the cause of any destruction of life. You shall bring neither hurt nor danger to any living thing, nor strike anyone without just cause, but you shall feel kindly towards all and live in harmony with others [all religions].

5. THOU SHALT ABSTAIN FROM UNCHASTITY [Buddhism].

You shall not commit adultery [Judaism], nor indulge in any form of unlawful sexual intercourse. You must refrain from all sensuality [Buddhism], and maintain control over the organs at all times [Hinduism], being free from aversion to or regard for the body [Jainism]. You shall be continent and pure [Hinduism], seek the society of the good, maintain uprightness of heart [Shinto].

6. THOU SHALT TAKE ONLY THAT WHICH IS GIVEN [Buddhism].

You shall not steal [all religions], nor take by force anything which is not given willingly. Neither shall you take anything by trickery [Buddhism], nor by persuasion of the innocent or ignorant to release their substance into your keeping [Islam]. You shall repay what you have borrowed [Taoism].

7. THOU SHALT SPEAK TRUTH AT ALL TIMES.

You shall not bear false witness against your neighbor [Judaism], nor shall you speak ill of anyone [Hinduism]. You shall not tell lies. You shall not be double-faced, nor speak in such a way as to deceive anyone [Buddhism].

8. THOU SHALT KEEP FAR FROM COVETING [Buddhism].

You shall not covet anything that belongs to your neighbor. You shall free yourself from the desire for worldly comforts, and shall amass virtue, accumulate deeds of credit, feel kindly towards all [all religions]. Covet not even the good opinion of the world; give your alms in secret, and God who sees in secret will recompense you [Christianity]. Speak no vanity, nor show pride [Buddhism].

9. THOU SHALT BE HONEST IN ALL THY DEALINGS. USE A FULL MEASURE AND A JUST BALANCE [Islam].

Do not use a short foot or an unfair measure, a light balance or a small pint [Taoism]. You shall make yourself correct, and so transform others [Taoism]. In all judgments you shall observe justice [Islam].

10. THOU SHALT MAINTAIN A HEALTHY BODY AND A CLEAR MIND [Zoroastrianism].

You shall be diligent in study and in the investigation of things, that your knowledge may be complete [Confucianism]. You shall maintain an active, watchful mind through meditation upon good thoughts. You shall maintain bodily health. Eat temperately, and only pure food [Jainism]. Abstain from drinking intoxicating liquors [Buddhism, Sikhism, Islam]. Do nothing which will cloud the mind or distress the body. There is no tranquil sleep without a good conscience [Hinduism].

This synthetic decalogue probably would not be accepted by any one religious group in substitution for the existing law of the group. However, any person who lives in accordance with the ten laws outlined above should be recognized as good by followers of the world's eleven living religions. In all of the religions, the body is fundamentally the same; it is the raiment that differentiates them. The body is the law, the principles of conduct, ethical and moral, which determines the character of the individual and of the group. The raiment is the ritual and ceremony which is the outward manifestation of the religious cult.

NOTES

1. See J. M. P. Smith, *The Origin and History of Hebrew Law* (Chicago: University of Chicago Press, 1931).
2. See Ferm, *An Encyclopedia of Religion*, p. 484.
3. Smith, *The Origin and History of Hebrew Law*, p. 181.

4. Exodus 20:1–17.
5. Deuteronomy 6:4–9.
6. Matthew 22:37–40.
7. Matthew 6:1,3,4.
8. Ephesians 6:14–17.
9. S. G. Champion, *The Eleven Religions* (New York: Dutton, 1945), p. 161.
10. Ibid., p. 158.
11. Ibid., p. 166.
12. E. D. Soper, *The Religions of Mankind* (New York: Abington, 1921), p. 191.
13. Ibid., p. 191.
14. Ibid., p. 196.
15. Champion, *The Eleven Religions*, p. 19.
16. Ibid., p. 12.
17. Ibid., p. 12.
18. Ibid., p. 219.
19. Ibid., p. 221.
20. Ibid., p. 215.
21. Ibid., p. 216.
22. Ibid., p. 257.
23. Ibid., p. 263.
24. Ibid., p. 239.
25. Ibid., p. 240.
26. R. E. Hume, *The World's Living Religions* (New York: Scribner's, 1944), p. 136.
27. Ibid., p. 137.
28. R. O. Ballou, *The Bible of the World*, (New York: Viking, 1939), p. 240.
29. Soper, *The Religions of Mankind*, pp. 141–2.
30. Champion, *The Eleven Religions*, p. 304.

CHAPTER XI
CONCLUSIONS

In the study of the eleven living religions, it becomes increasingly evident that each one has something of immense value to contribute to the religious life of the world. Evident also is the fact that one cannot benefit by that valuable contribution unless one has an understanding of the religions which are not a part of one's own heritage.

When we pause to think about the definition of the "foreigner," we may say that anyone who is of a different nationality from us is a foreigner. However, our first thought when the term is brought to our attention is, a foreigner is anyone whose religion is different from ours. He is the real "stranger" in the sense in which that term is used in the various sacred writings, and he is the foreigner in fact because it is his religion and not his geographical habitat which is strange or unfamiliar to us.

The foregoing chapters have endeavored to dispel some of this strangeness and to open new vistas of religious thought. The light of understanding guides our minds to an appreciation of truth and beauty and devotion existing in regions which we once considered pagan. The wealth of beauty and the sum of truth is only hinted at in this brief writing and the reader is urged to follow up this introduction with contemplative journeys through the pages of the sacred books of the East.

It is well to recapitulate briefly our findings in this

short pilgrimage. We have touched upon only ten of the many common denominators in religion, yet in these ten facets of the jewel which the whole world holds sacred, we have found a unanimity of faith and purpose that can become the firm foundation of a better world.

The world is one, and the creator of the world is one, regardless of the names or designations made by the different religions. The prayers in mosque and temple, in cathedral and before a wayside shrine, are directed to the same supreme essence.

The duty of the Christian is no more sacred than that of the Muslim or the Taoist. The love which the Buddhist demonstrates is of the same quality as that of the Jew. There is no place for hatred or distrust in any faith.

Good and evil mean the same to all followers of the truth. Good is that which uplifts and frees and strengthens. Evil is that which destroys, enslaves, or weakens.

Purity is essential to vital religious faith for everyone. Holy character is valued equally in East and West. The highest good cannot be attained without the acceptance of purity in thought, word, and deed.

Ignorance is the enemy of religious life, and knowledge is regarded as a requirement for perfection, as well as a mark of the quality of goodness.

Thoughtful and responsible conduct is the mark of the religious man. He shall be clean, honest, just, and merciful in all his dealings, and he shall have compassion in his heart for others. He will not take advantage of his position as a member of the faithful, but will endeavor to bring others into an understanding of the right by his precept and example.

The believer lives to serve, not to be served. He must do good and help those who come within the range of his experience. The welfare of man as an individual is determined very largely by the welfare of all men, the responsibility for which rests upon the individual.

There is no religion without hope and aspiration to give it the motivating energy of dynamic life. Aspiration is the upward pull which keeps religion alive and gives it the urge to progress toward perfection.

Life is more than simple physical existence to the religious man. There is a transcendent quality that continues beyond the death of the body, carrying the spirit into the limitless area of eternity. Man is uncertain of the form or extent of the transference but not of the fact, or of the possibility of the fact.

Man must be guided by certain fundamental laws or principles in his religious life. He may follow his own desires as to the intensity with which he pursues the religious life, but he must maintain definite minimum standards of living to be considered one of the faithful.

With these fundamental principles as a background, it seems logical to assume that some common ground can be found for world understanding in religion. Since every religion in the world is seeking to improve the condition of man, to increase his physical health and his spiritual welfare (his mental health, if you prefer), such a community of interest should be implemented by the organization of a world council of religion.

Such a representative group could, through study and open discussion, remove much of the misunderstanding which clouds the minds of religious leaders at the present time. Valuable and time-tested principles which will enhance the effectiveness of all religious teaching can be made available to every group. No single religion has all of the best thought, nor all truth, yet each group has a vital contribution to make to the others.

Religious understanding and cooperation on a worldwide basis will bring about the elimination of wasteful duplication and the eradication of the present competition which is so bewildering to the uninitiated observer. The forces of good, working together, will bring about the greatest advance in world welfare in the history of religion.

Whether a man is Buddhist, Christian, Muslim, or Hindu matters little so long as he observes the basic principles of his faith. What does matter much is that there are millions of people who have no faith, no hope, no directing influence that will improve their lives and increase their influence for good in the world. The paramount task of the world's living religions is to give these millions an adequate reason for living.

APPENDIX
THE GOLDEN RULE

Confucianism

When one cultivates to the utmost the principles of his nature, and exercises them on the principle of reciprocity, he is not far from the path. What you do not like when done to yourself, do not do to others (Doctrine of the Steadfast Mean).

—The Bible of The World, p. 423

Taoism

Rejoice at the success of others. And sympathize with their reverses, even as though you were in their place.

—THLR 223

Shinto

All ye under heaven! Regard heaven as your father, earth as your mother and all things as your brothers and sisters. You will then enjoy this divine country, free from hate and sorrow.

—Oracle of the Deity Atsuta, TER 239

Hinduism

This is the sum of duty: Do naught to others which, if done to thee, would cause thee pain.

—THLR 222

Jainism

A religionist who is possessed of carefulness should wander about, giving no offense to any creature. Having mastered the Law, and got rid of carelessness, he should treat all beings as he himself would be treated.

—THLR 223

Buddhism

Minister to friends and familiars in five ways: by generosity, courtesy and benevolence, by treating them as one treats himself, and by being as good as his word.

—THLR 221

Sikhism

As thou deemest thyself, so deem others. Then shalt thou become a partner in heaven.

—THLR 223

Judaism

Do that to no man which thou hatest: . . . and let not thine eye be envious, when thou givest alms.

—Tobit, Ch. 4
—Komroff, Apocrypha, p. 80

Zoroastrianism

Whatever thou dost not approve for thyself, do not approve for any one else. When thou hast acted in this manner, thou art righteous.

—SBE, 24:330
WLR 266

Christianity

All things whatsoever ye would that men should do unto you, do ye even so to them; for this is the law and the prophets.

—Matthew 7:12,
American Revised Bible.

Islam

No one of you is a believer until he loves for his brother what he loves for himself.

—Traditions, TER xviii

BIBLIOGRAPHY

Albright, W. F. *From the Stone Age to Christianity*, Baltimore: Johns Hopkins, 1940.

Ames, E. S. *Religion*. New York: Holt, 1929.

Archer, J. C. *Faiths Men Live By* New York: Nelson, 1934.

————. *The Sikhs*. Princeton, N.J.: Princeton University Press, 1946.

Aston, W. G. *Shinto (The Way of the Gods)*. London: Longmans, Green, & Co., 1905.

Ballou, Robert O. *The Bible of the World*. New York: Viking, 1939.

Bergson, Henri. *The Two Sources of Morality and Religion*. New York: Holt, 1935.

Breasted, J. H. *The Dawn of Conscience*. New York: Scribner's, 1933.

Brinton, D. C. *Religions of Primitive Peoples*. New York: Putnams, 1897.

Browne, Lewis. *This Believing World*. New York: Macmillan, 1928.

Carpenter, J. E. *The Place of Christianity Among the Religions of the World*. London: Philip Green, 1904.

Cave, Sidney, *Introduction to Some Living Religions of the East*. New York: Scribner's, 1922.

Champion, S. G. *The Eleven Religions*. New York: Dutton, 1945.

Edwards, D. Maill. *The Philosophy of Religion*. New York: Doran, 1924.

Ferm, Vergilius. *An Encyclopedia of Religion*. New York: Philosophical Library, 1945.

Greene, Wm. C. *Moira*. Cambridge: Harvard University Press, 1944.

Hocking, W. E. *The Meaning of God in Human Experience*. New Haven: Yale University Press, 1939.

Hume, R. E. *Treasurehouse of Living Religions*. New York: Scribner's, 1932.

————. *The World's Living Religions*. New York: Scribner's, 1944.

Jacobson, D. *Social Background of the Old Testament*. Cincinnati: Hebrew College Press, 1942.

Jaeger, Werner. *Paideia: The Ideals of Greek Culture*. New York: Oxford, 1939.

James, Wm. *Varieties of Religious Experience*. **New York: Longmans, Green, 1903.**

Lessa, William A. and Vogt, Evon Z. *Reader in Comparative Religion*. New York: Harper & Row, 1958.

McCown, C. C. *Genesis of the Social Gospel*. New York: Knopf, 1924.

Marett, R. R. *The Threshold of Religion*. New York: Macmillan, 1914.

Matheson, Geo. *Distinctive Messages of the Old Religions*. New York: Randolph, 1903.

Moore, G. F. *Birth and Growth of Religion*. New York: Scribner's, 1923.

————. *History of Religion*. 2 vol. New York: Scribner's, 1946.

Morgan, W. *The Nature and Right of Religion*. Edinburgh: Clark, 1926.

Nilsson, M. P. *Greek Popular Religion*. New York: Columbia University Press, 1940.

Paulsen, Friedrich. *Immanuel Kant, His Life and Doctrine*. New York: Scribner's 1902.

Pfeiffer, R. H. *Introduction to the Old Testament*. New York: Harper, 1941.

Pratt, J. B. *The Religious Consciousness*. New York: Macmillan, 1920.

Rylaarsdam, J. C. *Revelation in Jewish Wisdom Literature*. Chicago, University of Chicago Press, 1946.

Schweitzer, Albert. *Christianity and the Religions of the World*. London: Allwell, 1923.

Smith, J. M. P. *The Origin and History of Hebrew Law*. Chicago: University of Chicago Press, 1931.

Soper, E. D. *The Religions of Mankind*. New York: Abingdon, 1921.

Tisdall, W. C. T. *Christianity and Other Faiths*. New York: Revell, 1912.

Toy, C. H. *Introduction to the History of Religions*. Boston: Ginn & Co., 1913.

———. *Judaism and Christianity*. Boston, 1890. Ginn & Co.

Underwood, H. G. *Religions of Eastern Asia*. New York: Macmillan, 1910.

Wach, Joachim. *Sociology of Religion*. Chicago: University of Chicago Press, 1944.

Widgery, A. G. *Comparative Study of Religions*. London: Williams & Norgate, 1923.

WORKS OF REFERENCE

Apocrypha, The. The King James Version. Edited by Manuel Komroff. New York: Tudor, 1937.

Hasting, J. *A Dictionary of the Bible*. 5 vols. New York: Scribner's, 1902.

———. *Encyclopedia of Religion and Ethics*. New York: Scribner's, 1913–22.

Holy Bible, The. Edited by the American Revision Committee of 1901. New York: Nelson, 1901.

National Encyclopedia, The. Edited by Henry Suzzallo. New York: Collier, 1935.

New Century Dictionary, The. Edited by H. G. Emery and K. G. Brewster. New York: Appleton-Century, 1927–34.

Sacred Books of the East. Edited by Max Muller. New York: Oxford, 1879–1910.

BOOK II
THE TRUTH THAT
MAKES US FREE

INTRODUCTION

When one views the Judeo-Christian scriptures, the Holy Bible, as a human document rather than as the "revealed word of God," there are several points of difference between the recorded words and the traditional interpretation of the writings. I have been asked to document my sources, or proofs, of the statements made herein. Documentation is impossible because there were no complementary sources of information which survived the centuries. What is contained within this document is the result of inductive and deductive reasoning, stemming from a lifetime of investigation and comparison.

The biblical writings are evaluated in the light of the anthropological and sociological conditions and customs of the times and peoples whose history is recorded in the documents which have been collected into the libraries known to us as the Old Testament and the New Testament. Consideration is given also to the wisdom literature of the inter-testamentary period.

Consideration of this material as the production of human minds recording history, philosophy, and theology in response to the human needs of the period, leads one to the conclusion that the recorders set down the events and ideas which supported one basic concept. The recording of concepts which opposed this idea was not preserved except as manifestations of error that were thwarted by the supporters of the desired concept.

Consequently, we have only fragmented reference to Baal worship and the philosophy of those who held this belief, although this was the religious form indigenous to the geographical area of Palestine when Abraham entered. The monotheism of Abraham was maintained as superior to the polytheistic mythology of Palestine, Egypt, and later of the Greeks. The issue of monotheism brought about a serious split within the early Christian movements; a controversy which has continued in one form or another to the present day.

The material in this treatise points up the highlights of religious development from the time of Abraham forward, comparing the biblical record with the situation which is known to have existed at the time the record describes. Each highlight would require another book to detail, and this task is left for others to undertake. This treatise is presented to stimulate thought and discussion, and is not intended to contradict those who look upon the Bible as the revealed word of God rather than as a human document. There can be no basic relationship between the two positions. No rational or logical conclusions can be drawn from a text which was dictated by God. The most illogical conclusion can be "justified by faith" and there is no possibility of applying logic to the conclusion, nor is there any way that a mere mortal can interpret or evaluate a statement "dictated by God."

But, if you are the one who can be inspired by the dedicated actions of those who truly had the best interests of humanity at heart, and who spent their lives improving the human condition, this material will help you to see and appreciate the highest and best in human nature. The human record is even more inspiring to me than the "revelation" could be.

184

CHAPTER I
THE YAHWEH CULT

The Yahweh Cult is a religious movement which you would recognize if it were labeled "Judaism." It was a very definite religious development in the geographical area of Palestine during a period of approximately one thousand years prior to the birth of Jesus. This religious movement was not indigenous to Palestine. As a matter of fact it was brought into the region from an area of the Middle East where civilization had been developing for a very long time: the Tigris-Euphrates valley.

Before I go into this matter I wish to make one thing clear to you. I am not treating this matter as it is treated customarily, even by Old Testament scholars. For the purpose of this treatise I am assuming that the Bible is a human instrument. That is to say, it was written by men who were dedicated to an idea which they held to be supremely important for man's welfare and for his progress toward perfection.

I hope the reader will set aside any prejudgment of my departure from tradition in this matter. I do not question the writing being inspired, if you will permit me to define my use of the word "inspiration." I mean that the writers had imagination, foresight, and insight, and through this inspired presentation of the facts created something which has lasted for thousands of years. It is obvious that the writing of the Bible was inspired in this sense because it has lasted, and has inspired its readers; but that the Bible was verbally dictated by God for the edification of man is, in my opinion, open to very serious question.

I do not believe, nor do I wish you to believe, that God handed Moses the Ten Commandments in a thunderstorm on Mount Sinai. Historical facts and archeological findings prove that to be a legend, as we shall point out in a later chapter.

The assumption that the Bible is the result of human scholarship and insight permits us to make an evaluation which would be impossible otherwise. We can look into the reasons for the presence of certain elements that would be out of place in a divinely offered revelation. As we trace the development of God consciousness within the culture of ancient Palestine, we can see the growing structure of a group or cult, which I call the Yahweh Cult: that group of prophetic thinkers who sincerely believed in a special God-man relationship. This is described as the covenant relationship, and its development is the most important fact in the history of Judaism.

When you study the Old Testament book of Genesis as the product of man's creative writing, one fact stands out clearly. The sequence of events, the record of human progress, the comparison of recorded events in the document with known human and natural development in the region as discovered through archeological digs alone, proves that the portion of Genesis preceding the appearance of Abraham is purely speculative writing. Nobody was recording events at the time of Adam and Eve, and Cain and Abel, and Seth, and Noah. This was a projection into the past by those who believed in the God-man relationship, which Abraham introduced into the area.

The first eleven chapters of Genesis were probably written considerably after the time of Moses. In fact, I believe that the evidence proves Genesis to have been written following the writing of the book of Deuteronomy. The first known scroll in our archeological file was the scroll of Deuteronomy. Whether there was an older scroll which was lost, nobody knows. But from the style of writing, we believe that early Genesis was written later than the scroll of Deuteronomy.

This early portion was produced to lend authenticity to the position of the Yahweh cult, to the God-man relationship which the Yahweh cult accepted, as opposed to the mythological origin of man that was accepted by the Baal cult. The philosophy of man's relationship to God and to his fellow men was correlated with his religious evolution. Responsibility or the lack of same is central in religious evaluation.

In the Palestine area there was obviously strong conflict between two major concepts of the God-man relationship. In the Baal cult the relationship was casual to the point of indifference. In the Yahweh cult the relationship was personal; God was responsible for man and man was responsible to God. This covenant relationship is original with the Yahweh cult and its predecessors. Modern research and archeological discoveries point to the fact that the Judeo-Christian Bible, and especially the Old Testament, contains the record of the growth of this particular cultus. The written account is consistently in support of one stream of religious development, that which is designated here as the Yahweh cult.

When Abraham brought his beliefs and culture with him from his Chaldean origins, he did not bring them into a void. He and his retinue were not the only religiously oriented people in Palestine. There was a well-defined culture and an established religious consciousness in the land of his adoption. Many of the squabbles he had with his

187

neighbors in Canaan, as Palestine was called at that time, could well have stemmed from the religious difference existing between Abraham and his new neighbors. His many experiences of persecution have their counterpart in much more modern history, where one religious culture impinges upon another.

Undoubtedly there were many religious ideas current in this area at the time of Abraham. The strip of seacoast known then as Canaan, along the eastern shore of the Mediterranean, was the connecting link and overland route between Egypt to the south and the Mesopotamian valley to the east; as well as Asia Minor to the north. Known then as the fertile crescent, this area was the crossroads of the caravan routes of commerce and trade. It is only natural to suppose that many religious ideas came along these routes with the commercial travelers who brought their religious customs as well as their trade goods.

As a matter of fact, much of their trade goods consisted of religious artifacts—statues of Diana of the Ephesians, of Isis and Osiris from Egypt—which they couldn't sell unless they convinced the local populace that the statues represented gods and goddesses. They were not the last to bring religious ideas into an area in order to sell their merchandise.

The one religious form which appears to have been the most popular, the most widespread, and the most actively opposed to the development of the Yahweh cult, was of a mythological type similar to that of the Greeks, but of earlier origin than the Greek pantheon. This is the form which we have already referred to as Baal worship, because the name of Baal is the name most frequently found in biblical accounts.

This mythology consisted of more than the one god Baal. It was a pantheon which included four major god figures as well as many sub-gods recognized in specific geographical areas. The major god was El, who was the semitic equivalent of Zeus or Jupiter in the Greek and Roman mythology. El was the ruler of the semitic pantheon and Asherah was his goddess wife, who also had her counterparts in Greek and Roman mythology. The favorite son of El and Asherah was Baal, who was the god of fertility. As such, Baal was most closely in contact with the people because he supplied mortals with their sustenance. Baal must be propitiated for abundant crops, plentiful rainfall, protection from blight and insects. Therefore the altars were erected to Baal, rather than to El or Asherah, throughout Canaan.

The pantheon would not be complete without a villain, whose name was Mot. Mot was the god of death who killed Baal every year during the dry season, only to see Baal resurrected again as soon as the rains came. This concept of death and resurrection has been credited as the forerunner of the resurrection idea which was adopted by the Pharisaic branch of the Yahweh cult.

The cycle of the seasons in an area where there were only two, rainy and dry, is found in many cultures to symbolize death and resurrection just as it did in the Baal tradition. So whether the Pharisaic concept of the resurrection of man came from the Baal tradition or another is difficult to determine. Rather than yield to the temptation to speculate on this matter, we must continue to evaluate the struggle which unfolds upon the pages of the Torah; the struggle between the supporters of many gods and believers in one God.

This struggle was not confined to Palestine or Canaan, nor was it limited to the time of Abraham. The evolution of religious loyalties from polydaemonism to the Great Spirit which we have seen in American Indian culture, and from polytheism to the one God which we have seen in many cultures throughout the world, has spread controversy and dissension wherever man is found.

The development of the monotheistic concept in the great valley of the Tigris and Euphrates rivers, from which Abraham migrated, was at least three thousand years in progress at the time of his migration. The Mesopotamian valley was one of the incubators of civilization, as was the valley of the Nile. Man's moral responsibility had been established and codified into written law by the ancient Sumerians who occupied the delta of the Tigris and Euphrates rivers, known as Mesopotamia, at least three thousand years before the common era (B.C.E.).

Known as the Sumerian Code, this listing of rules of behavior and specific punishments for violation of each rule governed the behavior of the Sumerians among themselves and in their relations with foreigners as well. By the time of Abraham, the Babylonian civilization had replaced the Sumerian and had refined and expanded the Sumerian Code. Known to us as the Code of Hammurabi, the Babylonian equivalent of the Sumerian Code made the punishments more severe for a violation of the code. These codes were sources from which the Mosaic Code of the Yahweh Cult was developed to guide and govern the behavior of the faithful followers of Yahweh.

But to get back to the source of the monotheism which Abraham brought into Canaan we have to go back to Ur of the Chaldeans (Gen. 11:31), which was located in the delta of the Tigris and Euphrates rivers in the lower Mesopotamian valley. These descendants of the Sumerian culture had not been absorbed by the Babylonian culture, and did not recognize the king as a god, which made them quite unpopular with him and prompted them to migrate from Chaldea to the upper valley between the Tigris and

Euphrates where they established the towns of Haran and Urfa.

When you study the Mesopotamian valley (which is now Iraq and Kuwait) at the confluence of the two great rivers, you realize that the area is one of the most fertile in the Eurasian continent from the very beginnings of human history. This and the delta of the Nile are the two areas of human settlement and development, the two sources of western culture and civilization. In Mesopotamia, the Babylonian and Sumerian cultures overlapped. The residual Sumerian culture remained in the delta, centering around Chaldea, while the Babylonian culture centered around the city of Babylon farther up the river valley.

The more ancient culture was found in the Chaldean area and Abraham, being a Chaldean, was trained in this ancient monotheistic type of religious consciousness. The civilization was extremely well developed and the culture and religious beliefs were thoroughly defined to the point where they were documented. Written records existed, which have been found by archeologists in the form of clay tablets containing cuneiform writing. By this evidence we know that there was a culture in this area which was developing and growing, having written memory to assist its growth.

The struggle between monotheism and polytheism was one of long standing throughout the lower valley. The monotheistic position was highly moral and ethical in its development. The monotheistic religious idea included direct individual responsibility; direct responsibility of the individual for his condition and for his relationships, not only with god but also with his fellow men. Polytheism was more permissive, and that had a tendency to increase its popularity. One who wished to indulge himself at the expense of others chose polytheism because, as a polytheist,

191

he could do as he pleased. The polytheistic loyalties could be shifted and manipulated to support almost any desired position. One could propitiate one god, but if that god didn't approve of the needs or wants presented one could select another god who would bless the desire to steal the neighbor's sheep or cattle, or to take his land, or his wife, or his servants. Polytheism was permissive, capable of manipulation not only by the ordinary people but by the priests themselves. The keepers of the temples made a very tidy profit at the expense of the people, telling them what they wanted to hear as long as their gifts at the altar were adequate. One who brought a nice fat steer as a sacrifice could be sure of a favorable augury because the priests enjoyed eating well.

The monotheists in Chaldea were strict moralists, and resisted the threat of adulteration of their principle by the influence of the polytheists. Here was a real battle of principle and belief, and the leaders of Chaldea decided to migrate, rather than to be exposed continuously to this pernicious environmental influence which was tempting the children. So Terah, the father of Nahor and Abraham, took his whole clan and journeyed upriver to Haran and Urfa. Here the families settled and prospered.

Nahor was the older brother and would inherit the land where Terah had settled, so Terah gave Abraham all of the land from the south bank of the river to the great sea (which we know as the Mediterranean). When Abraham started out to claim his patrimony he took with him his whole family and Lot and his family. Lot was the son of Haran, Abraham's brother who died before the migration and left Lot without any claim to home lands.

ABRAHAM IN PALESTINE

When Abraham and Lot entered Canaan they brought several hundred of their family members and servants, including a private army of at least three hundred and eighteen trained men (Gen. 14:14), and their flocks and herds. Abraham may have expected to find a free and open area where there would be no culture to compete with his beliefs and where he could establish his own monotheistic ideas without competition.

We can trace Abraham's progress through Canaan to some extent because he was a digger of wells. He knew how to find water beneath the surface of the land and his servants supplied the whole retinue with water. They lined the wells with rocks, and archeologists were able to find the wells even after they were filled in and abandoned.

The discovery of the wells of Abraham gave us the information relative to the route he travelled through Canaan, as well as the relative time he spent in each section of the country. His conviction that God was close to him, and that he was responsible to God for his actions, inhibited his relationship to the residents of Canaan. He wasn't indifferent to the needs of his people in the way that the Canaanites were.

If your god is indifferent to you and considers you a plaything to be used for his amusement; if he must be bribed, propitiated, supplicated, in order to grant you a favor or notice your needs in a favorable light; your attitude toward your fellow men is apt to reflect that same attitude. If your god doesn't care about you, why should you care about your neighbor? This was the philosophy of the followers of Baal.

So the inhabitants of Canaan were very callous and unfeeling in their treatment of Abraham and his followers.

If he dug a well and obtained sweet water, they drove him and his servants away from the well so that they could have the water. They didn't want to do the work of digging the well, but they certainly enjoyed the benefits of the water. The record in the Torah shows that Abraham dug several wells in some areas before he found enough water for both the natives and himself. His persistence permitted him and his family to live in peace, and Abraham was not contentious unless pressed beyond his limits.

It was at about this period in Abraham's travels through Canaan that there was a severe drought in Canaan, and Abraham took his retinue down into Egypt for a period. He was in Eygpt as the guest of the Pharaoh during the period of famine in Canaan, and the Pharaoh presented Abraham with many servants and a great deal of livestock. When Abraham and Lot returned to Canaan, their combined holdings of servants and animals were so great that the land would not support all of them.

Abraham gave Lot the choice of locations, and Lot chose the valley of the Jordan river, leaving Abraham to continue his occupation of Canaan. Lot had not occupied his place in the valley very long before there was war between several kings, or leaders of the various tribes residing in the area and Lot was captured. Abraham led his private army into battle and rescued Lot with all of the cattle and servants.

We need to pause here in the account of the Yahweh cult's development to point out some of the inconsistencies in the text which make it difficult to be sure of the accuracy of the reporting, but which make it impossible to accept the text as revelation rather than strictly human authorship. In the report of God's revelation to Abraham in Genesis 15, for example, his descendants will be oppressed "in a land that is not theirs" for four hundred years (15:13) "and they shall come back here in the fourth generation" (15:16).

Another puzzler concerns Lot, who separated from Abraham because their combined families and livestock were so great that the land could not support them together; Lot was taken prisoner and was rescued by Abraham, "with his goods, and the women and the people" (14:16); then Lot fled from Sodom with his two daughters who seduced him because "there is not a man on earth to come in to us after the manner of all the earth," (19:31). One must use logical reasoning to bring out the anthropological and sociological development of the period as it must have happened.

The primary fallacy exposed by the present study is that of the Bible teaching of orthodox Christianity, from personal experience, which had Abraham coming into Canaan accompanied by Sarah on a donkey; going into the realm of Pharaoh and kings as a mendicant wayfarer, who was entertained by the ruler as an honored guest. Such things were socially impossible during that period. One had to have the rank equal to that of a king to be entertained and given gifts upon departure by the Pharaoh and the kings visited by Abraham.

At this point let us recapitulate the God concept of Abraham as it has been described in the Genesis text, in contrast to the theological concepts of the natives of Canaan in their Baal worship. Abraham accepted a direct individual relationship with God. He was God's child, and God was responsible for him just as he was responsible to God. He could talk with God just as he could talk with his wife or any member of his family. This personal relationship carried over into his relationships to other human beings. In some ways Abraham accepted responsibility for the condition and welfare of his fellow men. This was a completely new idea in Canaan, a radical principle.

The importance of this principle is reinforced by the development of the covenant concept, which was central to the theology of the Yahweh cult. Abraham showed a respect for human life missing in the Baal cult, which led to a significent development. The first indication was the plea of Abraham that God save Sodom and Gomorrah, introducing the concept that human beings could be redeemed if given the chance.

The second indication was an important development in the man-god relationship, as shown in the story of Abraham's intent to sacrifice Isaac. Many early religious practices in various parts of the world included human sacrifice, either of a first-born son or of a young maiden. This includes the cult of Molech in later Jewish history (Leviticus 20:1–5).

Abraham was ready to sacrifice Isaac as a guilt offering when, for the first time in the record of this particular religious development, there was a substitution. Abraham's attention was drawn to a ram caught in the brambles beside the place of sacrifice, and the ram was substituted for the first-born son. This was the origin of the expression "scape-goat" and is the first time substitution is mentioned in the account of this particular religious development.

This was a significant step forward in the man-god relationship. Not only did it preserve the first-born for the purposes of propagation, but it also brought man a step forward in his parental responsibilities not only for the first-born son, but for all of the family. The first born did not escape entirely from his unique position in society, however, because he was dedicated to God rather than being sacrificed. The rabbis of ancient Israel were all first-born sons.

The dedication of the first born has an interesting history that can be traced through centuries of religious development. For centuries religious tradition demanded that the first-born son be dedicated to God. As a matter of record, the rabbinical group made certain their own survival by including animal dedication as well; "The Lord said to Moses, 'Consecrate to me all the first-born; whatever is the first to open the womb among the people of Israel, both of man and of beast, is mine' " (Exodus 13:1–2). This assured the priests a constant source of food, as well as recruits. The basic concept is repeated in the New Testament; "Every male that opens the womb shall be called holy to the Lord" (Luke 2:23).

Another tradition that lasted through three generations of those Chaldeans who were settling in Palestine was purity of family blood lines. Abraham was already married to a daughter of the Chaldean families that had moved from the delta country of Mesopotamia to the upper reaches of the great valley, at Haran and Urfa, when he undertook the journey south into Palestine. The moral heritage and monotheistic belief of the Chaldeans was handed down to Abraham's son, Isaac.

Isaac was a peace-loving man who avoided contention with his neighbors whenever he could. He redug the wells of Abraham, which had been filled in by Abraham's enemies after Abraham had fled to Egypt. Then Isaac dug more wells when contention arose over the wells that he had restored. Isaac wished to be at peace with those who lived in his vicinity, but he did not wish to be too intimately related to them.

It is significant that Isaac did not take a Canaanite woman for his wife when the time came for him to marry. He returned to the upper Mesopotamian valley and found his wife, Rebecca, among his father's kindred in Haran. Thus was the continuation of the cultural tradition of the

Chaldeans assured, since Rebecca was reared in that same cultural environment. This also meant that Esau and Jacob, the children of Isaac and Rebecca, were brought up in this same tradition.

The importance of this factor is that it shows the continuing nature of the introduction of a high and ancient culture into the Palestine area. This culture was introduced by strong minds, by people who were very wealthy from a worldly standpoint. Their independence was assured through their ability to support themselves and their whole clan without any assistance from the local residents. In fact, they brought more into the area than they received from it. The contention of this cultural tradition brings into focus an interesting legend concerning the sons of Isaac.

Tradition dictated that the first-born son inherited the family estates. Observe the biblical record: "When her days to be delivered were fulfilled, behold, there were twins in her womb. The first came forth red, all his body like a hairy mantle; so they called him Esau. Afterward his brother came forth, and his hand had taken hold of Esau's heel; so his name was called Jacob" (Genesis 25:24–26). So Esau was first-born by only a moment of time.

As the two sons matured, Esau became the favorite of his mother; that is, until Esau decided to choose his wives from among the local girls. Whether this action on the part of Esau prompted the account of the bartered birthright is difficult to determine with any degree of accuracy, but the factor of family culture undoubtedly entered into the situation.

Esau's marriage was outside the family cultural limits. His children were only half Chaldean. Jacob returned to Haran and married Leah and Rachel, both descendants of Chaldean stock, and so continued for the third generation the culture of the founders and developers of the

Yahweh cult, of the monotheistic tradition as we know it today. The monotheism of Abraham, Isaac, and Jacob was carried into Egypt by Joseph and the others sons of Jacob, where it barely survived the long sojourn of the Israelites in the land of Goshen.

Esau was not "read out" of the family because of his marriage to non-Chaldean wives. He established what we would term a collateral line, which became extremely important to the survival of the monotheistic concept and the Yahweh cult. This importance will be understood when we come to a discussion of the relationship of Jethro and Moses during the wilderness journey.

THE SONS OF ABRAHAM

In connection with the development of the Yahweh cult, we must not overlook the input of Ishmael, son of Hagar and Abraham. Ishmael became very important in the development of the Yahweh cult in a different format. He is the traditional ancestor of all the Arabs, and thus is the linkage between Abraham and the Moslems. Islam is a branch of the Yahweh cult, a development of the same Chaldean concept of the god-man relationship; man responsible to god, god responsible for man. This idea is somewhat watered down in the Koran, but it is definitely present.

After Jacob had spent fourteen years in Haran in order to win Leah and Rachel, he returned to Palestine with his wives and children and flocks and herds and servants. Here he established the dynasty which was to become Israel. Leah was the fertile wife, even though she was not the favorite. She gave Jacob ten sons, and I don't know how many daughters. Rachel was not as fortunate, since the record says she produced only two sons for Jacob. But these two were very important for the development of the Yahweh cult because they were Joseph and Benjamin, and Joseph is the linkage between Jacob and Moses, the linkage throughout the whole period of the exile while Israel was in Egypt.

Jacob's return to Palestine brought about a condition which was very significant to the development of the Yahweh Cult. Jacob and Esau could not live together in the same area, and Esau agreed to move east of the Jordan. This move placed Esau between the people of Ishmael and those of Jacob, and gave three population concentrations where the covenant relationship between God and man as taught by Abraham was central to the religious teachings. This meant that Judaism, Christianity, and Islam were all "covenant faiths," following the teachings of the Yahweh Cult. Muhammad traced his spiritual ancestry back to Abraham through Ismael. The Edomites (descendants of Esau who settled in the hill country of Seir) traced their spiritual ancestry to Abraham through Esau. The Israelites traced their spiritual ancestry to Abraham through Jacob, so the belief in one God, and in the covenant relationship, was common to all three population groups.

One additional factor must be taken into consideration at this point and that is the development of a code of behavior, a code of law. There is no real evidence that a written code was available to Abraham, although a written code had been in existence for centuries at the time of Abraham. We are fairly certain that Abraham's instruction was entirely oral, that Abraham did not have access to the libraries that existed in both Nineveh and Alexandria during his lifetime.

Both of these great reservoirs of ancient learning were destroyed later, unfortunately for us, but they were available to the scholars of that period. However, it is probable that no scrolls were circulated in Palestine at the time of Abraham and Isaac. Palestine was not as advanced in culture as was the Mesopotamian valley or the valley of the lower Nile, and instruction was in the oral tradition there. Yet the evolution of the legal code can be traced through surviving documents which were in existence at the time of Abraham.

The Sumerian Code was discovered, inscribed on tablets of baked clay. The code of Hammurabi is almost a copy of the Sumerian Code, except for the fact that punishments for violations of the code have been made more severe. We assume from existing evidence that the Sumerian Code was the first democratic code to be formulated for social control. That would be about three thousand years before the common era. Then, at about 2000 B.C. or even later, the Babylonians overran the Sumerian civilization and adopted the Sumerian Code as their own.

At the height of the Babylonian development they expanded to the west and south and their laws followed their expansion. It is logical to assume that the Assyrian Code, the Hittite Code, and the Canaanitish Code all evolved from the Code of Hammurabi. Since all of these moral and legal codes were in existence before Moses was banished from Egypt, and since the Canaanitish Code had been adopted by the Edomites among whom Moses lived for some years, we can assume that the Mosaic Code was a refinement of these evolving moral and legal codes.

The source of moral and legal authority throughout the whole area was the king or the pharaoh or the deity, personified in some traditions by the king or pharaoh. There was competition between the monotheistic position and the traditions of local mythology as well, and this competition did not stem from a single source. Competition between Baal and Yahweh in Palestine had no traceable relationship to the competition between the mythological deities of Egypt and Aton, the one god of the sun worshipers.

Thus Ishmael and Esau and Jacob may not have been the communicators of the covenant relationship to the people living to the east and south of Palestine through the Negev, the Seir mountain range, and around the Gulf of Aqaba. But the biblical tradition gives them the credit for spreading the Chaldean concept throughout the region. Certainly there were settled communities east of the Jordan, along the shores of the Dead Sea, throughout the Negev and the area of the Seir mountains, and around the Gulf of Aqaba. And the culture that had been established in Chaldea, and transplanted to Palestine, came into this whole area with the sons and grandsons of Esau and with the inheritors of Hagar and Ishmael. The concept of the covenant relationship had a great deal of influence upon the development of the culture in the area.

BRIDGING THE GAP IN THE RECORD

There is a gap in the biblical record from the period of Joseph's Egyptian experience to the appearance of Moses. There are references to the fate of the Israelites, but the history of the period has to be drawn by inference. When Abraham's son Ishmael was banished from Canaan, he travelled south and is reported to have settled into the central plateau of the Sinai. There is no hard evidence of this, but we know that the Sinaitic peninsula was arable land at that time. There were running streams of water as well as ponds and wetlands.

Before Hagar and Ishmael were banished from Abraham's family, there was plenty of time for Ishmael to have been thoroughly trained in the religion of his father. This would have made Ishmael a monotheist, trained in the Yahweh tradition. It is very obvious from the later history of Islam that Ishmael passed these teachings on to his descendants. The basis of Islam is Judaic and the Koran is approximately 75 percent Torah. Ishmael is the link through whom the followers of Islam trace their heritage to Abraham, and is considered to be the founder of Islam. All Arabs trace their ancestry to Abraham, as do all Jews; the Arabs through Ishmael and the Jews through Isaac.

One generation from Isaac brings us to Esau and Jacob, who were thoroughly trained in the religious beliefs of Abraham and Isaac; i.e., the Yahweh tradition of monotheism. Esau, although he was the older brother, was not accepted as the pure line of descent of the Yahweh tradition because he married outside the Chaldean tribal family. Esau married a Canaanitish woman, while Jacob went back to Haran to find a wife from the family of his uncle. But Esau and his family were also monotheists, and their descendants were devotees of the Yahweh tradition (Gen. 28).

The geographical situation of Esau and his family, as outlined in Genesis, shows that the name Esau was synonymous with Edom and that his people were situated primarily in the hill country of Seir, which is to the south of the Canaan that Isaac occupied and that Jacob returned to occupy. The significance for us is that the whole area, including the Sinaitic peninsula and the northern Hejaz to the Gulf of Aqaba, was settled by people who believed in one God. The region east of the Jordan River, and that between the Dead Sea and the Gulf of Aqaba, had not been denuded of its topsoil at that time. There were streams of water available to the flocks and herds.

The account indicates that the famine which drove Jacob and his family into Eygpt was not as severe in the land of the Edomites; the hill country of Seir and the Negev. It was to this southern area that Moses fled when he was banished from Egypt. We know from history that the region was populated at the time of Solomon, whose navy was based at Aqaba and whose mines were located in the southern area. We can assume that the laps of generations between Joseph and Moses did not indicate a static period in the development of the culture of this area.

The biblical account ignores all activity not directly affecting the Hebrews who were living in the land of Goshen under the protection and the domination of the Egyptian Pharaoh, but the other people were actively living and developing their own culture. They were thinking and writing. They were teaching and learning. And all of this activity was going on while the Hebrews who were descended from Jacob were being stultified by slavery in Egypt.

Since we have filled in the blank period in the biblical account by speculation and inference, let us take another speculative journey with regard to Moses. Here we have a man whose exploits were as great as those of any leader in history. Moses was the greatest Hebrew of the period, if he was a Hebrew. I have a tendency to believe that he was an Egyptian. The independent identification recorded in Exodus 2:19 states: "An Egyptian delivered us out of the hand of the shepherds. . . ." The ethnic differences between the Hebrews and the Egyptians were so marked that one could not mistake them, especially when the daughters of Jethro were themselves Semitic.

born to her or adopted being open to question, and was wet-nursed by one of the Hebrew slaves. This led to speculation that Moses was actually the son of the wet-nurse, even though the custom of having a baby nursed by a servant was widespread among the high born and wealthy. As the Pharaoh's grandson, Moses was educated at the palace and schooled in the administrative and martial arts which were required of one who might become the Pharaoh.

There are accounts found in Egyptian sources that give us reason to believe that Moses actually became the Pharaoh for a short period before being deposed and forced into exile by a collateral relative who was also eligible to be the Pharaoh and who was jealous of Moses' ability and of his selection as the Pharaoh.

This speculation is based upon two pertinent facts. First, there is a blank space in the recorded history in one of the pyramids during this exact period, where the following Pharaoh destroyed the historical record of his predecessor. This was done by Ramses II. Second, Moses was evidently one of the royal faction who followed the religious position of Ikhnaton (Amenhotep IV), which was monotheistic belief, at variance with the many gods of Egyptian mythology. Ramses II returned to the worship of the traditional gods. Such a religious position on the part of Moses would make him receptive to the monotheism of Jethro, who was a worshiper of Yahweh.

MOSES, THE EGYPTIAN

The first hidden years that we have to fill in for Moses are the years between the time that he was weaned and when he appeared as a young man. His whole educational preparation for life is a blank. All that we know of that period must be assumed from the record of his abilities after his reappearance as a young man. He disappeared from the Torah when he was weaned from his wet-nurse, and he reappeared in the Torah only when he was banished from the Egyptian court. However, we know that his early training and education would have been completely Egyptian. We know that if he were educated in the Egyptian court, his education would have been for leadership in Egypt.

As a member of the royal family, Moses would have had all of the privileges and the social position of that membership. His killing of an Egyptian overseer of the Hebrew slaves would not have caused a ripple in the society of that period because life was cheap and the royal household could act on impulse without endangering either life or status.

The fact that there was competition in the royal family for the power position, as well as religious loyalties which were incompatible, gave the rival of Moses the excuse to force him into exile. Moses was very young at this stage, and unsure of himself to the point that he could be frightened by his scheming rival. Much can be read into the passage found in Exodus 2:11–15, including the inference that the majority of the royal family followed the mythological tradition rather than the faith of Ikhnaton.

Present-day students have a tendency to think of past history in the context of the present, especially in the matter of age and time of maturity. Moses was undoubtedly under twenty years of age when he fled from the Egyptian palace. Average life expectancy was less than forty, and there was much less value placed on human life then than now. Life was short and hard and people were ruthless in their struggle to gain power and position in the short span available to them. Moses, being a progressive in his approach to life and religion, threatened the security of the conservatives in the royal family and they rid themselves of the threat by finding an excuse to banish him.

His Egyptian training would not have included principles or concepts of the Yahweh teaching. He would be trained and thoroughly grounded in the Egyptian religious beliefs, not the Semitic. Also, he would be thoroughly trained in Egyptian military strategy and tactics because, as the Pharaoh or as a prince of the realm, he would be a commanding officer in the military establishment. There was no source in his early educational period for the inspiration which made Moses the leader of the Hebrews; made him come back to Egypt after his banishment and court death in order to free the Jewish slaves. This inspiration came from elsewhere.

Where did Moses get this other training? There is very little in the biblical record. We know that Moses went to Midian. We know that he married a daughter of Jethro. We know that he and his wife had at least two children, and we know that there was considerable lapse between his leaving Egypt and his return. This second period of "hidden years" started with the phrase, "Moses fled from Pharaoh and stayed in the land of Midian." This is our first clue.

Geographically, Midian was located on the eastern shore and northern tip of the Gulf of Aqaba, east of the Sinaiatic peninsula, which is the northern Hejaz. (In the latter half of the twentieth century, this area is a part of Saudi Arabia.) To get from the palace of the Pharaoh to Midian, Moses had to cross the Sinai peninsula while avoiding concentrations of the Egyptian military units who would be alerted to watch for him. This meant that he could not use either the route along the shoreline of the Mediterranean, which was the busy route of that period, or the route along the shore of the Gulf of Suez and the Red Sea where the Egyptians were operating mines.

This left the central route through the wilderness as the safest way for Moses to escape the threat of capture, and he undoubtedly took this direct route to the land of Midian. There is evidence that the central route was feasible at that time, although it would be very difficult in modern times, because Pompey led his Roman legions directly across the peninsula when he left Egypt to invade Palestine. This meant that water must have been available in sufficient quantity as late as the first century of the common era.

If Pompey used this central route to take his legion from Egypt to the land of Palestine, it is obvious that it was an established trade or caravan route which had been used for some length of time. And it is logical to assume that Moses used this direct route to get him out of the area which was controlled by Egypt. Upon entering the land of Midian, Moses came into contact with descendants of Abraham, who were Yehweh worshippers. Thus he was exposed for the first time to the Yahweh teachings that had not been influenced or corrupted by Egyptian beliefs.

The Midianites would have been sympathetic to Moses, since they would be natural enemies of Egypt, and the priest of Midian would have been the natural person for Moses to approach since, even in the early days of the Yahweh tradition the priest afforded sanctuary. Wherever a priest of Yahweh or a temple altar was available, when one made contact he was protected from his enemies. This was sanctuary and Moses was a fugitive, but his contact with Jethro, the priest of Midian, was fortuitous. We turn to the book of Exodus for the story.

MOSES, THE SON-IN-LAW OF JETHRO

The early life of Moses is a mystery that can only be solved by inference. It is claimed that Moses was born of a Jewish mother and a Jewish father of the house of Levi. Yet he was raised in the house of Pharaoh by the daughter of Pharaoh, as a prince of the realm. His youthful activities are not recorded, but it should be obvious that he would receive the same preparation and training and education that any son of the family of the Pharaoh had. That means he would be skilled in military and administrative methods so that he could discharge the duties of the Pharaoh should he be elevated to that position.

There is some evidence that Moses did indeed become the Pharaoh, and that he was later deposed by another prince of the realm during the struggle between the followers of Amon and those of Aton for supremacy. A hundred years before the birth of Moses the Pharaoh Ikhnaton eliminated the priests of Amon and established the worship of Aton (the sun) as the official religion of Egypt. Ramses II was the Pharoah who reigned during the period of Moses' life, and who restored the worship of Amon and the ancient gods.

If Moses had adopted the monotheistic tendency of Ikhnaton, he would be interested in the monotheistic position of Jethro, his father-in-law, who was the priest of Midian and a worshiper of Yahweh. That Moses was an Egyptian rather than an Israelite was attested by the daughters of Jethro who told their father that "an Egyptian delivered us out of the hand of shepherds" (Exodus 2:19). There was enough racial difference so that a Semite would not mistake another Semite for an Egyptian, regardless of the dress and manner.

The daughters of Jethro, having been saved by Moses from the unwanted attentions of the shepherds, invited Moses to come home with them and their father invited him to remain. Moses stayed with Jethro and married Zipporah, one of the seven daughters, and remained working for Jethro long enough to sire at least two sons and to become thoroughly familiar with the philosophy and religious beliefs of Jethro.

The age of Moses which is mentioned in the Torah cannot be accepted as years of the Gregorian calendar. The way of telling time in the days of Moses was completely different and probably made use of a lunar calendar, although no calendar has survived. We know that their year and ours were entirely different measurements of time. Their year may have been a growing season and in a subtropical area that could mean two or three crops in one of our years. Exodus 7:7 has Moses eighty years old when he appeared before the Pharaoh to plead for the release of the Israelites. That would make him 120 years old when he died and we know that the average life span at that time was less than forty years.

Moses probably fled from Egypt when he was in his later teens. This is the time when he could be considered "grown up" in that culture. Living with Jethro for the years while he lived in Midian and sired at least two sons, Moses was exposed to the teachings of Jethro concerning the God of Abraham, since Jethro was a priest of Yahweh. Whatever the reason Moses had for attempting to rescue the Israelites from Egyptian bondage, his return from Midian would have been the same path he took going across the Sinai peninsula in the first place. It would also be natural to assume that he would use this avenue of escape from Egypt when he brought the Israelites into the wilderness from Goshen. He would naturally lead them across territory with which he was already familiar. I think it only logical to assume that Moses used the same course to bring the Israelites out of Egypt that he used in his flight from Egypt and in his return to Egypt from Midian.

First he took the central course across the peninsula

to avoid the concentrations of Egyptian soldiers and traders who would be encountered along the shores of the Mediterranean or of the Red Sea. He returned by that route because it was the shortest distance and he already knew the route. When he brought the Israelites out he wanted to have the advantage of familiar territory. Remember that Moses was trained early in Egyptian policy and strategy. His familiarity with Egyptian court protocol helped him tremendously in his pleading for the release of the Israelites. He knew the Egyptian weaknesses as well as their strengths. He knew their superstitions and could play upon them. He knew their military strategy, knew how they used their chariots, how they ranked their cavalry and their foot soldiers. When he took the Israelites out of Egypt he could use tactics that were unfamiliar to the Egyptians in order to confuse the army. The Israelites, having no tradition or previous experience which had proved effective, used tactics and strategy unfamiliar to the Egyptians to confound them and to escape from them.

This opens up a whole new area of speculation, which I will leave the reader to pursue. Suppose that while Moses was in Midian he raised a small but mobile army with which he made a surprise attack upon the Egyptians. The pestilences visited upon the Egyptians were not visited by a miracle from Yahweh, but were initiated by the army under the leadership of Moses. This is very possible, because the legendary pestilences were the picturesque way in which the ancient writers depicted the results of war, especially upon the defeated. It was visitation of Yahweh which could have been.

We do know from the record in Exodus (chapter 18) that when Moses brought the Israelites out of Egypt into the wilderness he was met by Jethro who brought him his wife and children. When Jethro reunited the family he stayed in Moses' tent and became his most trusted advisor. Moses was having difficulty handling the Israelites. This statement is heresy to the orthodox Jew, but I think it is perfectly obvious to an objective reader of the Exodus story. Moses was making mistakes and was not efficient as he could be.

Jethro prompted Moses to delegate authority and showed him how to delegate it, how to assign specific responsibilities to the captains of hundreds and of thousands, and to retain the policy-making function in his own hands. Remember that Jethro was the high priest of Midian, the devout disciple of Yahweh and it was with Jethro's advice and counsel that Moses drew up the whole constitution and bylaws of the Israelites. The moral code of Moses was practically dictated by Jethro, and was the moral code of Yahweh. It was the foundation of the morality of the Midianites and of all the followers of the monotheistic idea represented by the Yahweh cult. Jethro reinforced his influence for Yahweh through Moses, and this period in the wilderness, as it is called in Exodus, firmly established the principles and philosophy of the Yahweh cult in the life of the Israelites. It gave impetus to the Yahweh cult which secured its historical tenacity to the present day.

When we try to locate Mount Sinai geographically we are in trouble. The traditional location is the southern part of the Sinai peninsula, in the Department of Horeb. Some maps refer to the mountain as Mount Horeb, while others name it Sinai. There is another mountain which figures in the history of this period, referred to as Mount Seir, in the Seir mountain range which is located south of the Dead Sea in the land of Edom. On Mount Seir there was an ancient rock city, sometime known as Petra; a center of habitation, a center of culture, a center of study where a monastery was located. If Moses ascended Mount Seir it

212

could be assumed that he went to the monastery and had a long conference with the abbot or the leader of the monastic group. It was this same monastic group that assisted Elijah when he fled from Ahab, which we will go into later in this account.

The "wilderness" in which Moses and the Israelites are supposed to have spent forty years comprised the whole of the Sinai peninsula, including the Wilderness of Sin and the Wilderness of Paran. It is questionable that the Israelites went into the Wilderness of Sin or the Wilderness of Sinai because that area of the coastline of the Gulf of Suez was where the Egyptian mines were located and would have been patrolled by the Eygptian military.

A much more logical area for the Israelites to have visited early in their wilderness journey was the northern Hejaz where the Midianites, the descendants of Esau, had settled and were currently under the direction of Jethro. We must stress once more the importance of Jethro, the priest of Midian, because he supplied the impetus of the Yahweh philosophy and morality to the Israelite culture. He was responsible for the delineation, the explanation, and the detailed development of the Mosaic law. Whether Jethro was the original spokesman for the Mosaic Code, or whether the Mosaic Code was developed from the Canaanitish code after the Israelites conquered Canaan, we do not know. But we do know that Jethro was the source of the rules which were established within Moses' camp, and given to the Israelites on Mount Sinai. We also know that the trek from Midian to Jericho followed an established caravan route to the east of the Dead Sea which was later a military road used by Pompey when the Roman legions invaded the territory.

We also know that there was contact between the Israelites and the inhabitants of this area. In fact, there was so much contact that two of the tribes of Israel decided to settle in the area, rather than go into the land of Canaan with Joshua. When the Israelites left the wilderness area of the Sinai and went north to cross the Jordan river at Jericho, they left two tribes behind.

ENTRY INTO CANAAN

The conquest of Jericho initiated a new phase in the life of Israel. Canaan worshipped Baal, and some of the Israelites found Baal attractive. This was the most serious challenge to the Yahweh cult, and it led to a struggle for domination which continued for many centuries. After a long struggle, the Yahweh cult became dominant and was established as the primary religious philosophy of all of Palestine.

Moses had brought the Israelites from Egypt through the wilderness and Midian north to the east of the Dead Sea and to the Jordan river opposite Jericho. There he turned over the leadership of the Israelites to Joshua, his successor. Moses, as the law giver, had established the fundamentals of the moral and ethical position of the Yahweh cult, with the assistance of his father-in-law, Jethro. Moses was not a priest, as Jethro was, but he certainly was a student of theology, philosophy, and psychology as we would classify them today.

Beginning with Joshua, the successors of Moses were not priests or theologians, but warriors. For many years the leadership of the Israelites was in the hands of fighting men because that is what the conquest of Canaan required. The Talmud refers to them as Judges, but they would be termed more properly Generals. It is important to note that since the leaders were warriors skilled in battle, in tactics and strategy, in conquest of land and in control of peoples, and not skilled in religious ideas or in philosophical contemplation, the development of the philosophy of the Yahweh cult remained at a standstill during this period.

Progress in philosophical thought and religious development do not occur during periods of stress and conflict such as were present during the conquest of Canaan by the Israelites. As we know from our experience during the 1970s and 1980s in the United States, even a so-called cold war period stifles philosophical development. We are now concentrating, not on philosophy and the humanities, but on science and atomic energy. The major emphasis in scholarship in the United States today is a scientific emphasis. We feel it necessary to "win" the cold war, and while we are so engaged we can't take too much time out for the humanities, or for our religious philosophy. We have to take what we have already developed and make it suffice during this period of stress and danger.

This is exactly what happened to the Israelites during the period of the conquest of Canaan. The warrior chiefs were more interested in the geographical than in the philosophical situation. They had to consolidate their ranks to withstand the attacks of their enemies. In securing their geographical position they had to have a reasonably static and reliable philosophical and religious position upon which to depend. This static position was represented by the Ark of the Covenant, which accompanied them into battle and on the march.

The Israelites had a fundamental loyalty and responsibility to Yahweh. The law was there, set down by Moses. This was something that was absolutely reliable. It was there always, no matter whether they were triumphant or defeated. Whether they were conquering Canaan or being driven from their position, they had their religion, their belief in Yahweh, and this was their security. It became a dogmatic position, but dogma was necessary at this point. There are points in history when a dogmatic position is psychologically necessary for the welfare of a community. This was also a necessary situation when the Israelites came into contact with the Baal cult in Canaan.

The Baal cult was indigenous to the Palestine region. There were four principal deities: El was the father-god; Asherah was the mother-goddess; Baal, the son, was the god of fertility; and Mot was the god of evil or death. Mot killed Baal each year during the dry season, and Baal was resurrected at the beginning of each rainy season. The gods created humans as their playthings, to furnish them amusement at their whim. The humans were entirely dependent upon the gods for their food, and must propitiate them constantly to ensure a continued harvest.

The position of the Baal cult was traditional, dogmatic, unchangeable. It was the established religious idea in the area, and had been dominant for many generations. Thus the Yahweh cult needed an equally static, unyielding position in order to maintain its hold on the Israelites, who were not too secure in their allegiance to the Yahweh tradition. During the wilderness sojourn the Yahweh principle had barely outlasted the Egyptian mythology which had been so familiar to the Israelites during their captivity. It was on the crossing of the Jordan River above the Dead Sea, the invasion of Canaan and the conquest of Jericho, that the people of Israel came into close assocation with an established religious idea which was not their own. The Baal worshippers were followers of the ancient Semitic mythology which had been in the ascendency in this area for several hundred years. Historically, it was a perfectly valid religion. It was just as sound as the Greek or Roman mythologies were during the period of development of these later civilizations.

216

But Joshua was the champion of Yahweh, the up-holder of the law of Moses and the inheritor of that law. He was the inheritor of the social structure which had been built up and supported by the Mosaic law. He knew the judgments which could be handed down under the Mosaic law and this was the law by which he controlled his people. He had been thoroughly indoctrinated with the Yahweh idea, both by Moses and by Jethro, and he was convinced of the value of the Mosaic principles. So he brooked no desertion of these principles on the part of his followers. He insisted that all of the Israelites be worshippers of Yahweh. Joshua made sure that the altars of Yahweh were erected in the high places at the crest of the hills. The crest was the place closest to Yahweh, closest to heaven, so this had to be the earthly dwelling place of Yahweh. When the people needed the instructions of Moses regarding sacrifices it was necessary that they build altars, and these altars must be built on the high places. The following instructions make plain the tradition, and are found in Judges 6:25–26: "That night the Lord said to him, 'Take your father's bull, the second bull, seven years old, and pull down the altar of Baal which your father has and cut down the Asherah that is beside it and build an altar to the Lord your God on top of the stronghold here, with stones laid in due order. Then take the second bull and offer it as a burnt offering with the wood of the Asherah which you shall cut down.' "

In other words, the religious symbolism of the Baal worshipers was used as the kindling wood for the sacrifice to the true God, Yahweh. This support of the Yahweh cult was the basic attitude of the Israelites as they invaded Canaan. But the Israelites were tempted by the Baal worship. After all, the Canaanites were well educated; they had fine cities; they had very good commerce with their neighbors; they seemed to enjoy life; and yet they worshiped Baal.

217

The Israelites did not particularly like the restrictions placed upon the followers of the Yahweh cult. The law of Moses was a strict code of conduct, and did not permit the Israelites to do many things which they would enjoy doing. The reason that the Israelites resisted the law of Moses all the way through the wilderness campaign, and through the conquest of Canaan, was not that they thought it was wrong, but they thought that it was too strict. The discipline of the Mosaic Code was too much for these half-wild, nomadic people to accept.

The Mosaic law was not only more severe than the law of Baal, but the law of Baal had certain loopholes that couldn't be found in the Mosaic Code. And the Baal worshipers, in spite of making use of these loopholes, seemed to prosper even more than the Israelites did. Obviously, Israel was influenced by the civilization of Egypt, an older and more developed civilization than their own, and the so-called wilderness generation had been exposed to this civilization during their early years. The Israelites had been without any definite contact with an urban-centered civilization during their sojourn in Midian, because the Midianites were a nomadic people rather than city dwellers. They were tent dwellers, who followed their flocks and herds from one grazing area to another.

The civilization of Canaan was a relatively static one, with a well-established trade policy and with considerable culture. In other words, the Israelites were intruding on a well organized community. It is a fact of history that a conqueror often absorbs the philosophy and the mores of the conquered, and the conquest of Canaan followed this pattern. The Israelites absorbed the philosophy and the mores of the Canaanites, and were greatly influenced by the culture of Canaan.

The conquest of Canaan, as recorded in Judges and

218

in other sections of the Talmud, is a cyclic running account of the Israelites following the Lord, forsaking the Lord, et cetera, over and over and over again. The strength of the Yahweh concept was such that the faith in Yahweh came back stronger with each cycle of enslavement and redemption and renewed following of the Lord. It might take a generation or more to complete the cycle; to have the apostasy and enslavement, the redemption and the regeneration; but every regeneration and return to the pattern of the Mosaic law was stronger than the one before, at least a slight advancement, a little progress.

The people usually returned to the observance of the Mosaic law, to the symbol of the Ark of the Covenant, under the leadership of a warrior chief who was a champion of Yahweh. This warrior chief had strength of ten like Sir Galahad because his heart was pure. He was an uncorrupted follower of Yahweh and, as such, could lick his weight in wildcats, or Philistines, or Amonites, or whomever the opposition happened to be. The early champions of Yahweh were all warrior leaders, most of whom were known as Judges. Today we would refer to them as military dictators. Israel was the aggressor during this whole period in their history because Israel was the invader of Canaan and conquest was the order of the period.

When the Israelites failed to conquer, when they failed to win the battle, then came disaster because as soon as they were defeated they became the slaves of the victorious warrior chief. And, of course, when they met disaster, when they were defeated, it was not because they had met a superior force and had been outmaneuvered in the field. It was because one of two conditions caused the defeat: Either Yahweh had turned his face away from them and so had withdrawn his support; or else Israel had forsaken Yahweh's instructions and so was defeated because of forsaking them. These were the only two reasons for the defeat of Israel, because Yahweh had promised Israel the land; that they could just walk in and take it. If they couldn't take it, then it was either Yahweh's fault or their fault because they hadn't adhered to the covenant relationship firmly enough.

In Canaan there was a rivalry for the loyalties of the people, with the Baal cult being the most persistent rival of the Yahweh cult. Altars to Baal were found wherever the Israelites turned, on all the high places, and with the Asherah standing beside the altar. But Yahweh must be worshiped in the high places, and so the altars of Baal usurped the position reserved for the altars of Yahweh. Joshua, Gideon, and all of the early leaders had to tear down the altars of Baal and erect altars to Yahweh. This didn't make for very good neighborly feelings between the Canaanites and the Israelites. In fact there was a bitter strife between the two groups over control of the high places.

The record shows that Israel deserted Yahweh for Baal at rather frequent intervals, because it was the line of least resistance and constant strife was wearying. In reading the book of Judges you can see that chapter after chapter begins with the words, "Israel did what was evil in the sight of the Lord." That phrase means that Israel deserted Yahweh for Baal, and it seems that every time they deserted Yahweh they were defeated in battle by the Canaanites. It is difficult to tell from the record in Judges whether the apostasy came first, or whether the defeat brought on the desertion of Yahweh. Sometimes it appears that the defeat came first and that the desertion was used as an explanation of the defeat. But the cycle was clear; the Israelites deserted Yahweh, they were defeated in battle, they were taken as slaves, they repented, they were rescued by a champion, they were free to return to the worship of Yahweh. And that cycle was repeated from the time of Joshua until the time of David, through many generations.

Who were these champions of Yahweh? Many are legendary folk heros of Western culture. Joshua led the Israelites into Canaan, and through many of their conquests. Gideon was the one who used lights in pitchers to bring about a surprise night attack and rout the enemy. Samson came along later, and was the original Nazarite who would not let his hair be cut nor his face shaven because this was his strength, and demonstrated his devotion to the Lord. Samson was the mighty example of individual rectitude who was suborned by a treacherous wife who happened to be a Baal worshiper and who wanted Samson to forsake Yahweh and join her in Baal worship.

The struggle for the loyalty of the people which was represented by the story of Samson was a most unequal struggle. Baal was in the ascendancy, with a well-organized priesthood and great follower acceptance. The Yahweh cult was unorganized. The champions were loyal but the people did not support the champions as they should have done. The Israelites didn't uphold Gideon and Samson and the others. There was no organization to uphold the leadership. The champions were isolated devotees who believed so strongly in the Mosaic teachings that, regardless of social pressure, they were going to be true to what they understood to be the law of Yahweh.

The hereditary priesthood of the Yahweh cult was very weak and vacillating. It was from the tribe of Levi that the priesthood was drawn, and they took their responsibilities as a routine matter. Thus it was fairly easy for them to be corrupted by the followers of Baal. The biblical account points out that they often took bribes. They even vacillated between serving the altars of Yahweh and the altars of Baal. They were much more interested in the quantity and quality of the sacrifice which was brought to the altar than they were in the sincerity of the worship with which the sacrifice was given to the deity.

The meat which was offered to Baal was just as succulent as that which was offered to Yahweh, and the quantity of meat offered to Baal was much greater because there were so many more worshipers of Baal. So, if a priest became hungry enough for good meat, he might very well turn to sacrifice a bull to Baal so that he could have the hind quarter for his own table, rather than to wait for a chicken or a sparrow to be sacrificed to Yahweh. The existence of this situation was responsible for bringing about a very significant change in the organization of the Yahweh priesthood.

The corruption of the hereditary Yahweh priesthood brought into the situation the first nonhereditary priest, the first of the priest-prophets, which brought about a profound change in the fortunes of the Yahweh cult. Back in the time of Moses, the Levites were designated as the tribe of the priests. Only a Levite could serve Yahweh in the sanctuary, and the Levites were responsible for the care of the Ark of the Covenant. All non-Levites among the Israelites left the leadership of the worship to the Levites. But now came a change which made the contest between Yahweh and Baal less onesided, because the priesthood became a chosen profession rather than merely hereditary.

THE YAHWEH PRIESTHOOD CHANGES

For the first time in generations something other than heredity entered into the selection of the men who would serve Yahweh. The basic qualifications for the new priesthood were quality of service, intelligence, dedication, and sincerity of purpose. According to the Torah, the firstborn were "holy unto the Lord," and Samuel was the first-born son who was pledged by his mother as a sacrifice to Yahweh of the firstborn. Samuel and his parents were members of the tribe of Ephraim, rather than Levi, so Samuel was the first of a tribe other than the tribe of Levi to attempt to qualify for the priesthood of Yahweh.

Abraham, by his willingness to sacrifice his son, established the tradition that the firstborn was sacred to Yahweh. Here was a mother, not of the tribe of Levi, who said, "I am a follower of Yahweh. My firstborn shall be dedicated to Yahweh because Yahweh has been good to me and to my family." So she brought Samuel as a boy to the house of Eli, a Levitic priest, and asked Eli to train Samuel to be a priest of Yahweh.

Eli took Samuel into his household as a tutorial student. The only qualification for the priesthood which Samuel possessed was his dedication, that was given by his mother but accepted by him. He had no other claim to the priestly office because all of the duties of the priesthood had been reserved for the Levites.

Samuel became the best-prepared priest in the history of Israel since the time of Moses. He not only studied all of the priestcraft that was known to Eli, but he also studied the people who came in to Eli for help. He became knowledgeable in the ways in which he could help people to solve their problems. He concentrated upon his vocation, as the sons of Eli did not.

The sons of Eli didn't have to concentrate because, as Levites, they were automatically qualified for the priesthood. Samuel, the Ephriamite, had to qualify. His application and concentration qualified him as a priest who exceeded all expectations. His perceptive advice was available to any Israelite leader who sought it, and Samuel became known as a prophet as well as a priest.

So Samuel became the first priest-prophet. This made him the most influential priest since Moses and Aaron, and he became even more influential as he grew older. As priest-prophet, Samuel introduced a decisive alteration of procedure in the selection of Israel's leader. Previously, according to tradition, Yahweh had selected the leader by direct intervention. Yahweh spoke to Moses from the burning bush, and chose Aaron to accompany Moses back to Egypt to free the Israelites. Moses selected Joshua as his successor with guidance from Yahweh, and the same guidance influenced the selection of Gideon and Samson and the other leaders until the time of Samuel.

But Samuel selected the next leader. As the priest of Yahweh, Samuel went out and selected Saul, who was the son of a rich and powerful family of the tribe of Benjamin to which Samuel himself belonged. Saul was a young man who had not been tried in battle, who had no qualifications other than that his family was a leading family and he was a giant of a man, standing head and shoulders above the average Israelite. Samuel chose Saul to be king of Israel by designating him king and anointing him in the name of Yahweh.

This is the first time that a leader of Israel had been anointed king by a priest of Yahweh. Being anointed by a priest made Saul the representative of Yahweh as king of Israel. It also made Samuel the selector of the representative of Yahweh, and the right-hand supporter of Saul. So Samuel, by this one act, placed the Yahweh cult and the Yahweh idea at the center of the life of Israel, since Yahweh selected the king and Samuel was logically the Yahweh-selected advisor to the king.

The ninth and tenth chapters of the First Book of

Samuel contain the story of the selection of Saul to be king of Israel. Samuel's selection of Saul was no hit-or-miss accident. Saul had been sent out by his parents to recapture a number of mules that had escaped from their corral. Saul was managing the men who were pursuing the mules so skillfully that his actions attracted the attention of Samuel. Saul was very good at tracking, but was also intelligent enough to seek information and to put it to the best possible use, and Samuel noted this as he observed Saul in action.

It was easy for Samuel to make other observations and assumptions as well. Samuel observed that the family must have considerable livestock if they sent only one son and a few servants to recapture the escaped mules. This indicated that Saul's family was rich. The fact that they sent Saul out to recover the mules indicated that they trusted their son and relied on his ability. Samuel was also impressed by the size of Saul, who stood head and shoulders above anyone around him. In other words, he towered. So Samuel said to himself, "This man would make a good king for Israel."

Nobody else thought that Saul should be king until Samuel pursuaded them through certain machinations which are outlined in the tenth chapter. The people were led to believe that they selected Saul by lot, but Samuel had seen to it that the lots would fall to Saul. By clever manipulation, Samuel made sure that Saul was the one selected by chance. Samuel showed wisdom, not only in his choice of the man, but in his political maneuvering to make sure that the people would accept Saul as their own chosen leader.

Samuel proved by this action that Yahweh, and Yahweh's representative, were more powerful than the king because Yahweh selected the king. This was the first political application of a basic principle of the Yahweh cult; that Yahweh is responsible for man and that man is responsible to Yahweh. This principle was established by Abraham and carried on personally and individually by Moses. Here, for the first time, the principle became a national relationship. The king and all of his subjects were included. This was a new step in the development of the Yahweh cult; the belief that God was responsible for the nation, and that the nation was responsible to God. This was a logical extension of the individual relationship that had obtained since the time of Abraham.

Not only did Samuel choose Saul and make Saul responsible to Yahweh, but Samuel also organized the priests of Yahweh into a well-knit, well-defined organization. There is not very much direct evidence of this organization, but one passage which shows it is found in the first book of Samuel (I Sam. 10:1–8):

> Then Samuel took a vial of oil and poured it on his [Saul's] head, and kissed him and said, "Has not the Lord anointed you to be prince over his people of Israel? And you shall reign over the people of the Lord and you will save them from the hand of their enemies round about. And this shall be a sign to you that the Lord has anointed you to be prince over his heritage. When you depart from me today you will meet two men by Rachel's tomb in the territory of Benjamin at Zelzah, and they will say to you, 'The asses which you went to seek are found, and now your father has ceased to care about the asses and is anxious about you, saying, "What shall I do about my son?" Then you shall go on from there further and come to the oak of Tabor; three men going up to God at Bethel will meet you there, one carrying three kids, another carrying three loaves of bread, and another carrying a skin of wine. And they will greet you and give you two loaves of bread, which

you shall accept from their hand. After that you shall come to Gibeathelohim, where there is a garrison of the Philistines; and there, as you come to the city, you will meet a band of prophets coming down from the high place with harp, tambourine, flute, and lyre before them, prophesying. Then the spirit of the Lord will come mightily upon you, and you shall prophesy with them and be turned into another man. Now when these signs meet you, do whatever your hands find to do, for God is with you. And you shall go down before me to Gilgal; and behold, I am coming to you to offer burnt offerings and to sacrifice peace offerings. Seven days you shall wait, until I come to you and show you what you shall do."

Observe that Samuel had everything organized. He had the priests alerted. He told the priests exactly what to do. And then he told Samuel exactly what he would find, so that Saul would be absolutely convinced that God had selected him, and would wait for Samuel's instructions at the end of seven days. This was a beautifully organized plan to secure Saul for the Yahweh cult. Was there anything wrong in that? This is the way that bright planners do things at all times. It was for the good of Saul, and for the good of Israel. It was just organizing the good so that it would be most effective, and Samuel used the medium of the times, which any good Jesuit will tell you is perfectly proper procedure, even today.

Samuel, by evidence of the passage quoted, established communication with all of the priests of Yahweh in the vicinity. He used the priests in furtherance of the development of the Yahweh cult. He used them to impress young Saul with the power and insight of Yahweh, and the cooperation of the priests at Bethel and Gibea gives the first real evidence that the Yahweh cult had now actually reached cult status. The organization of the priesthood was evident, and the action in concert for a desired result showed structure beyond anything that had been shown up to this time.

The priesthood of Yahweh was a very important post, and the man who was the priest of Yahweh must establish himself in the eyes of the political leadership. Therefore the priesthood of Yahweh was a very self-centered activity. One must build oneself up, one could not give anyone else credit because to do so would be to weaken one's own influence.

Now, for the first time, one sees a change which served to introduce a new era. One priest cooperated to bolster the position of another priest, making the position of the Yahweh cult more secure in the life of Israel. The subordination of self-advancement on the part of the priest to the advancement of the whole Yahweh cult was unique at that time. It marked the beginning of real cooperation among the tribes of Israel in Canaan, and was a giant step forward in the development of the Yahweh cult.

Samuel established a code of personal conduct for the priests of Yahweh and this, more than any other one factor, turned the tide in the struggle between the Yahweh cult and the Baal cult. It tipped the scales in favor of the Yahweh cult when Samuel established an ethical code for the priests of Yahweh which lifted them above the ordinary association of men and made them morally responsible for their actions. The code made the priests responsible, not only for their actions, but also for the morale of the people over whom they watched.

This code was accepted as the standard for the priests of the Yahweh cult. It gave the rules of conduct for all priests, and its acceptance established Samuel as the priestly leader. It was a strict rule that prohibited rapacity on the part of those who served the people. The main points of the code are found in I Samuel 12:1–3:

> And Samuel said to all Israel, "Behold, I have hearkened to your voice in all that you have said to me, and have made a king over you. And now, behold, the king walks before you; and I am old and gray, and behold, my sons are with you; and I have walked before you from my youth until this day. Here I am; testify against me before the Lord and before his anointed. Whose ox have I taken? Or whose ass have I taken? Or whom have I defrauded. Whom have I oppressed? Or from whose hand have I taken a bribe to blind my eyes with it? Testify against me and I will restore it to you."

Samuel personalized his code of ethics, but it is obvious that he was speaking for his sons and all members of the Yahweh priesthood when he spoke the words, "Whose ox have I taken?" He was saying that a priest of Yahweh would not take anything from the people for his personal use. Samuel had never taken an ox, nor would a priest of Yahweh take the possessions of any person. It was the same with the ass. "Whom have I defrauded?" A priest of Yahweh will never defraud the Israelite. "Whom have I oppressed?" A priest of Yahweh will never enslave anyone, nor permit oppression in the land. And the reference to bribe-taking is plainly a prohibition as far as the priests of Yahweh are concerned. This outlined the moral code of the Yahweh cult when Samuel was its leader.

Samuel was the first leader of the Yahweh cult to select the leader of the people, the king, in his anointing of Saul to be king of Israel. One must remember that, when Samuel was operating, Palestine was united. The entire area was Canaan, and had not been separated into Galilee, Samaria, and Judea. This separation came quite a bit later; in fact, not until after the reign of Solomon. At the time of Saul as king, the Jews were operating within the area of Canaanitish civilization.

But it wasn't very long before the Jews became dominant in the area of Canaan. And it was during the rise of Jewish influence in Canaan that Samuel realized the inadequacy of Saul as leader of Israel. Samuel realized the need to have a king who was stronger than either Saul or Saul's sons. Samuel searched for a successor to Saul, and found him in the family of Jesse; his son David.

THE DAVIDIC LINE APPEARS

David was chosen by Samuel because he was very alert. He was not a giant as Saul was, but he could think for himself. In present-day parlance he would be referred to as "a brain." David was one who could reason, could figure things out, was clever. When Samuel anointed David, he established a line of kings that was important in the history of Israel for many, many years.

Samuel not only established a line of kings for Israel, but he also established the primacy of the Yahweh cult. For David was a devotee of the Yahweh cult, most of the time, during his reign. Sometimes he slipped in his allegiance, but usually he was actively supportive of the Yahweh cult.

Although David, the warrior king, established the line of kings known as the Davidic line, his successor was a matter of much controversy. The kings of those days were by no means monogamous. They had plural wives; and they had plural children by their plural wives; and those children, particularly the first-born of each wife, had a certain significant place in the family.

When David was old and had ceased to be effective as the leader of his people, there was quite a struggle between two of David's wives as to who should be the successor to David. The succession rested between two of David's sons, Adonijah and Solomon. The mother of Adonijah was a Baal worshiper and the mother of Solomon was a Yahweh worshiper. So the ultimate question was: which religious group would be dominant in Israel under the successor to David?

There was a bitter struggle between the followers of Baal and the followers of Yahweh. All of the Baal worshipers supported Adonijah, and all of the Yahweh worshipers supported Solomon. It took a very adroit piece of political finagling to have Solomon selected as David's successor. The followers of Yahweh were triumphant, and the followers of Baal had to bide their time until a king more favorable to the Baal cult should ascend the throne.

Solomon was a devotee, a very strong supporter of the Yahweh cult, and he established a priesthood which continued in Judah through the centuries until the destruction of Jerusalem, and Zadok founded the priestly cult which included all those who considered the high priest to be the authoritarian religious interpreter of Yahweh.

The religious party of Zadok was known as the Sadducean party, and was the first tightly organized party of the Yahweh cult. Later the party of the Pharisees was organized to challenge the authority of the Sadducees, and to present a somewhat different interpretation of the Yahweh principles. And it was not long before the priesthood included a monastic group which became the Essenes.

The Sadducean party was the temple party, believing that the temple in Jerusalem was the center of the religious life of the Jews and that the high priest was the unquestioned authority. This anticipates the Roman Catholic idea of the hierarchy, because the high priest in Jerusaelm had exactly the same position in Judaism as the pope has in Christianity. He was the authoritarian head of one main branch of Judaism, and this is mentioned to show that it was at this juncture—with the introduction of Solomon as king and the building of the temple in Jerusalem by Hiram, king of Tyre, and his workers—that the priestly group within the Yahweh cult was established.

There were two priests who contended for the top spot in the religious life of Judaism. Adonijah supported, as high priest, Abiathar who was in contention with Zadok for the religious leadership. They were caught up in the rivalry between Adonijah and Solomon. The rivalry reached a point where it could not be tolerated any longer, and Adonijah and Abiathar disappeared from the scene. The record suggests that their disappearance was rather violent, and it is evident that civilization had not reached the point where ostracism was the solution. If people became too annoying they were eliminated. This is all a part of our human history.

After Solomon's reign there was another struggle for succession to the throne. This struggle also carried religious overtones, since one of the competing successors was loyal to the Baal cult and the other to the Yahweh cult. The Yahweh cult had a majority of followers in the southern province, Judea. Those who were Baal cultists in the majority were found in the central and northern sections, Samaria and Galilee.

The sons of two of Solomon's many wives emerged as the contenders for Solomon's throne. Their names were Jeroboam and Rehoboam and they went to war against each other to determine who would be king. Rehoboam was strongest in the south and Jeroboam was strongest in the north. Neither could subdue the other's stronghold, and this led to the establishment of the divided kingdom, with Judah in the south taking Rehoboam as king and Israel in the north taking Jeroboam. Israel was comprised of Samaria and Galilee.

There was a bitter struggle between the kingdom of the south and the kingdom of the north for many, many years, in fact for generations. This was also evident in the religious struggle between the Baal cult and the Yahweh cult because the struggle between Baal and Yahweh was an important part of the political struggle between Israel and Judah. Israel had a majority of Baal worshipers, with a militant minority of Yahwehites, and Judah had a majority of Yahweh worshipers, with a militant minority of Baalites.

The significance of the religious situation becomes crucial in the record of the Yahweh cult when Ahab replaces Jeroboam as king of Israel. Ahab was a good, conscientious king, but he was also a good, conscientious husband and he was married to one of those women that men who are conscientious and loyal sometimes marry. Jezebel, the wife of Ahab, was a tyrant with the courage of her convictions, and her convictions were much more important to her than Ahab's. So Jezebel became, in fact, the king of Israel with Ahab tagging along. Jezebel not only bossed the family, but also she bossed the country. She was a loyal follower of Baal and she had a whole retinue of the priests of Baal in her household. This was a privilege of royalty which we do not find very often so early in our history, but it is very much like the feudal period in Europe when the lords of the manor had priests who were on their payroll, so to speak. These priests ate at the lord's table, lived in the castle, and were beneficiaries of their largesse as they tried to assist them in ruling their fiefdom.

This custom was introduced by Jezebel when she had the priests of Baal entertained in the palace, had them supported by the royal treasury, keeping them under control as her personal emissaries. Obviously, Jezebel influenced Ahab religiously, as she did in many other areas, and she established Baal as the favorite of Israel. Ahab couldn't stand up against her; probably didn't wish to do so.

All this was the prelude to the establishment of a seat of religious devotion in Samaria, which meant a continuation of the conflict over the location of the high places which were religiously significant to the people of Israel. Jerusalem had been selected as the center of religion by the tribes of Judah. The tribes of Israel did not have access to Jerusalem because they were warring with Judah. They had to establish one such area at Sychar, or Schechem, and another at Dan in the north. One of the kings of Israel constructed two golden calves, harking back to the time of Aaron and the people coming out of Egypt. These two golden bulls were located, one at Sychar and the other at Dan, and became the centers for the religious observances of the Israelites. But there was another very important high place which had been selected many years before in the northern part of Samaria, named Mount Carmel, and

234

it became an area of dispute between the Baal cult and the Yahweh cult.

The Baal cult had already established an altar and a place of worship on Mount Carmel, and the Yahweh cult wanted to establish an altar on the same spot. This was the high place that was most bitterly contested between the followers of Baal and the followers of Yahweh. It was during this period that Elijah appeared before Ahab, king of Israel. Elijah, the Tishbite, appeared as the prophet of Yahweh in the court of Ahab and predicted a drought which would bring famine to Samaria and Galilee.

After he had predicted the drought, and the rain stopped, Elijah was persuaded by members of the Yahweh cult to flee from the court. Jezebel, the queen, had told Ahab, "If you get rid of Elijah you will get rid of the drought. The priests of Baal don't seem to be able to overcome his strong magic, but just get rid of him and the priests of Baal will bring you rain."

Elijah fled from the court into the countryside and came to the brook Cherith, east of the Jordan. I have never seen the geographical location of the brook of Cherith, but it was undoubtedly a tributary of the Jordan which came into the Jordan valley somewhere between the lake of Galilee and the Dead Sea. We suspect that it was near an enclave of the monastic members of the Yahweh cult because the account says that Elijah was fed by the ravens. If the ravens were actually birds, that is one thing, but if they were some of the black-robed monastics of the Yahweh cult (so-called by the Baal cult as a term of derision) the situation is entirely different.

There were many unexplained happenings in the entire area at the time of Elijah, and some were very interesting from an historical point of view. Picture the area in and around Palestine at the time of Ahab. The whole area to the north and East, comprising Samaria, Galilee, and Syria with its capital of Damascus; the area to the South and West, comprising the Negev, Sinai, and Egypt; and including Judea which was separated from Israel at this point in time; was fairly thickly populated by rather intelligent people. Ahab's people were not nomads, wandering around in a vacuum with no neighbors. This area was more thickly settled at this time than all of Europe, although there were semibarbaric tribes throughout Europe at the time of Ahab.

When Elijah fled from the wrath of Ahab, or rather the wrath of Jezebel, he was evidently in touch with the underground of the Yahweh cult. The ravens who fed Elijah might have been birds, but it is doubtful that such was the case. The Yahweh cult at that time was a cult whose distinctive garb was the black robe, rather than the white robe of the Essenes who carried on the monastic tradition in later times. The black-robed priests were dubbed "ravens" as a nickname by their enemies of the Baal cult.

Rather than birds, the ravens who fed Elijah were members of the Yahweh cult who saw to it that Elijah, an important prophet of Yahweh, did not suffer. The evidence of cult intervention was even stronger in the case of the widow of Zarephath, who took Elijah into her home for a period. Although she had nothing when Elijah came, the meal and oil did not become exhausted during the period of Elijah's stay with her. This could have been a miracle, but I like to think that the Yahweh cult was taking care of its own, and that members of the cult had been instructed to supply food and oil to the widow as long as she harbored Elijah. This interpretation is more logical than the "miracle" explanation.

Zarephath was a coastal city half way between Tyre and Sidon in Phoenicia. This indiciates that the Yahweh cult had members throughout the region. We know that there were many members of the cult in Damascus and throughout Syria. So the cult members were able to care for Elijah outside of Ahab's realm during the period when Ahab was searching for him. But there were many Yahweh supporters in Israel, and even in Ahab's household.

Even though the Israelites were Baal worshipers in the majority during the reign of Ahab and Jezebel, there were Yahweh worshipers within Ahab's household. Ahab had a general manager, or a head of household, named Obadiah. Obadiah was a devout follower of Yahweh, despite the fact that Ahab and Jezebel were trying to eliminate the Yahweh cult so that the Baal cult would have no opposition.

From his vantage point as the general overseer of Ahab's household, in charge of the granaries and all of the functioning areas, Obadiah decided that he personally would be responsible for the saving of members of the Yahweh cult so that the cult would not be eliminated from Israel. He made it possible for a hundred members of the cult to hide and be fed from the king's storehouses during this period of persecution. He hid the hundred in caves near the city and fed them from the king's granary during the entire period of persecution when Ahab was trying to eliminate the Yahweh cult from the land of Israel.

During this entire period Elijah was out of the jurisdiction of Ahab. While he was at the brook Cherith he was across the Jordan River from the land of Israel. When he went to the city of Zarephath he was half way between Tyre and Sidon on the coast of the land of Phoenicia. But he realized that he could not be effective in support of Yahweh unless he could be back at the court of Ahab. In pursuit of this purpose he contacted Obadiah and asked him to tell Ahab that Elijah was coming. Obadiah was fearful that Elijah would flee again and leave him to bear the brunt of Ahab's wrath, but Elijah convinced Obadiah that he would meet Ahab.

When Ahab saw Elijah he cried out, "Is it you, you troubler of Israel?" Elijah replied, "I have not troubled Israel; but you have, and your father's house, because you have forsaken the commandments of the Lord and followed the Baals. Now, therefore send and gather all Israel to me at Mount Carmel, and the four hundred and fifty prophets of Baal and the four hundred prophets of Asherah, who eat at Jezebel's table" (I Kings 18:17–19, RSV). Thus did Elijah lead up to the challenge on Mount Carmel.

Elijah's familiarity with the nature of Ahab led him to attempt something dramatic in order to save the day for the Yahweh cult. The Baal cult had too many advantages, and so Elijah decided to "go for broke" as the modern expression puts it. How he had the nerve to challenge four hundred and fifty priests of Baal is a mystery, because Elijah thought that he was all alone against them. He didn't seem to know about the hundred hidden by Obadiah, or the thousands throughout the area who were loyal to Yahweh.

You know the story of the contest: how Elijah gave the priests of Baal the first chance. They erected an altar to Baal, slaughtered a bullock and placed it on the wood atop the altar. But Elijah was right there to make sure they did not slip glowing coals under the wood to start the fire so that they could claim that Baal had brought fire to the sacrifice. Elijah gave them all day to call upon Baal, but there was no fire and the sacrifice was not consumed.

And you remember how Elijah, at the close of the day when he saw a storm coming, built up the altar of Yahweh with the twelve stones which represented the twelve tribes of Israel. After he placed the wood on the altar and the slain bullock on the wood he did a very smart thing, if one remembers the natural laws, and thoroughly soaked the sacrifice and the wood and the altar, including a ditch around the altar which he had dug, with water. The trench guaranteed that the altar would be thoroughly wet. The altar was at the highest point on Mount Carmel, which was the highest mountain in the area, and there was a storm coming. If Elijah knew his physics he knew very well that he was inviting God to strike the altar and set it afire, because lightning would naturally strike the highest point, particularly if it was well grounded as it was with the water soaking.

Whether the sacrifice to Yahweh was consumed by lightning, or whether it ever happened at all we cannot prove at this point in time. But I like to think that Elijah was canny enough to have nature work for him; and I like to think that the breaking of the drought was signaled by the bolt of lightning striking the altar and consuming the sacrifice. Whatever happened, we know that Elijah won the contest and came very close to losing his head.

When Ahab reported to Jezebel the results of the contest on Mount Carmel—how the Yahweh cult was triumphant, and that the priests of Baal had been slaughtered by the newly won followers of Yahweh after their failure—Jezebel threatened Elijah with the same fate that had overcome the priests of Baal. This caused Elijah to flee from Israel into the land of Judah, where the majority of the people were followers of Yahweh. Elijah would have been accepted in Judah, but he was an Israelite and the Judeans were enemies of the Israelites. He went down to Beersheba, at the southern extreme of the land of Judah, and continued his journey southward.

The biblical account of Elijah's journey through the Negev has the angels feeding him, but he was going into an area that had been settled by at least two of the tribes who were released from Egypt when Moses led the Israelites out and was taking them to Canaan. So the area had been settled before the conquest of Canaan by followers of Yahweh. These people had constructed a rock city in the hills southeast of the Dead Sea.

In this range of hills is a mountain, the name of which is in question. Scholars cannot agree whether the mountain was named Mount Sinai, Mount Horeb, Mount Nebo, or Mount Seir. From the account it is called the sacred mountain. Also from the account, when Elijah left Beersheba he went a day's journey into the wilderness and lay down and went to sleep. He was awakened by an angel who said, "Elijah, rise and eat."

It was the custom during this period in history for the faithful to make pilgrimages to the sacred spots. Certainly, one of the most sacred spots for followers of the Yahweh cult would be the mountain of Yahweh, where the law had been handed down. This would have been the logical spot to establish a retreat for the monastics who served Yahweh. They would abide here to search out the scriptures, the laws of Yahweh governing his people.

It would be very possible and logical for the devotees of Yahweh who lived in Judah to make the pilgrimage to the sacred mountain in the Negev. It would be logical, also, for the monastics of the Yahweh cult to maintain waystations, each a day's journey from the last, through the wilderness. These waystations, or hostels, were places established so that the pilgrims could get refreshment and rest to enable them to continue the journey on foot to the mountain of Seir from Judah.

Elijah could very well have come to the first of these hostels, and have fallen exhausted into a deep sleep; and to have a devotee of Yahweh awaken him with food, which refreshed him and made it possible for him to resume his journey. The account says he went forty days and forty nights into the wilderness, which is the biblical way of saying that he took a long trip. A survey of that region on the map shows that the distance from Beersheba to Seir was not far enough to take the time recorded, and anyone could walk it in a week or less.

When Elijah came to the holy mountain, having been assisted in his journey by devotees of Yahweh, he discovered that there were instructions awaiting him. Who gave these instructions? Here again we come into the area of speculation. It wasn't "The Lord God Almighty." It was "The Lord." Was the reference to the Lord a reference to the abbot of the monastery, to the leader of the Yahweh cult of that period, to the prophet of righteousness that we find reference to in the Dead Sea Scrolls?

It could very well have been. Certainly Elijah consulted someone; whether it was Yahweh, or the leader of the Yahweh cult who was the abbot of the monastery, we can only speculate. But the fact is plain that Elijah came into contact with someone who knew the situation, not only in Judah, but also in Israel and Syria and Phoenicia. This meant that there had to be communication among various parts of Palestine, the surrounding territory, and Mount Seir. There must have been runners to bring information to headquarters, and to take information and instructions from headquarters back out into the field.

The mountain of the Lord may have been in the unpopulated wilderness, and Elijah may have been there all by himself, but I doubt it very much. In the first place Elijah wouldn't have had to go that far to be by himself. He wouldn't have to travel forty days and forty nights. Just a day's journey below Beersheba he would have been safe from any enemies, and yet he took this pilgrimage. And note the results.

After he had taken the pilgrimage he was no longer

discouraged. He had fled Ahab and Jezebel, had given up hope for any assistance from anyone, any member of the Yahweh cult. He was convinced that his life was over and that he had no further contribution to make. Yet, after his journey into the wilderness, he returned so thoroughly inspired by the strength of the Yahweh cult that he went right back into the area from which he had fled. He continued to prophesy and to admonish, where once he was afraid to open his mouth.

What happened? I think that he consulted the head of the Yahweh cult. I think that he had conferences with the leaders of a monastic group who were in possession of a great deal of information that Elijah didn't have. I think that when he went to the mountain of the Lord he received orders, and also received assurances. I Kings 19 shows that Elijah was completely discouraged. He is quoted as saying, "I, even I only am left, and they seek my life, to take it away." Yet, after he goes into the Negev he is assured that there are seven thousand in Israel, not in Judah, but in Samaria and Galilee, still loyal to Yahweh. His informant says, "There are seven thousand who have not bowed the knee to Baal, who have not kissed him."

Who would know that figure? Of course, if you believe in the miraculous communication between God and man, God would have known the figure, being the omniscient deity, and could have told Elijah. But I think it was the head of the Yahweh cult who had that information, and who told Elijah. And if it were the leader of the Yahweh cult, certainly he knew a lot about what was going on. And if he knew a lot about what was going on, he had representatives in the whole area who were giving him periodic reports on the state of things.

After Elijah had visited the mountain retreat and had been assured by the leader that things were under control, he left the area south of the Dead Sea and returned to Israel and contacted Elisha on a farm in the area south of the Sea of Galilee. How could Elijah have found Elisha if he had not been instructed as to the location of Elisha in Galilee? But he walked out into the field where Elisha was plowing with a yoke of oxen, and "cast his mantle upon him." Elisha did not order Elijah off the land, as he would have if Elijah came upon him unannounced.

What happened was that Elisha began immediately to follow Elijah, and made preparation by slaughtering the oxen and cooking them for his family. He didn't desert his family, but left them well provided for with food and the farm and livestock. And when he followed Elijah, he did not do so blindly and without preparation. He immediately became a spokesman for Yahweh and he didn't just start out speaking as a mature individual. Obviously he had been schooled in the Yahweh tradition, knew the principles of the Yahweh cult, was thoroughly educated to it, knew what to say and how to say it.

How did this happen? Miraculously, perhaps! God entered into the mind of Elisha and made him the spokesman of the Yahweh cult. That is the only way it could have happened—unless Elisha had been prepared as a student and a member of the Yahweh cult, thoroughly educated and indoctrinated in the principles of the cult. It had to happen one way or the other. You can take your choice. I choose to maintain that the organization existed, that Elisha was thoroughly oriented to the Yahweh principles before Elijah ever appeared and "cast his mantle upon him."

HISTORICAL REPRISE

Before we trace the development of the Yahweh cult any further, I wish to reprise the events of the life of Elijah. We would do well to examine very closely the story of Elijah as one of the most intriguing stories in the whole of the biblical account; as a basis for speculation there is no more suggestive account than that of Elijah. He was apparently standing alone, or virtually alone, against the resurgance of the Baal cult in the life of Israel. Ahab, a weak king, had married Jezebel, a strong queen, who was a follower of Baal. Baal worship was indigenous to Palestine, to Canaan, while the Yahweh cult carried on the tradition of the Chaldean monotheism that Abraham brought into Palestine from the upper Mesopotamian valley, where his father had migrated during the Babylonian reign of Hammurabi.

Jezebel had persuaded Ahab to erase the Yahweh cult by killing all of the prophets and priests of Yahweh. Elijah was the one prophet of Yahweh who seemed to be immune to Ahab's designs. He was the spokesman for the cult, and was protected by the cult members so that his usefulness would not be lost. Note the subtle difference in the reporting of "the Lord's" instructions to Elijah from that of earlier pronouncements. Here it is "the word of the Lord," which could very well indicate that the word was transmitted by a human emissary. The ravens who fed Elijah at the brook Cherith could well be members of the Yahweh priesthood in black robes, whose garb had caused the followers of Baal to dub them "ravens" as a term of derision.

A similar interpretation fits the incident concerning the widow of Zerapheth who had been commanded to care for Elijah, and who was supplied with additional food as long as Elijah was with her. This would have been a logical arrangement for the leader of the Yahweh cult to have made, knowing as he must how little extra such a person would have under normal circumstances. Another illustration of the organization of the Yahweh cult is given by Obadiah, manager of Ahab's household, who was shown by the record to have saved a hundred followers of Yahweh during the attempted extermination of the entire group by Jezebel. But the crowning hint of organization and power comes following the contest on Mount Carmel, when Elijah bested the priests of Baal and then fled from the wrath of the queen.

According to the record, Elijah fled to Beersheba at the southern border of Judah and then went a day's journey into the wilderness where an angel of the Lord (or a devotee of the Yahweh cult) fed him. Thence he traveled a long way into the wilderness (forty days and forty nights is the way a long time is indicated) to the sacred mountain. Whether that mountain was Sinai, Horeb, Nebo, or Seir is open to question; but Elijah was cared for on the journey. One must surmise that the way was traveled often by members of the Yahweh cult, and that there were way stations manned and supplied by devotees of the cult.

At the sacred mountain Elijah was evidently in conference with the leader of the Yahweh cult, or at least with the director of the community maintained on the mountain in the rock city, evidence of which still exists. The instructions were most specific, showing that the leader had a thorough knowledge of what was transpiring in Palestine and Syria. He also knew that there were seven thousand devotees of Yahweh who had not deserted the ranks.

Here for the second time in the record a Yahweh priest is commissioned to anoint a political leader. Samuel was the first priest on record to have done so, and now Elijah is commissioned to anoint not one but two kings who would be favorable to Yahweh. Note how the power and influence of the Yahweh cult has grown and spread since the time of Samuel. Elijah is not only to anoint Jehu to be king of Israel, but also Hazael to be king of Syria which indicated that the Yahweh cult was strong in the Damascus area.

One last speculation from the story of Elijah is pertinent at this point, showing both organization and communication. From the sacred mountain somewhere to the south of Palestine, the leader told Elijah to anoint Elisha as his successor in the role of spokesman for Yahweh in Israel. The exact location of this new prophet was described so that Elijah could walk out into a field to the south of the Sea of Galilee and pick out the man. And when this farmer was chosen he neither questioned nor objected. In other words, he was fully trained and ready for the appointment, knowing that it was coming. He didn't question Elijah's authority, nor did he hesitate to accept the responsibility. Such actions do not come spontaneously.

So, from the story of Elijah, we are able to make certain basic assumptions: first, that there was a well-organized cult or party or monastic order of those dedicated to Yahweh; second, they were underground in Israel but openly in operation at other locations, including Syria; third, they had means of fairly rapid and effective communication; fourth, they took care of their own, and had ways of guaranteeing survival under most circumstances; fifth, they had some effective method of instruction which prepared a succession of dedicated men to assume leadership in the cult order.

The assumption that there was a monastic group somewhere outside of Palestine with a static headquarters is made by inference only, yet it would not surprise me if an archeological expedition should discover concrete evi-

246

dence of the existence of just such a monastery. Certainly the span from Samuel to Elijah had indicated tremendous growth in organization and effectiveness on the part of the Yahweh cult.

THREE-PRONGED DEVELOPMENT OF THE PRIESTHOOD

It is very difficult to trace the development of the Yahweh cult in the Old Testament account of the Jewish people because after Solomon Palestine was split into two political entities. Israel, in the north, was made up of Galilee and Samaria. Judea, in the south, was separate and centered on Jerusalem. The record takes you from Israel to Judah, back and forth, and from king to king and invasion to invasion until it is virtually impossible to trace a continuous thread of development.

It would take a separate volume to trace the development of the Yahweh cult from Samuel to Hillel, through all of the vicissitudes of the political life of Palestine. But the central idea has never changed. The force and power of the Yahweh cult rests in the core principle that God is responsible for man and man is responsible to God. This concept of God's responsibility for man and man's responsibility to God has guided Judaism from the time of Abraham to the present day. This concept has been the unifying, activating, dynamic force in the development of Judaism as well as of Christianity.

The casual designation to the Levites, the tribe of Levi, made them the priestly tribe, having been so designated at the time of Moses. We have many references to the tribe of Levi and to the Levites in later Judaism, but it doesn't carry the same connotation that it did at the time of Moses.

247

As you recall from a previous reference, Samuel broke the continuity because he was an Ephriamite rather than a Levite, and he became the first priest-prophet of the Yahweh cult.

Beginning with Samuel, priests became independent; independent of their ancestry, independent of the political situation, completely self-contained in their authority. This is a very important point. The Yahweh cult took authority unto itself. No authority was given to Samuel or to the Yahweh cult by the king or by the people or by anyone. The cult established its own authority (and you will realize a very close parallel between the Yahweh cult and the Roman Catholic Church in Christian development as we sketch the history of this development).

The priesthood of the Yahweh cult was self-perpetuating. One priest would have disciples, and these disciples would become priests. The priest would anoint or ordain his disciples to take his place when he retired, or when he died. In this way the priesthood was not only self-perpetuating, but the priests were responsible only to themselves, to their own religious tradition, apart from the political situation.

Palestine was a theocratic state, whether it be Israel or Judea, and it was a theocracy where the priesthood, the religious group, delegated authority to the political group, and the high priest became the counsellor of the king. No one could tell the high priest what to do but the high priest could tell the king what to do. The king might not follow the instructions of the high priest, but the high priest was in the dominant position. This was the true theocracy, with the priests responsible only to their own traditions and responsible for their religious duties. They could be held accountable by everyone for the faithful performance of their religious duties, but no one could challenge them on any other phase of their leadership.

The organizational structure of the Yahweh cult instituted by Samuel became fairly evident at the time of Solomon. You recall that Samuel anointed Saul to be king when Samuel was just a young priest. After Saul had reigned for several years, Samuel anointed David to succeed Saul as king. This shifted the succession from Saul and his sons to the sons of Jesse, an entirely different family grouping. Samuel anointed David as a young shepherd lad out in the fields while Saul was still king and leader of the Jewish nation and of the army. Samuel died before David became king.

David had been anointed by Samuel before he fought Goliath, before he became a helper of Saul in the palace, before he became friendly with Jonathan, the eldest son of Saul. Not only was David not king when he was anointed, he did not become king until much later after a great struggle with Saul which developed into a civil war.

When David became king he had to choose a successor to Samuel to be his spiritual guide. Abiathar, the son of Ahimalech, travelled with David as his priest before David replaced Saul as king. When Saul was killed David made Abiathar high priest of the realm. During David's reign there was much agitation over his successor. Absolom tried to displace David during his lifetime and, as the eldest son, was in line for the throne whenever David died or abdicated. But David had no thought of permitting Absolom to replace him as king, even though Absolom was David's favorite.

With Absolom eliminated, Adonijah became the heir apparent and was supported by Abiathar the high priest, as well as several others in the king's household. But the son of David's favorite wife, Bathsheba, was supported by Zadok the priest and Nathan the prophet as David's successor. This son was Solomon and was the favorite of most of the king's household to succeed David as king. Since

249

Abiathar supported Adonijah, he lost his position as high priest when Solomon was named king, and Zadok became the high priest and Nathan continued as prophet because he also supported Solomon.

Zadok and Abiathar were both priests of the Yahweh cult during the reign of David, and they were rivals as well because they supported different candidates for the throne. But when the situation was resolved politically by Solomon being placed on the throne, the Yahweh cult was strong enough and well organized enough so that they maintained their leadership regardless of who became king. The successful supporter became the chief priest and the other became the assistant. They worked together and Zadok made the priestly group a very strong and exclusive temple-centered group of religious leaders.

After the building of the temple, which was erected during Solomon's reign, the priests became the caretakers of the temple and the Yahweh cult took on the responsibility for the administration of temple affairs. The administration included not only the celebrating of sacrifices on feast days, attending the altar, preaching to the people, teaching the leaders of the people, and communing with God in the Holy of Holies, but also keeping the temple repaired and repointing the stone work. The priests had to collect taxes for this responsibility and this prompted emphasis on tithing. The tithe was a tax levied on the people, not only to maintain the priestly group but also to maintain the temple. The kings had all they could do to collect enough money to spend on their several wives and to maintain their armies. The king did not want the responsibility of maintaining the temple so the priestly group accepted this responsibility with the right to collect a temple tax which permitted them to maintain the temple and their organization.

When the temple was built, the use of the high places declined in popularity because God appeared only in the Holy of Holies in the temple of Jersualem. As far as the Judeans were concerned, God did not appear in the high places anymore. The Zadokian priesthood maintained the Jerusalem-centered worship in the temple, and Zadok withdrew the sanction of the Yahweh cult for the use of the high places which had been the holy places prior to the erection of the temple. During Solomon's reign everything was centered in Jerusalem. Baal worship was in eclipse and Zadok was in command of the Yahweh worship.

After Solomon's death the Judeans and the Israelites formed two kingdoms again. Judah maintained the attitude that there were no valid centers of worship outside the temple in Jerusalem, but the northern kingdom returned to the use of the high places, particularly Mount Carmel which had witnessed the triumph of Elijah over the priests of Baal. The Israelites had no access to the Jerusalem temple while the area was divided because Jerusalem was enemy territory. This led to a resurgence of Baal worship in the northern kingdom, with a resumption of the rivalry for command of the high places between the Baal and Yahweh cults.

The division of the Jewish group into two kingdoms required a change in the leadership of the Yahweh cult. Samuel was a priest-prophet who performed both functions for Saul and David. When Abiathar became the high priest, Nathan filled the role of prophet, but when Zadok assumed leadership of the Yahweh cult he established the priesthood as the dominant portion of the leadership. The priests became so involved with the administrative detail and religious functions in the temple that they had no time for the prophetic functions. They didn't have the time to pursue knowledge, or to go out through the country to study the mood and the needs of the people. This led to the development of a prophetic group that was mobile, not tied to the temple of Jerusalem. This was a part of the leadership of the Yahweh cult, but a mobile group whose members could move with the people.

THE SADDUCEES

Zadok established himself as the high priest in the temple at Jerusalem and formed the beginnings of a priestly group that became known as the Sadducees, or the sons of Zadok (Sadok). The Sadducees were the representatives of the ruling class and the aristocracy. They were the chief supporters of the theocratic state, and their power was evident in the political decisions of the king and his court. They concentrated on the temple as the center of religious worship and God's leadership of the people since God could be contacted only in the Holy of Holies in Solomon's Temple and only the high priest could enter the sacred heart of the temple to receive God's commands.

The worship of Baal had ended with the total destruction of the followers of Baal by Jehu, while he was king of Israel. He also saw to it that Jezebel was destroyed. Thus, the Yahweh cult became dominant in the life of Palestine without any opposition. This brought power and responsibility to the Yahweh cult which was felt throughout the political and sociological structure of Palestine.

The priests of the Sadducean party, being temple-oriented and temple-bound, became very conservative to the point of being dogmatic. The Sadducees were not only a religious party, but also a political party and a social party. They were a party made up of the priests and the aristocracy and the rich merchants, and were the ruling group in Judah but not in the northern section.

THE PHARISEES

The Sadducees were the lineal and spiritual descendants of Zadok. They were conservative and temple-bound. But the Hebrews of the northern section of Palestine could not come to Jerusalem for their religious instruction or for worship. This situation made it imperative that religious leadership be supplied to the people outside of Jerusalem and Judah. This in turn led to the development of a prophetic line which did not center in Jerusalem but circulated throughout the length and breadth of Palestine. The prophetic line became known as the party of the people, called the Pharisees.

These leaders of the people established synagogues in the towns and cities of Israel for the worship and instruction of the people. Being close to the people, the prophetic line progressed as the people developed, as they evolved. As ideas changed, as new experiences changed the thinking of the people and as new invasions changed the conditions under which the people lived, the prophets adjusted to the new horizons, to the new ideas.

The prophets shared the exile of the Hebrews when they were taken into the land of Assyria, and when they were captives in Babylonia. The prophets were with them to care for them and to give them religious services. So the Pharisees were a liberal group, evolving as conditions changed. They saw that the Mosaic law needed to be interpreted in the light of the conditions under which the people existed, so they ventured new ideas in the interpretation of the law.

Where the priestly group had frozen the interpretation of the law, the prophetic group continually expanded and reinterpreted the application of the law. The priestly group maintained that God could be worshiped only in Jerusalem, but that was of small comfort to the exiles in

Babylonia. As a matter of fact, it was the activity of Ezekiel who was the prophet with the Hebrews during their Babylonian exile that brought about a significant advance in the concept of God.

The exiles in Babylonia were far from their Palestinian homeland. They felt that the protection of Yahweh was unavailable in this foreign land. They had reason for that feeling because Yahweh had always been present in the experience of the people. From the time of the giving of the law to Moses to the time of the Babylonian exile, the presence was seen. During the wilderness years the presence was the ark of the covenant which was carried with them on their journey. During the period of the Judges the presence was available on the high places, such as Bethel and Carmel. With the building of the temple of Jerusalem, the presence was in the Holy of Holies at the heart of the temple. It was up to Ezekiel to convince the Hebrews that Yahweh was available in a foreign land, even without the presence of the ark or of a twelve-stone altar on a high place.

Prior to Ezekiel the thought was that the local God protected a specified geographical area. The God of Palestine did not intrude upon the territory of the God of Babylonia or of the God of Egypt, and the Hebrews could not depend upon Yahweh when they were in a territory protected by another God. This is known as Henotheism, which is another way of saying territorial monotheism. Ezekiel was probably the first Jew to use the phrase "King of the Universe" to describe Yahweh. He certainly convinced the Hebrews in Babylonia that Yahweh could take care of them by the waters of Babylon as well as in the land of Palestine. This turned Judaism into a truly monotheistic religion for the first time in the experience of the Hebrews.

While the Sadducees continued to insist that Yahweh

254

could be reached only in the Holy of Holies in the temple at Jerusalem, the Pharisees claimed that Yahweh was reachable anywhere, and by any one of the faithful regardless of social, economic or political position. The Pharisees constituted the liberal party in Judaism, the party of the prophets and of the people. The Pharisaic party had the impetus of the prophetic line of thought and the outreach of the synagogue, whereas the Sadducees insisted upon the primacy of the temple of worship and the exclusiveness of the Torah as the sole source of the interpretation of God's law.

The difference between the Sadducees and the Pharisees, and the difference between orthodox and conservative Judaism today, is the difference in the documentary base of Judaism that is acceptable. The Sadducees held to the five books of Moses, the Torah, as the only truly authentic statement of the law. The Pharisees maintained that not only the Torah but also the Talmud and the Mishna, the written and oral traditions, revealed and interpreted the word of God. This much broader acceptance of interpretive writing the Sadducees rejected. The oral traditions in particular comprised the teachings of the prophets and the rabbis throughout the centuries. This made up a whole body of religious research and interpretation which was noncanonical as far as the Sadducees were concerned but which was accepted as authentic by the Pharisees.

Thus the sacred writings of the Pharisees included the interpretations of the Torah which were included in the Talmud and the Mishna. And to carry the interpretation one step farther, when Jesus began his ministry he reinterpreted the Talmud and the Mishna. Jesus was representative of the reform tradition which we recognize as a part of Judaism today. And it is interesting to observe that, while the orthodox (Sadducees) tolerated the conservative (Pharisees), neither group would accept the position of the Reform movement.

The only form of religious worship banned from the state of Israel today is Reform Judaism. This is difficult to understand, although Unitarianism and Universalism is in much the same situation within the Christian tradition. The Pharisees were more conservative than the Reform movement, but much more liberal than the Orthodox. Why the Reform movement was rejected is a mystery, since the Torah is the center of worship in Reform as well as Conservative and Orthodox Judaism. The Reform movement did not develop to any extent until after the advent of the Common Era, which corresponded to the advent of Christianity. Prior to this period the two branches of Judaism were Sadducean and Pharisaic, until the reintroduction of the monastic movement with the development of the Essenes during the intertestamentary period.

The Pharisees were the supporters of the synagogues as centers for the worship and study of Jews, as distinct from the temple-centered worship of the Sadducees. Today we call the Jewish centers of worship and study temples, but they are actually synagogues. The center of their worship is the Ark of the Covenant, which contains the Torah or the scroll of the law. The eternal flame or light burns over the Torah or the Ark in the syngogue, and represents the Holy of Holies, the eternal presence of God.

The Pharisees had no high priests, no single person designated as the one who communed with God, as was the case with the Sadducees. The center of their worship was the Torah, which was elevated at every service in the synagogue, and which has been read through once a year for thousands of years. The ark replaced the Holy of Holies, even in the Old Testament period, and a good Jew did not have to go to the temple at Jerusalem although it was well if he did.

Judaism and Christianity differed from Islam in the requirement to go to the center of their religious faith. The Jew desires to go the Temple in Jerusalem at some time, just as the Roman Catholic desires to go to Rome for a blessing by the pope, but this is not a requirement as the journey to Mecca, the Haj, is for the Moslem.

The division came between the Sadducees and the Pharisees in this matter, with the Sadducees concentrating on the Temple in Jerusalem and the Pharisees centering on the local synagogue with the Torah on the altar under the holy lamp. There was no split in the Yahweh cult and its core principle which was God's responsibility for man and man's responsibility to God. In fact, the Pharisees felt that their interpretation was much closer to the basic attitude that God expected of man. In many respects this attitude is similar to the attitude of the Unitarians, who believe that their approach is much closer to primitive Christian teachings than any of the orthodox churches.

There was reason for this attitude on the part of the Pharisees. They were the younger of the two religious groups, and they were the party with a much broader base of social respresentation. The Pharisees were the party of the common people, as opposed to the Sadducees, who represented the aristocracy. The Pharisaic party was every man's party. The rich had no more voice in the party than the poor, and the Pharisaic party did not discriminate in favor of those who were high-born, or members of the first families of Judea as the Sadducees did. The leaders of the Pharisees came from the common people. They worked their way up from the ranks, elevating themselves through their education, their devotion, their earnestness, their eagerness to learn and to produce and to serve.

The leaders of the Pharisees came up from the ranks just as modern rabbis come up and just as the clergy comes up in our congregational system today; through the congregation, from the broad base of the community that was the primary concern of the Pharisees. Thus the Pharisees represented the religious beliefs and social outlook of the common people and not of the aristocracy. The religious concern of the Pharisees was the total community, not just the aristocracy. The aim of the Pharisees was to democratize Judaism, to bring it out of the Holy of Holies, out of the Temple environs, into the home and the family group.

The Pharisees wanted to take Judaism out of the exclusive hands of the Sadducees, just as the Protestant Christians want to take Christianity out of the hands of the Roman Catholics. That is to say, we do not accept the idea that Christianity is the exclusive property of the Roman Catholics, as they believe it is. The Pharisaic party changed the worship pattern of Judaism by taking it out of the Temple and placing it in the home and the synagogue. Such family-centered worship brought conflict within the Yahweh cult. One branch of Judaism claimed that God resided in the Holy of Holies in the Temple, just as one part of Christianity claims that God is present only at the altar of the church. This presence is represented by the Host, which is kept on the altar and is shared by communicants during celebration of the Eucharist. That is why some Christians tip their hats or cross themselves when they pass the church. This is not out of respect for the church as such, but because God is there and that is where they must go if they wish to commune with God.

The Pharisees insisted that God was with everyone, that God was in every home, that God partook of every meal with the family. He partook more carefully of certain meals than he did of others, but he was there in the home and in the family relationship which was a very close personal relationship. This was still the Yahweh cult, but it was a far cry from the interpretation of the priestly group, the Sadducees.

The vicissitudes of Judaism through the period following the first Isaiah are difficult to categorize without getting into the political arena. There was no clear delineation of groups or parties within the Yahweh cult, particularly during the Babylonian captivity. Ezekiel was the prophet of the exile in Babylon while Jeremiah remained in Jerusalem. The prophets of the restoration were concentrating on the restoration of the temple and the redeeming of Israel from foreign influences. But the two major segments of the priesthood, the Pharisees and the Sadducees, were joined during this period by the resurgent monastic order called the Essenes. This was the later equivalent of the monastic group that was active during the reign of Ahab and Jezebel and the religious leadership of Elijah.

It was during this period of turmoil and captivity that the idea of God developed within Judaic culture. Prior to the Babylonian captivity the Israelites had the same concept that other groups had, of a geographically limited God whose power was effective only within the boundaries of the homeland. Theologically, this is referred to as henotheism rather than monotheism. What happened when the people had no homeland?

Moses had the problem of keeping God within reach of the Israelites during their forty years in the wilderness. When they went out of Egypt, God led them as a pillar of cloud by day and a pillar of fire by night. When Moses received the Ten Commandments on Mount Sinai he placed the tablets in the Ark of the Covenant and took the ark with him at the head of the column as it advanced. Moses taught the people that Yahweh was the Lord of Hosts; the strictly just God who had righteous anger, and who could smite his people as well as help them. Yahweh assisted the Israelites to victory in battle when they were good, and defeated them through use of the enemy when they were bad.

After the conquest of Canaan the altar was located on a high place, and there the Ark rested for the worship of the Israelites. Yahweh could be found in the high place, and his influence extended throughout the land of Canaan, but not beyond. When the kingdom was divided there had to be two high places; Carmel for the Israelites and Jerusalem for the Judeans. But the influence of Yahweh was confined to the territory of Palestine. This posed a problem for Ezekiel.

Ezekiel went with his people into Babylonian exile. During that period the Jews felt that Yahweh was powerless to assist them, since Babylonia had its own God in the person of King Nebuchadnezzar. Ezekiel persuaded the people that Yahweh was the God of the people, wherever they were, and that his influence was everywhere, not confined to a geographical setting. This was the first indication of a monotheistic concept. The later prophets expanded the concept of God in many ways, but Ezekiel was the first to introduce the concept of universality and so became the first true monotheist within the Jewish tradition.

Isaiah introduced the beautiful servant passages which showed God serving the people; ready to help, ready to serve, ready to guide; patient, not imperious, not humble, but cooperative. One can readily recognize the importance of seeing in Deity a cooperativeness, a willingness to tolerate the frailty of human nature, to make allowances for human weakness.

Micah developed the servant concept to the point

where God became a merciful God, not just a righteous God, not merely a just God, but a God of mercy, a God who would not punish irrevocably but who would condone in part, who would make concessions. God would not compromise but he would make concessions to human frailty, he would be merciful in his judgment of human error.

Hosea brought the concept of God and his relation to humanity to its highest point in Jewish tradition. Hosea pictured God as the God of love who could not reject man even though man rejected him. Here was a depth concept which we do not reach today, in many instances. Hosea saw God as so pervasive that even though man was an utter rotter, even though he ignored God, God would not ignore him. Nor would God hold man accountable (strictly accountable, that is) and would not destroy man, even though man ignored him.

By the time one arrives at Hosea's interpretation of God in the prophetic line of religious leaders, the divergence between the Pharisaic interpretation and the Sadducean interpretation was as great as anything one can imagine in religious history. The priestly group maintained the historical tradition and steadily retrogressed in its contact with the people. The prophetic group was progressive and humanizing in the active development of it religious concepts. It was continuously evolving and it be came the progressive group within Judaism. The broa differences between the two parties brought about schis'

One could not have a situation where the liberal gro insisted on the primacy of the home and the importa of the synagogue, while the conservative group insistec the primacy of the Temple centered in Jerusalem, witl a serious break and a violent reaction. The diverg between the priestly and prophetic groups brought ; a bitter and divisive situation.

During this period, which antedated the birth o'

by about a hundred and fifty years, the more serious and devout students of Judaism had a tendency to withdraw. They withdrew from both the Pharisaic and the Sadducean parties, but they were still loyal members of the Yahweh cult.

Those who withdrew were still true to the basic ideal of Judaism—God's responsibility for man and man's responsibility to God—but they did not like the controversy and the strife which was abroad. They withdrew for contemplation, for study, for calmness and lack of discord. They became monastics and built monastic communities away from the population centers where they could study undisturbed by the friction of the outside world. They became known as the Essenes, and they were a most interesting development in the history of the Yahweh cult.

CHAPTER II
THE ESSENES

At the outset it is useful to point out the differences between the Essenes and the monastic order active at the time of Ahab. The earlier order was secret, with the members remaining in the mainstream of society and working with the Baal worshipers in everything except Baal worship. The Essenes withdrew from the mainstream of society to the point that they would not even eat with anyone who was not an Essene.

The earlier order had only one monastery and that was on Mount Seir. The Essenes had their enclaves outside several of the larger centers of population in Palestine, so that they could come into the cities to tutor the children of the wealthy and still return to their enclave for the evening meal. The Essenes were never a large percentage of the general population, while the earlier order was extremely influential in the political life of both Israel and Syria and consisted of a relatively large number.

Note the power of their earlier order. The Abbot was commanding Elijah to return from Mount Seir: "Go, return on your way to the wilderness of Damascus; and when you arrive, you shall anoint Hazael to be king over Syria; and Jehu the son of Nimshi you shall anoint to be king over Israel; and Elisha the son of Shaphat of Abelmeholah you shall anoint to be prophet in your place." And he indicated the number of members of the order when he said, "Yet I will leave seven thousand in Israel, all the knees that have not bowed to Baal, and every mouth that has not kissed him." The Essenes had no such political clout.

When we discuss the Essenes, we actually depart from canonical scriptures because the Essenes were not recognized as a separate branch of the Yahweh cult by the Jews themselves. In the Talmud we recognize many individual Essenes, those who rose above the group and became great leaders in both the religious and the political field, but Judaism did not recognize any separateness. As a matter of fact there was no real separation between the Essenes, the Sadducees, and the Pharisees that the selection of the Essenes for separate treatment might imply. The cultus was one and the same; all were members of the Yahweh cult.

The sole difference is that the Sadducees and the Pharisees are recorded in the canonical scriptures and the Essenes are not. At the point when the Essenic movement developed the Yahweh cult was pervasive in Palestine. This cult was not challenged by any other group. The Baal cult had disappeared and there was no competing religious or philosophic orientation for the Jewish people. All were within the mainstream of Judaism and followers of Yahweh.

It may be that the dominance of the Yahweh cult in Jewish life at this period was due to the political situation. The Jews had been invaded, captured, taken into slavery, first by the Assyrians and later by the Babylonians. When the Roman legions conquered the entire Mediterranean, the political control of Palestine came under Roman domination. The only independence left to the Jews was in their religious life, which the Romans left undisturbed.

So it was during this period that the religious beliefs of the Jewish people were made an integral part of their individual and family life. It was the Yahweh cult that took complete control of Hebrew life at this period. The Yahweh cult controled the politics, the economics, the religious and social life that was not affected by the Roman occupation.

What divisiveness there was during the Maccabean period and continuing to the destruction of Jerusalem in 70 of the common era concentrated on the application of the precepts of the Mosaic law, rather than the acceptance of these precepts. All Jews accepted the law. The difference came in the interpretation of that law. One observes a similar situation in the fact that Roman Catholics, Episcopalians, Lutherans, and Unitarian Universalists accept the teachings of Jesus but are divided on the interpretation and application of those teachings.

This was the situation in Palestine during the Maccabean period and beyond. At this point the Sadducees were the authoritarian party. They were in control of the social, political, and economic life of Palestine. They represented the rich merchants, the aristocracy, and the priestly caste. They could be termed the party of the privileged.

The Pharisees were the party of the common people, the home-centered party, the broadly based democratic party. They were diffused and pragmatic in their application of the Mosaic law. The Pharisees chose their leaders from among the common people, and the leaders wrestled with the problem of law and order, morals and ethics, requirements of the religious life, in the local community and the village synagogue.

The third movement which came into prominence at this time was neither temple centered nor home centered. It centered upon the individual rather than the family and practiced celibacy. This third movement, the Essenes, was

265

contemplative and withdrawn from the mainstream of society. The Essenes postdated the Pharisees just as the Pharisees postdated the Sadducees, and for a similar reason. The Pharisees were established when the Sadducees became separated from the common people and became the exclusive party of the privileged class. When the Pharisees became too highly organized, too pragmatic, too worldly in their application of religious principles for the satisfaction of certain ascetics, the Essenes came into being. The Essenes were individuals who felt that being withdrawn from the vices and superfluities of life in the world was a mark of religious attainment.

The Essenes are first mentioned during the Maccabean period, and most of the information about the Essenes as a group or order comes to us from extrabiblical sources, from the philosophical and historical writers of the period. For example, Philo, the writer during the period just preceding the common era, orients the Essenes and the Essenic movement with the Persian Magi, or Wise Men, and with the Indian Gymnosophists. The Gymnosophists were the very early antecedents of the Brahmo-Somaj, the philosophical movement within Hinduism. The philosophical perspective of the Essenes is very similar to that of the two oriental groups mentioned, and it is quite interesting to many of us that Philo should equate the Essenes with these rather metaphysical and mystical orders of the East.

On the other hand, Pliny describes the customs of the Essenes in a much different vein. He writes to a considerable extent about their habits, their habitat, and about their influence upon the life around them. And Josephus, an historian of this period who was himself Jewish and who wrote extensively about the Jews, did considerable historical research on the Essenes. As a matter of fact, we believe that Josephus became an Essene novice, entering the novitiate with the intention of becoming a monastic. It seems that he endured almost the entire three-year period of the novitiate, and then resigned because he could not take the rigorous discipline.

He did not resign because he was in opposition to the movement. He simply resigned because it was too ascetic for his taste and too stark for his feelings and his beliefs. But he became an apologist for the Essenes and a very accurate historian of the external story and the history of the order. He could not describe the internal workings because the Essenes were a secret order, a monastic order, keeping their secrets from the uninitiated. But his writings shed considerable light on the principles and tenets of the Essenes.

The Talmud and the Midrash, the canonical and extracanonical writings of Judaism during this period, give indirect information on the Essenes because they contain very valuable information concerning certain individuals who were loyal Essenes and who became politically important in the life of Judaism.

Our chief source of information concerning the Essenes comes from the Dead Sea Scrolls, and especially from the Book of Discipline, which was discovered among other scrolls found in the caves at Qumran. The Book of Discipline gives a great deal of internal information concerning the life and habits of the Essenes. Obviously, it was never anticipated that the Book of Discipline would pass from the hands of Essenic scholars into the general field of information.

The Essenes were not allowed to destroy a scroll. When the word of God was written, when a scroll was transcribed, that writing was holy and could not be destroyed. When a scroll was copied because it had become so worn that it had to be replaced, the worn scroll was sealed in a pottery jar, or container, and stored forever. It was just set aside in a safe place. Like the American flag here in the United States that is stored away when it becomes worn or frayed, the worn scroll could not be destroyed. It was thought to be not only sacred but imperishable.

We are very fortunate that the Essenes felt that way about the scrolls, because otherwise we would never have access to them for study. We would have had only the archeological relics of the Qumran community as a record of their existence. Our scholars have found a great deal of information about the Essenes from the excavations on the shores of the Dead Sea. These excavations, coupled with the translation of some of the scrolls, give us an insight into the Essenic community life and activity.

From the excavation of the site, we can get a great deal of information concerning the living standards and the major activities within this one Essenic community. There was a library where the current scrolls were kept for the use of the members of the community. There was a scriptorium where the scrolls were copied when they became worn. There was a common dining hall and a common kitchen where the food was prepared. Obviously the Essenes lived together as a communistic group, holding all things in common. No one member of the order had more than any other member. This is an obvious inference from the archeological findings on the shores of the Dead Sea.

From the material available it is possible to draw up an inferential description of the typical Essene. First of all, the Essenes were obviously very pious or virtuous Jews who lived in their own communities in both Palestine and Syria. It is equally obvious that the Essenes were very similar to the monastic order that was active in the time of Elijah and Ahab. Remember that Elijah was instructed by the leader of the Yahweh cult to anoint the king of Syria as well as the king of Israel. Philo records the presence of Essenes in Syria as well as in Palestine, showing that the monastic element in the Yahweh cult had impact in relatively non-Jewish areas as well as in Palestine itself. In the Essenic culture there were groups or communities in Syria as well as in various sections of Palestine.

According to Philo there were about four thousand Essenes living in Syria and Palestine at this time, as nearly as a census could be taken. This compared with seven thousand at the time of Elijah. The total of four thousand Essenes was a relatively small group, yet I believe that the number would compare favorably with the number of Dominicans in the Roman Catholic church in recent times. The Dominicans have exerted tremendous influence in Western Europe in political as well as ecclesiastical matters. I don't believe that any order, with the possible exception of the Society of Jesus (Jesuits), would have a larger membership than the Essenes had during this period.

It doesn't take too many dedicated individuals, working in concert, to make an impact upon a culture. I think as we proceed, you will realize the extent of the impact that the Essenes made upon Judaism and Christianity during the years of active participation in the life and thought of Palestine. The Essenes were communists, holding all things in common. They fulfilled the basic tenet of communism, which is "from each according to his ability, to each according to his need." They were not dialectical materialists, as the Soviets are, but were definitely socially and politically communistic.

The Essenes supported themselves by manual labor, and they would hire out to anyone who would pay their wages. Their manual labor was primarily concentrated in agriculture because they were agrarians by choice. One thing they never did was to make weapons of war. No matter how much they were importuned or how high the wages were, they would never go into the so-called defense industry. And all proceeds from their labor were turned into a common fund to be used equally for the benefit of all.

The Essenes were devoted to study and prayer, being primarily a contemplative order. They believed study of the scriptures to be the highest virtue, and were continuously striving to get the deepest possible meaning from the scriptures. Their prayer was not merely contemplation, but a sincere attempt to achieve direct personal communication with God, with nature, and with their environment. "With the center of thought," is a phrase that they used quite frequently.

And while they were devoted to study and prayer, they carried out acts of benevolence. They were a kindly order, much like the Franciscans in the Roman Catholic church. Their interest was centered primarily on the aged and the sick, and they would nurse them and care for them and make sure that everything was done for them that could be done.

The Essenes were generally celibate; they did not marry because they did not feel that the family unit was the important unit. Some of them had marriage relationships for the sole purpose of procreation. When the children were born the conjugal relationship was dissolved and the children were brought up by the whole community, which accepted the responsibility for the rearing of the children. Only a small number of Essenes entered into these marital relationships for the production of children.

Most of the children who became members of the

Essenic group were adopted. This was the generally accepted recruiting policy. Members of the order would go through the communities near their enclaves and find children who were not wanted by their natural parents. They would adopt these children and raise them in the Essenic community, training them for the life of an Essene.

The Essenes also accepted proselytes; mature people who were fed up with the world, who wanted to adopt a meditative life, who wanted to withdraw from the competition of the secular world. In line with this movement you may recall that the Roman Catholic church set up a special order some time ago that would take older novices, permitting men over fifty to begin their vocation and to prepare for the priesthood.

The Essenes condemned slavery, categorically and absolutely, both in principle and in practice. They were the strongest proponents of free society in the world at that time. They were so strong in their espousal of freedom, and in their antagonism toward and hatred of slavery, that they influenced the whole Jewish community. In fact, they influenced the civilization of the Near East to eschew slavery as a national policy.

Slavery had become a natural result of conquest. If one nation conquered another, the vanquished became the slaves of the victors. This practice was sociologically acceptable as a part of the spoils of war. But the Essenes refused to recognize the acceptability of this social custom and eliminated slavery from the Jewish community.

Within the Essenic community the younger ministered to the elders. The young Essenes did the hard work, the manual labor, and the elders did the teaching and the research and study. The respect accorded seniority replaced any thought of rank. There was no social stratification within the group. Profound respect was shown the elders, an attitude which was observable in the sociological impact of Confucius upon the Chinese society of his period.

The respect for the elders was accompanied by a willingness on the part of the younger generation to defer to them, to learn from them, to support them and to see to it that their life was as pleasant as possible. This teacher-pupil relationship was the sociological pattern of the Essenic community.

The rulers of the Essenes were the elders, selected by seniority. The chief elder was the leader of the community. The Essenes were a secret order, not open in their teachings. Their Book of Discipline was a closed book, and even their innermost thoughts were closed to the world and reserved for the community in which they lived.

The Essenes did not occupy one geographical area in Palestine, nor were they limited to Palestine. They were found wherever Jews congregated but were found in areas where there were few Jews because the Essenes attracted non-Jews to their ranks. There were many Egyptians who joined the Essenes who lived on the outskirts of Alexandria and Cairo.

The Essenes had no separate city of their own but tended to congregate in certain districts of established cities. There were Essenic communities within or just outside Damascus, Jerusalem, Cairo, and Alexandria in addition to the large Essenic community at Qumran on the shore of the Dead Sea. It was unusual for the Essenes to occupy a relatively isolated spot and to have a large community isolated from the mainstream of the population.

Qumran had an unusually large number of Essenes living in the isolation of a prepared community. History shows that Qumran was important as the control center of the Essenic movement, and evidence indicates that the leadership of the entire movement was concentrated there. To that extent the Essenes did have one specific geographical location, although it was not the center of Essenic culture or of Essenic instruction. Their instruction was available all the way from Damascus to Cairo and Alexandria.

The Essenes preferred the country to the city because they were essentially agrarian. Thus they were found on the outskirts of large cities, rather than within the city limits. They were among the first suburbanites. They preferred to live on the edge of the city where they could be away from the noise and confusion of the central city, and yet close enough to the center of culture so that they would have access to the libraries and the collections of scrolls available to them. They were particularly interested in the great library at Alexandria.

The Essenic characteristics were very marked. They despised pleasure and luxury. They were not party-givers. They regarded anointing with oil as defiling. They wore simple white garments and they did not own a change of clothing. They would remove their garment and wash it as they bathed themselves, and then put it back on. Obviously they were not encumbered with luggage when they traveled.

The Essenes bathed daily in cold water. They never permitted themselves the luxury of a hot bath. At mealtime they ate a single item. They never had a dinner of several courses, and the one dish seemed to fill their need for food. They always worked from sunrise to sunset. They completed their worship when the first full rays of the sun came across the landscape, and they could not cease labor until the sun had disappeared over the horizon.

The leaders of the Essenes determined the procedures and assigned tasks to the members of the group just as a foreman would do today. They named the individuals to the task. The individuals had no choice in the matter, but they didn't care about having a choice. They were completely submissive to the will of the group as expressed by the leaders. If any leader became overbearing or domineering he ceased to be a leader, and was demoted to the ranks. The leader who had the best interests of the group at heart would replace any leader who became domineering in his attitude.

There was only one area in which independent action was allowed or encouraged, and in this area it was mandatory. This was the area of deeds of mercy or charity. Whenever an Essene saw something that needed to be done to help a fellow human being, whether or not that human was an Essene, he did it without any recourse or referral to the leader for guidance. Immediate and unquestioning assistance when needed was a cardinal principle, one of the foundation principles of the Essenes. One must help other people at all times, at all opportunities. Whenever a need appears, it is obligatory to assist.

The Essenes objected strenuously to oaths, to swearing. Their modern counterpart in this position is the Society of Friends. They both follow the teaching of Jesus, who undoubtedly received the instruction from his Essenic tutors. His statement was:

> You have heard that it was said to men of old, you shall not swear falsely, but shall perform to the Lord what you have sworn. But I say unto you, do not swear at all, either by heaven, for it is the throne of God, or by the earth, for it is his footstool, or by Jerusalem, for it is the city of the great king. and do not swear by your head, for you cannot make one hair white or black. Let what you say be simply "Yes" or "No"; anything more than this comes from evil.

> Matt. 5:33–37

The Essenes were very careful about the use of oaths because, once taken, an oath was immutable. It must be honored absolutely. And when the Essene took the oath of loyalty to the group he was bound forever after that by that loyalty, whether he departed from the group or not. This was the chief disciplinary tool available to the leaders because no Essene could eat food that was prepared by anyone except another Essene. Any food prepared by a non-Essene was impure. All Essenes ate in a common dining hall served from a common kitchen, and if a member was read out of the group by the leader he would starve to death because he could not eat any food prepared by anyone else. So there was very little falling away from the Essenes, but there was very little contention as far as we can observe.

The rules of the order were very strict, and each member had to observe the obligations set forth in the Book of Discipline. The rule for the novice was one of the important control factors of the order. The novice had to serve for three years, divided into two periods of approximately equal length. The asceticism demanded of the novice increased during the three-year period, so that the novice realized before he took his final vows whether he could actually adhere to the rigid life of the cult or not.

I imagine that the extreme asceticism and the exclusiveness of the Essenes was the reason why Josephus withdrew from the novitiate before the end of the three-year trial period. One could resign without prejudice at any time during the three-year period. The oath of the initiate is very interesting. This oath was taken by the initiate before he was allowed to share the common meal, before he was purified so that he could eat with the others. It is found in the *Encyclopedia Brittanica*, and reads as follows:

To be pious to the Deity, to practice justice toward

275

men, never to injure anyone, either of his own accord or under compulsion, always to hate the wicked and side with the just. Ever to show faithfulness to all mankind and to be true to those in authority, for all power comes from God. Never when in office to force his personal views or authority or to assume a special dress or luxury. To love truth and hate falsehood. To keep his hands pure from a theft and his soul from unrighteous gain. Not to have any secret from his brethren and never to betray one of theirs, even at the cost of his life. To pass on the traditions he himself had received. Never to be a brigand. To safeguard the sacred books and to preserve with care the names of the angels that had been taught to him.

This was the oath of the Essenes. You may recognize the similarity to the oath of Hippocrates, or the oath of allegiance to many of our secret orders. The Essenes took their oath very seriously. For them it was an absolute rule of behavior. They could not deviate one step from it, and even though they were compelled by threat of death to do an injury, they could not do it; they had to submit to being killed for refusal to obey an order which violated their oath. This is a part of their history.

This also gives us a very interesting insight into the dedication of the early Christians who allowed themselves to be torn apart by savage beasts in the Roman Arena rather than to violate their vows. This dedication carried over from the Essenes to their counterparts in the Christian movement. The Essenes were not a completely separate sect, or a different religious group. They provided the vital force in one segment of the Judeo-Christian movement. The Sabbath observance of the Essenes was very strict, and the whole group was divided into four grades based on seniority and on learning. This was the only differentiation permitted within the group.

276

We have outlined the tenets of the Essenes, and now should delve into the history of the movement a bit. Their origin was a branch of the Pharisees; they were a subgroup within the Pharisaic tradition. They conformed to the most rigid rules of Levitical purity and aspired to the highest degree of holiness. This was all within Judaism and within the Pharisaic group. The Essenes were from all walks of life; they were broadly democratic, as were the Pharisees. They were essentially Jewish. There is no doubt of this in the mind of any historian.

They were the *Hashain* in Hebrew; they were the silent ones, the reticent. They were the heirs of the Hassidic movement which was the ascetic movement within Judaism during the Maccabean period, but was definitely a part of the Pharisees. The Hassidic group was the very pious, dedicated group within the Pharisaic movement before and during the period of the Macabbees. The Essenes were successors to the Assideans, who flourished during the Hellenistic period of Jewish history from the fourth to the first century BCE. They were among the most ardent followers of Judas Maccabeus. They regarded the Oral or traditional Law as equally binding and authoritative to the Torah, which placed them in opposition to the Saducean party.

During this period there were also the Theraputae, who lived near Alexandria in Egypt. The Theraputae (meaning worshipers of God) were Essenes. They had connections with the Essenic groups in Palestine and Syria. They lived in separate houses rather than a communal dwelling because they wanted to be able to be alone to meditate, and yet come together in a group for discussion. They meditated in solitude during the week, and then they came together on the Sabbath and prayed and ate in common.

The feasts of the Theraputae were famous at this time. This was the Greek period, when the Greeks had their Bacchanalian festivals at which they ate and drank themselves into a stupor. In contrast, the Essenic feast was one at which no flesh, no meat, was served, where only cold water was drunk, and where the main feature was not food, but philosophical discourse. This was the greatest feast in the Essenic year, when they got together to eat just enough to sustain their energies, and where they had no stimulants whatever except the intellectual stimulation of a philosophical discussion.

The Essenes were philosophers and scientists, so noted by Philo and other reporters of that period. They were the intellectuals of that era. Another branch of the Essenes were called the Hemerobaptists, who believed in daily ablutions as a matter of ritual. Their baths were ritual baths, and instead of just washing their hands and feet as the good orthodox Jews did, they washed themselves from head to foot every day, as a part of their ritual purity. It is believed that John the Baptist was a member of this branch of the Essenes, that he was a Hemerobaptist.

The Essenes were contemplative Pharisees. They were not separate or divorced from the Pharisaic party and were well within the mainstream of Judaism. They were very pietistic, but they allowed all manner of divergencies within the group. Personal tastes were recognized and honored as long as the basic position of the group was maintained. Such flexibility was much more sensible than the hard-and-fast rules governing so many societies today.

The Essenes read the law diligently, but they accompanied the reading of the law with expository homilies, or sermons, just as the Reform Jews do today. Orthodox Jews have just the reading of the law, but the Essenes were not Orthodox in that they accepted the Haggadah, the Midrash, the oral tradition which has so enriched both Conservative and Reform Judaism.

Angelology was a very strong part of the Essenic tradition. They believed that the angels were the communicators between God and men. Angels were the messengers and were very real to the Essenes. It is very possible that the angelology of the Essenes contributed a great deal to the legends which gathered about the birth of Jesus. Certainly angels were a part of the tradition, and appeared as messengers, validating the message of Jesus as basic Essenic philosophy. This was to be expected since Jesus was tutored by the Essenes, and was initiated as a novice Essene by John the Baptist. More of this will be discussed in the following chapter.

The Essenes disappeared. They were a vital part of society for between two and three hundred years, and then they just disappeared from the face of the earth. The organization, the communities, everything faded out. They were not eliminated by an enemy, there was no cataclysmic reason for their disappearance. They just faded away, perhaps because they had assimilated their environment. Certainly they had not succumbed to it; rather, they conquered it. Their communistic form of government made it possible for them to concentrate on their goals for human betterment. When paganism was driven out of the Mediterranean area, the purpose of the Essenes was achieved. It appears that the Essene became the devout Christian and the law-abiding Jew; that the Essenes raised the general level of society to match their own standards. When this occurred the Essenes became one with the general level in the interpretation of values and ceased to exist separately. This is the story of the Essenes as a separate movement within the religious development of the eastern Mediterranean area.

CHAPTER III
THE HISTORICAL JESUS

I stated that we would have a more extensive treatment of Jesus as he appears in history, rather than in the myth concerning "the only begotten son of God." It is necessary to evaluate the little that is recorded concerning the birth and early life of Jesus. Only two of the four canonical gospels mention the birth and childhood, and these two disagree greatly. Matthew has Jesus born in a house in Bethlehem (Matt. 2:11) and Luke has him born in a stable attached to an inn (Luke 2:7). Luke has Joseph and Mary coming to Bethlehem from Nazareth (Luke 2:4) but Matthew has the family going to the city of Nazareth for the first time after the sojourn in Egypt (Matt. 2:23).

It is obvious to the reader that Matthew originally began with what is stated as chapter 2. Chapter 1 contains two obvious additions that are mutually incompatible because the line of David is traced through the male descendants, yet the second addition claims that Jesus was not the son of Joseph. Luke likewise could have begun with what is now listed as chapter 2. The first chapter primarily establishes the authenticity of John the Baptist as the prophet of the Most High.

It is interesting to observe that both Jesus and John were products of the Judean aristocracy and that they were both tutored by the Essene scholars. It is also a valid assumption that both Jesus and John were accepted as novices by the Essenes. John was attracted to the Hemerobaptist sect of the Essenes, while Jesus did not accept the restrictions of the cult and went out to challenge the establishment. The appearance and activity of the angels at the birth of Jesus indicates Essenic sources because the Essenes were the only segment of Judaism having a tradition of angelology.

If the flight into Egypt was actually undertaken by Joseph and his family, it could only have been as invited guests of the Pharaoh. There was no love lost between the Herodian kings of Israel and the Egyptian monarch, and the Pharaoh could have seen a possibility that he was assisting a future king of Israel in giving shelter to Joseph and his family. Had Joseph not been welcomed by the Pharaoh, he and his family would have become slaves in Egypt because the Egyptians had very little use for the Hebrews and were known to enslave any that they captured in border skirmishes.

When Joseph and his family moved into Nazareth, they were recognized immediately as the first family of the community. Joseph occupied a position which would correspond to being the mayor in modern parlance. He supplied the farmers with their farming implements, and was assuredly the richest man in the community. It would be only logical to assume that the education of Jesus and his younger brothers be provided by the Essenic tutors who taught the sons of the wealthy and the high-born.

With this as background we can make certain assumptions concerning Jesus and his early training. Since Jesus was the first-born son of the first-born son of the line of David, he was eligible to become king if the Herodians were replaced by the Davidic line. Because of this fact, Jesus had to be educated to assume leadership responsibilities, should such a shift occur. Consequently, Jesus was thoroughly grounded in both religion and politics so that he could lead the nation if the occasion arose.

As Jesus was being tutored by the Essenes, he absorbed much of their philosophy and accepted their basic rules of conduct as his own. He accepted responsibility for the welfare of humanity, and determined to do whatever he could to improve human conditions. He accepted the central theme of the Yahweh cult—God's responsibility for man and man's responsibility to God—as the basic rule for his own life. The Essenes were the religious group in Judaism that followed this principle most closely, and Jesus was completely faithful to the covenant relationship. His basic philosophy is brought out in what is termed "The Sermon on the Mount" (Matt. 5–7) and which I would describe as "The Christian Manifesto."

There is one element of the birth of Jesus that needs clarification. Later church authorities claimed that Jesus was born of a virgin. They based that assumption on a passage in Isaiah (Isaiah 7:14) in which Isaiah states that a temple virgin will conceive and bear a son. He follows up that prophecy by going in to the temple priestess and impregnating her (Isaiah 8:3), after which she bears a son who is called Immanuel (Isaiah 8:8) and who later rescues the Israelites from the yoke of Assyria, in fulfillment of the prophecy.

The role of the temple virgin or priestess was an honorable one. The fairest maidens were selected for this honor, and served for a specified term. They were not considered prostitutes, and were most acceptable as wives after their term in the temple was finished. While they served in the temple they were available to the priests and prophets, but this service was highly regarded rather than being frowned upon.

Luke supplied Jesus with a normal Jewish boyhood,

uninterrupted by a flight into Egypt. Luke rec[c] circumcision (2:21) and the Bar Mitzvah (2:41–47) required the presence of Jesus in Jerusalem, rath[er] in Egypt. Since Luke was not a Jew, and never [in] Palestine during the time he was physician to Paul, he would naturally assume that Jesus observed the orthodox Jewish customs. Paul was an orthodox Jew who followed the teachings of the Torah, and this was the source of Luke's information as to the customs of Judaism.

The next period of speculation concerning the life and training of Jesus is during the so-called "hidden years," when some claim that he sojourned in India and came under the influence of theosophy. It is much more realistic to assume that he followed the custom of high born Jews and was tutored by the Essenes. It is obvious that he must be prepared to take his place at the head of both church and state if the Davidic line of kings was restored in place of the Herodians. As crown prince, Jesus must be prepared to lead the nation. Consequently, his instruction must be most thorough.

It was during this instruction that Jesus became interested in the life and philosophy of the Essenes. He was not attracted in the same way as his cousin John, who adopted the strictest form of Essenic life, that of the Hemerobaptists. Jesus was much more realistic in his interpretation of the duties of individuals toward others. He obviously accepted and adopted the Essenic attitude toward people, that each human being was a child of God and worthy of his assistance. This finally led Jesus to reject his social position and dedicate himself to the service of humanity.

This is the explanation of the temptation story. Jesus knew that he had opportunities as well as responsibility in serving his nation and his class. He felt that he could become another Judas Maccabaeus and free his people from the yoke of Rome. He could become the head of the state or of the church, if the Davidic line replaced the Herodians. But his Essenic instruction had convinced him of the reality of the brotherhood of all believers. So he rejected his heritage and dedicated himself to the welfare of the common people.

Tradition had it that he started his ministry at the age of thirty. In terms of the life expectancy of his times, that would put him past middle age. His energy and enthusiasm would indicate that he was much younger. I would deem him no older than twenty-one. Certainly his disciples, those who followed him in his revolt against the uncaring social system of his day, were all young. His favorite disciples were teenagers whose fathers were still actively working in the fishing industry. Judas was probably the oldest and his age was twenty-seven. Of course, this does not square with the artistic depiction of the Last Supper by Leonardo da Vinci, in which some of the disciples are depicted as old men with bald heads and long beards.

A rather casual reference in Luke (8:19–21) shows Jesus rejecting the responsibility for the family estates that his brothers and mother requested him to assume. This is an indication that his father, Joseph, had died and that he as the first-born son was responsible for the family estates. His brothers could not legally accept the responsibility because he was the first-born son of the family.

The core of Jesus' message and purpose is put forward in three chapters of the Gospel of Matthew (5–7) referred to as "The Sermon on the Mount." One questions whether Jesus said all this at one time. It is more logical to assume that the principles enunciated here were the central part of his entire ministry. It is also interesting to note that there is a distinct parallel to the principles set forth in the

Book of Discipline of the Essenes. Jesus patterned his entire ministry on the philosophy of the Essenic cult.

Another evidence of Jesus' acceptance of the Essenic philosophy is his criticism of the Pharisees. The Essenes were the monastic branch of the Pharisees, or the people's party of Judaism, as contrasted with the Sadducees who were the Temple party of the aristocracy and the political power of the Jewish nation. Jesus obviously felt that the Pharisees were not sufficiently aware of the needs of the common people, and that they had a tendency to separate themselves from the needs and problems of the people. Consequently, the Pharisees did not come to the defense of Jesus when he was attacked by the Sadducees. The Essenes were the only group to stand by him during his trial, and to minister to him following his crucifixion.

It is rather obvious from the total record that Jesus did not die on the cross. The "men in white" mentioned in the accounts were Essenes in their usual white habits. They removed Jesus from the cross during the period when he was in a coma, and probably moved him to the nearest Essene community. There they attempted to restore him to health but he died later of septicemia, due to the infection of the spear thrust or the nail holes. It is entirely possible that Jesus was seen by his disciples following the crucifixion, and that he would have spoken to Thomas as it is said that he did.

There is one element in the life of Jesus where the Gospel of John is much more accurate than the other Gospels. This is in the matter of what the Christians call "Holy Week." John has Jesus in Jerusalem for at least six months prior to the Passover celebration. This makes sense in the progression of events in the Jewish religious calendar. Note the major events recorded.

The "triumphal entry" would be in keeping with the

autumn festival of First Fruits, or Succoth, or the Festival of Booths. This was the time when the Jews paraded with tree branches, or palm branches, and had a processional going to the temple in Jerusalem. It was the celebration of the harvest period and was observed by individuals and families alike.

Driving the money-changers from the temple could have occurred only when money-changers were in the temple courtyard. This would occur during the feast of Purim, or the time of the payment of the temple tax. The temple tax was traditionally paid in the shekel of Tyre, because King Hiram and the workmen of Tyre were the ones who constructed the temple. Since Judeans would not have a shekel of Tyre as a usual medium of exchange in Jerusalem, the money-changers were needed to supply the appropriate coins for the payment of the tax.

Passover was in late March or early April, according to our present calendar. This was a celebration within the family which was observed in the home. It started in the evening preceding the passover day with the family ritual meal called *seder*. This is the meal that Christians refer to as the last supper, which Jesus celebrated with his disciples because they had no family with whom to celebrate.

There are many inconsistencies in the account of "Holy Week," in addition to those mentioned above. For example even in the days of the Sanhedrin and the Roman courts, there would not have been four trial periods in the space of two days. Justice was never that swift in real life. And people could not have been turned from a celebrating, welcoming throng into a lynch mob in the space of four days. I doubt that it was accomplished in four months. Jesus had many champions, even in Jerusalem, and they would not turn on him without prolonged and insidious provocation by his enemies among the Sadducees. Even so, his enemies had to take him surreptitiously at night when his friends were not present to defend him.

Incidents of the activity of Jesus that indicate the depth of his training in the knowledge of the Essenes are evident throughout his ministry. His uncanny ability to recognize functional illness, and to cure it through the power of suggestion and the force of his personality, was manifested time and time again throughout his ministry. The Essenes were expert in their practice of folk medicine and Jesus was an apt student of the craft. He knew instinctively what Mary Baker Eddy discovered many centuries later, that psychosomatic medicine had its place in the care and cure of human beings. Many of his listed miracles were psychosomatic cures, in which he was highly skilled.

It was the aristocrat turned commoner, and not the humble carpenter's son, who attracted the young men who were restless and eager for new worlds to conquer. He promised them nothing but hardship and lean times, with a chance to improve human condition, and they bought it enthusiastically even though they did not fully understand it. His high-born station was evidenced in the contact with Zacheus in Jericho. Jesus invited himself to dinner with Zacheus, the richest man in Jericho. Had Jesus been an ordinary commoner he would have been killed for his effrontery. Society was not very flexible in that period and in that part of the world.

And so we have a glimpse of the real Jesus; the Essene who would not be circumscribed by the strict rules of the order, but who championed the common people in accordance with the Essenic teachings. This picture was later to be horribly distorted by the Roman bishops who were assisted by the Roman emperor. The Christology which emerged had no relationship to the sermon on the mount, or to the humanitarian emphasis Jesus gave to his teachings.

All the earth calleth upon Truth, and the heaven blesseth her; for with her is no unrighteous thing. Wine is wicked, the king is wicked, women are wicked; and they all pass away. But as for Truth, she abideth, and is strong forever; she liveth and conquereth forever more. With her there is no accepting of persons or rewards; but she doeth the things that are just, and refraineth from all unrighteousness and wicked things; and all men do like well of her works. Neither in her judgment is any unrighteousness; and she is the strength, and the kingdom, and the power, and the majesty, of all ages. Blessed be the God of Truth!

—I Esdras